On Being Free

FRITHJOF BERGMANN

On Being Free

UNIVERSITY OF NOTRE DAME PRESS

NOTRE DAME ~ LONDON

Library of Congress Cataloging in Publication Data
Bergmann, Frithjof.
    On being free.
    1. Liberty. I. Title.
JC571.B474   123   77-89760
ISBN 0-268-01492-2

For
Jandy and Lukas

*Publication of this volume
was assisted by a grant from
The American Council of Learned Societies
as a result of a grant from the Andrew W. Mellon Foundation*

Contents

Acknowledgments

ABOVE ALL I want to thank Walter Kaufmann for being my teacher and my friend. Among the many who have helped me I would like to mention especially John Bennett, Jack Meiland, George Rosenwald, William Schroeder, and the group that used to meet at Frederick Wyatt's house. Philippa Gordon's work on the book improved it as well as my own spirits greatly. Andrea Sankar lived through the stages of the manuscript. Jim Langford has been midwife as well as editor. I am grateful also to Taya. To the University of Michigan I am indebted for a sabbatical leave.

On Being Free

1

Opening the Question

I

OUR CULTURE HAS a schizophrenic view of freedom. Two schools of thought concerning liberty are simultaneously alive in it. These schools proceed from utterly different, almost contradictory assumptions to equally different and opposed conclusions—yet they do not argue with each other. The conflict is not brought out into the open. There is no exchange; not much communication. The two go their own separate ways as if there were a gentlemen's agreement to keep quiet.

For the first school it is axiomatic that freedom is wonderful: freedom separates man from the beasts, and raises him above nature; it is the *sine qua non* of his distinguished position. Liberty gives a man a unique and incommensurate status which is lost to him when it is forfeited. His claim to it is indisputable for it constitutes and defines his being; it is the essence of his manhood. To gain it is more mandatory than all other conquests; to lose it is final defeat.

This is the more "official" tradition. It views freedom as satisfying, as the natural and obvious object of every man's longing. People, according to it, want freedom as spontaneously and directly as babies want milk. All political faiths, no matter how sharply they may disagree on other matters, subscribe to this view—though in very different fashions. All sides fight for freedom. Every conquest is a "liberation." Even the Nazis declared that they were for it.

The divergences between the various political canons seem no greater on this score than those between the sectarian creeds of one religion. All invoke the same ancient text: that freedom is desirable. If

1

politics occupies in the modern age the place that religion held in the Middle Ages—if it now furnishes the basic framework of orientation, the instruments of salvation, and the only ideas that match the power then possessed by their more theological antecedents—then freedom holds now in this new framework the place that was formerly occupied by Grace. Only by entering into the Kingdom of Freedom will the new man be born from the old Adam.

This view of freedom helps to paint the general picture of history, which still orders the world for us in a drama of progress. We think mankind is attaining ever greater freedom. It was Hegel who first developed this hope into a system. He depicted history as mankind's difficult advance towards its own liberation and he placed an immense and radiant value upon freedom. He did not see in history a gratifying, steady climb but rather thought it addicted to the exploration of blind alleys and the paying of monstrous prices. He thought it, in his own famous phrase, "the slaughterbench on which whole nations are sacrificed." Yet he believed that it was, in spite of the carnage and the waste, somehow justified and redeemed. Why? Because it did lead to freedom. Freedom sufficed. It merited the cost.

From this school also, we learned to make freedom the final standard of adjudication for the superiority of "our way of life," and of our institutions, even our superiority as human beings. We are free, that is why we are better. This is rock bottom. It ends the debate. And the origin as well as the rationalization of many foreign and domestic policies follow the same pattern. The last resort to which one takes recourse is that this or that stratagem promotes freedom. Everyone knows that this invocation is often hypocritical. But the fact that one acts the devotee of freedom when one is not, shows only how unquestioned and sacrosanct the value of freedom has become. "Give me liberty or give me death!" might be the emblem of this first tradition.

If one had to choose a single motto for the second tradition, one might pick the phrase "escape from freedom." In that school Sartre and Kierkegaard are prominent, but Dostoyevsky wrote the formulation which has become classical for modern writers. It is The Grand Inquisitor chapter of *The Brothers Karamazov* and we shall look at it more closely.

In this chapter Ivan tells Alyosha a parable which is set in the sixteenth century in Spain at the height of the Inquisition: Jesus returns for one day to this earth, the day after the Grand Inquisitor presided over a large-scale execution of heretics, a splendid, spectacular *auto-da-fe* in which almost a hundred misbelievers were burnt at the stake. The crowd recognizes Jesus, and has already burst into Hosannahs, when the Grand Inquisitor, knowing that it is Jesus, orders his guards to arrest him. That night the Grand Inquisitor visits Jesus in the inquisitorial prison, and by far the largest part of the story records the conversation that occurs between them, in which the Grand Inquisitor justifies himself and his Inquisition and even his arrest of Jesus to Jesus himself. The heart of his argument is that Jesus tried to set mankind free, but mankind does not want and cannot bear freedom. He, the Grand Inquisitor, therefore took this terrible gift from them out of compassion and out of mercy. The freedom that Jesus bestowed upon man was an affliction and a scourge. Man suffers from it and cannot sustain it. It makes demands upon him that he cannot meet. He does not possess the dimensions, the stature and the strength to endure it. What mankind really wants, what it craves is mystery and authority. "Man strives for nothing so incessantly and so painfully as to find someone to worship."

In essence the Grand Inquisitor poses a dilemma: One can either grant to mankind what it wants, although that dispensation will be degrading, or one can offer noble values, but then one has to be cruel. One has only a choice between a compassion that concedes to mankind the vulgarities for which it hankers—and a will to raise and lift it, which is ultimately brutal. It is impossible to give both happiness and dignity at the same time. Faced with this either/or, the Grand Inquisitor elects to be gentle, and grant all mankind the mystery, the authority, the object of worship, the servitude it wants. He knows that what he does and gives is revolting, but the fact that he renders himself repulsive is a gauge of his compassion. To give only what is still consistent with one's own immaculateness is too sparing. The Grand Inquisitor makes a more strenuous sacrifice and Jesus stands accused, charged with lukewarmness.

For this tradition the first basic ground rule is that the options open to us are split. The terms are: one or the other—but not both. In the novel Ivan's outrage against this basic premise renders him incapable of action. He is too noble to give mankind what it wants, but too sensitive to afflict it with high values. His refusal of this choice holds him in the stocks in which he is tortured. And this same dilemma was faced by a whole line of thinkers, all the way from Plato down to Sartre (*Dirty Hands*).

From the point of this bifurcation, Liberalism looks like an impossible insistence on having both; it links happiness and freedom, satisfaction and nobility so that there need be no choice. It is amazing that Liberalism usually treats this as completely obvious, that it talks as if there never had been any question. But there is, at the very least, a problem which has to be faced.

The choice which Ivan poses runs directly counter to a structural thought-pattern that had dominant importance during the Enlightenment and that still governs much of our thinking: in essence it holds that the defects of societies and men are in the last accounting due to man's repression, to one or the other of the ways in which man is held down. Liberation, therefore, is *the* answer, and the political question reduces simply to the question of how a maximum of freedom can be won. One operates on the assumption that there is no upper limit to the amount of freedom that each individual wants (and that is good for him), and one believes that the need for limits is entirely external. This means that society should impose only that minimum of restraints required to safeguard other people, and it also means that other people and society are primarily perceived as something that sets limits.

To attack this thought-pattern challenges not just the foundations on which Liberalism rests. It threatens the whole spectrum of political discussion, and crosses sharply even the main hope that underpins most revolutions. Take the famous closing lines of Trotsky's *Literature and Revolution*. Once the revolution has been won,

> Man will become immeasurably stronger, wiser and subtler; his body will become more harmonized, his movements more rhythmic, his voice more musical. The forms of life will become dynamically dramatic. The average human type will rise to the heights of an Aristotle, a Goethe, or a Marx. And above this ridge new peaks will rise.

Why did man not attain these peaks before? Because something actively prevented it. Once he is free of hindrances the ascent will happen almost by itself. The capacities were in man all along; they only needed room in which they could unfold.

This view of man sees him mainly thwarted. It believes that his nobility only has to be released. In Dostoyevsky's parable we confront a very different vision: one which sees in man both more fragility and more evil.

II

To bring these two traditions into contact with each other settles nothing and our reason for doing so is precisely the reverse: to unsettle a few dogmas about freedom. But the notion that servitude may be granted from compassion may still strike us as a mere hyperbole. We shrug it off. We know that people basically do want freedom.

But do they?

Dostoyevsky obviously did not mean trivial choices. The Grand Inquisitor says that it is the need for miracles, for mystery and authority that concerns him; it was the hunger for an object of worship that he sought to relieve. But is this hunger so great? One measure of its intensity is the fast rise of the psychoanalytic movement. Even if we set aside the issue of the scientific merit of Freud's ideas (and disregard the fact that many have used them to abrogate responsibility in favor of the mysteries of their own unconscious); even if we consider nothing but the popularity of psychoanalytic treatment, we still get some indication of that appetite. The sheer fact that so many people find it necessary to submit their lives to an inspection, that so many are impelled to display their intimacies for an appraisal, and precisely that they do this in spite of their doubts and reservations is evidence enough of the reality of that need.

Or take totalitarianism: We repeat phrases like "people need an identity" and "people want a definition of themselves" in an absent-minded way. Yet the desires are as palpable as those for sex and food. To get some sense of their reality and power one must remember what people are prepared to do—the kind of hunger, suffering and denials they accept for an "insignia," for a "name," a "title" (for a button to pin on their lapel), and also how the whole tone and rhythm of someone's life is changed, how he no longer walks in the same way, because now there is a phrase, or an image, that applies to him.

Once one has thought concretely about the "need for an identity," one's picture of how totalitarianism grows may be reversed. Customarily we imagine that two forces pull in opposite directions: the desire for freedom, and the fear of going hungry. We think that these conflict and that freedom sometimes loses out. But often this is not what actually occurs. When someone joins a severely regimented group, he does not usually do so by a cautiously conducted barter. Two things are not weighed against each other. The urgency is all in one direction. There is a feeling of relief, almost of exultation. Independence was not wanted, freedom was feared.

In some contexts we accept this as a platitudinous fact. When suburbia or fraternities are the topic, no one needs to be reminded that people in general want "to fit in," want "to be part of the group," want "to be accepted," that there is a herd for every lone wolf. And yet these banalities are barred from other contexts. Virtually every political, philosophical or moral discussion of freedom in the abstract assumes the very opposite: that men demand individuality and freedom, that only measures such as repression and brainwashing can begin to curtail these desires, and that men will rebel if freedom is not granted. We have again the same schizophrenic segregation, and here it is reinforced with semantics. Instead of saying bluntly that people do not want freedom, we say that people need a sense of solidarity and of communion, or at worst that they need to "conform." Desires contrary to freedom are given other designations, thus preserving the illusion that the appetite for freedom is unqualified and absolute. This compartmentalization is carried to such extremes that even the theoretical and historical explanations of modern totalitarianism rigidly adhere to it. In the analysis of totalitarian movements the major question usually is: What constrained a people at this point to yield up their freedom and to submit to a more dictatorial rule? But this question is probably malposed. It assumes that there is a natural tendency towards freedom and the "explanation" of totalitarianism becomes in effect a list of the pressures that overrode this tendency. This may be the wrong way round; if men in general do not desire freedom then the important question would be, What at this point weakened the imposition of individuality and freedom and what allowed the natural drive towards conformity to go unchecked?

There is no reason why a man who dreads retirement cannot be said to fear a kind of freedom, or why a middle-aged mother who clings to her children cannot be said to hold on to a kind of servitude. Part of what makes these crises painful is the discovery that the exigencies of a job or of raising children, which so far were experienced as confinements, in fact provided one's life with structure and coherence. The sense of futility, the exasperation at not having anything outside oneself that demands one's service, the whole experience of having to live "for oneself"—for nothing but the prolongation of one's own existence—these are all the effects of a kind of freedom. Even the most hyperbolic-seeming dicta suddenly sound straightforward once they are placed into such circumstances. Sartre has said that "we are condemned to be free," and in one of his plays Orestes says that "freedom crashed down upon him." If this were said by a man whose life's work has just been taken from him, we would understand it right away.

One last example. Consider how we invoke for our actions the support and the endorsement of abstractions. We have a penchant for acting "in the name" of something. If nothing plausible is close to hand, we reach out for airy, dubious notions; we become the shield-bearers of Progress, of Enlightenment, of Order, of Good Judgment. It is as if we need something, even if it has to be a half-discarded fancy, to which our act can be subordinated; something that will give it the guise of an instrument that performs a service. It is possible to look at morality in this perspective and to imagine it as a kind of last recourse: if all else fails, we still invoke its blank and stony categories and act at least in the name of Goodness. This whole phenomenon constitutes still a different stratagem with which we avoid freedom. That we become so cunning, and palliate the threat of an autonomous bare action with such disguises, shows how deep our fear of freedom really is.

III

The recognition that freedom in any of its definitions is not unequivocally desired moves us only one step closer to the possibility of a genuine rethinking. Our next and also still preliminary step must be the shedding of some further preconceptions.

We posit freedom and slavery as opposites. We imagine a polarity and think that liberty represents the one extreme and slavery the other. That makes the case for freedom categorical and simple. Who wants to be a slave? But is the difference between the master and his slave simply that one has freedom which the other lacks? Doesn't the master live in a mansion, and the slave in quarters? Doesn't the slave toil while the master drinks mint julep? Doesn't the master wield the whip that cuts the other's back? A preference for the master's life proves therefore very little about freedom.

It is the requirement of any scientific method to isolate the property that one is testing. This means that one at least should not compare a life that is unfree, but is also dreadful in other ways, to one that includes freedom yet is also greatly advantaged on other scores. Even the ABC of fairness and of rationality requires that the two lives should be on other counts at least approximately equal. So we should compare to the master someone with an easy life, with similar other benefits and then ask, how much better this life would become if we still added freedom, and how much worse if the rest were the same and only freedom were subtracted.

Or we could make the comparison to monks. In certain very rigorous orders the rules require not only chastity, but abstinence from most foods, nearly unbroken silence, complete submission to superiors, and a strict disciplining even of one's private thoughts. There is, without question, far less freedom in such a life than there is even in the lives of slaves, and yet the lives of monks are at least sometimes impressive.

(The objection that monks choose to forfeit their freedom meets first the counter-question, Do they indeed? How many entered monasteries because their parents took a vow? What of the threats posed by this and the other world? But in any case, even if there were a choice, and even if a Trappist monk were in some sense free to cast off his habit (and on the same terms one could also argue that a slave has the freedom to rebel), this would only reinforce the point: for precisely that someone might choose such a life, and might choose to forfeit his freedom shows that the loss of freedom alone does not reduce life to a horror.)

This has several implications: for one, it means that slavery is not equivalent to the absence of freedom. The two concepts do not stand at polar opposites, and slavery does not represent the end-point on a continuum of decreasing liberties. It is possible to have less freedom than is possessed by a slave. One example of this is the monk. Another illustration of it would be your tying me like a dog to a post in your backyard. That again would take more freedom from me than is taken from most slaves—and yet it would not make me your slave. It is only the deprivation of other things, less equivocal and more debilitating than the diminishment of freedom, that reduces a man to that condition.

The other side of this is very plain: if taking someone's freedom does not make him a slave, then merely giving him his freedom back is also not sufficient to terminate that degradation. Setting him free may in fact be the easiest and smallest part of what has to be done to restore a man from that position.

The habit of juxtaposing Master and Slave on the individual level has its counterpart on the level of societies. We pit the worst examples of totalitarianism (especially Hitler's and Stalin's) against the best representatives of free societies, and freedom wins again without a fight. The point is once more the same: the difference between Hitler's Germany or Stalin's Russia on the one side and Switzerland or Sweden on the other is not simply that people in the former were "unfree," whereas those in the latter are "free." Regardless of how freedom is understood there are other and very major differences. Hitler's Germany was racist, jingoistic, murderous, militaristic, anti-intellectual and bent on destruction. These qualities may have had more to do with its horrors than did the absence of freedom alone, and may have been what made that society "totalitarian." The "totalitarian" therefore is not simply the opposite of the "free." There have been societies that offered little freedom without practicing these other vices. Why not compare the free societies to those—e.g., to most "primitive" societies, to Sparta or Medieval China?

Another tacit sleight-of-hand, partial to freedom and performed just as routinely, has to do with causes and effects. In general everyone agrees that ideologies and institutions must be assessed in a historical and social setting. When we appraise religions, say Buddhism or Islam, this is often done with subtlety and brilliance. But when it comes to freedom we often drag one foot—on the side of the benefits we move with confidence but on the disadvantages we put very little weight. How far we lean to one side will become graphic if for once, just for an exercise, we bend the other way and rehearse some of the negative effects that the faith in freedom may have had.

The framework for this would of course have to be very large. To do it at all justly one might have to take a panoramic look at the whole development of Western culture and sketch something like the following picture:

Western, or the white man's civilization was not clearly dominant during Antiquity and the Middle Ages. It was essentially confined to the small peninsula of Europe and was not, all in all, more advanced than the Indian or the Chinese or some South American civilizations. It also did not exercise a political hegemony over these others. In fact for centuries it held its own only with great difficulty, and sometimes it fell short even of that, as when it failed to defend its own territory against extensive Slavic and Mohammedan advances. The fabulous and unparalleled rise of the West to supreme power obviously cannot be neatly dated, but in a general way it did coincide with the evolution and the progressive institutionalization of the ideals of individual independence, and with the genesis of the superior technology and of the economic system that were fostered by these ideals and that in turn reinforced them.

Hence one might have to count this technology and this economic system with both their positive and their negative sides among the more distant consequences of the belief in individual freedom. The same would be true of the diverse phenomena that are now subsumed under the idea of alienation. They, if anything, are more immediately connected, being nearly the other side of the same coin: if individuality is extolled and one insists on the prerogatives of one's privacy and of one's individual inclinations—if each person conceives himself as ringed round by a fence of rights—then one is bound to feel isolated. Alienation may be a completely inevitable by-product of "freedom," and discussions of the modern "loss of community" will be mawkish as long as they do not acknowledge that individuality and community do tend to exclude each other, that the space occupied by one will be taken from the other.

One could argue further that the stress on individuality in the modern technological society starves certain fundamental appetites, which then progressively accumulate till they break the gates that dammed them in. Once out of control they glut themselves in an orgy of social coherence and interpersonal integration. An untrammeled sense of communion overcompensates for the exasperation of a hedged-in private life. So totalitarianism, too, might have to be included in this accounting—not, of course, simply on the con side of the ledger, but in a way that represents the more extended causative connections. And from totalitarianism it is only a step to the disastrous wars that began as factional conflicts inside the West before they embroiled most of the world. They, too, could appear in this calculation, and the First World War no less than the Second. For, as many writers have shown, the First World War was actively desired by precisely that large class of people that had been most influenced by the ideals of individual freedom. Much of the European middle class was exultant when that war broke out. As with totalitarianism later, they saw in it a chance to escape from their confined, cautious, individual existences; their impatience had mounted slowly till it finally vented itself with unexpected force.

And with these wars we still have not mentioned the one fact that stands out like a tower for all those who judge this from the outside: the fact that the idea of individual freedom was an organic part of the culture that developed such capacities and such needs for expansion that it destroyed all other civilizations—some by annihilation, the rest by making them Western.

To see in these qualities of the West only "temporary aberrations," "accidents," "corrigible imperfections" is precisely the main device with which we slant this whole adjudication. What entitles us to the faith that the dark sides can somehow be omitted, that eventually nothing but what one hoped from freedom, and what one intended with that idea can be realized—without side-effects, and with no compensating losses? Why assume that the terrifying and daemonic features of the West are only incidental, temporary flaws? Their roots may be as deep as those of its magnificent achievements. Both, the splendid and the appalling, may be tied with equal strength to the idea of freedom.

In the end this could be one of the arch-reasons for the reluctance of other people to receive this gift from us—they are not apt to see in "freedom" an unalloyed, "pure" value, but rather, in our version of it, an organic arm of the West. And they are right. If it has made its contribution to our glories, then it also shares the responsibility for our crimes. It is not innocent. It lent a hand when the West made lepers of two-thirds of mankind.

Maybe a kind of story will give a first, approximate idea of the whys and wheretos of what is to follow:

Imagine a very isolated, meticulously cared for village. Everything is at right angles, not a stick is out of place. The people that inhabit it are much more civilized than ordinary peasants. Hundreds of years ago they spoke with very quiet and melodious voices, and now they have reached a point of delicacy that imposes almost complete silence. They do most of their communicating through exquisitely subtle ritual gestures. There are, let us say, at least a hundred different ways of shielding one's eyes from the sun and each one of them has its own meaning.

In the center of this village stands an ancient straw-thatched temple, and in that temple hangs an enormous gong of polished brass, large as the surface of a pond. When anything of concern to the whole village happens, if the river floods, or an enemy has crossed the border, or a cloud of grasshoppers casts a shadow, then someone runs to the temple, and after months and sometimes years of dignified severity and silence there rises then the booming of that gong. After the long quiet this noise produces a great shock. Some—admittedly, the most refined—fall to the ground, their arms vined round their heads. The rest tremble too much to be able still to execute their deaf-mute language gestures, and whispering in that noise is of course in vain. That makes it very difficult for anyone to find out why the gong is being sounded, and every threat, or enemy, or danger finds the village an easy half-lame prey.

The point is that the sound of "freedom" deafens us, as does that gong those peasants. If we want a general denominator, something that gathers up the multiple deficiencies of our own society, then to declare that "we are oppressed" has the same effect that the gong noise has in this story: it fills our ears till our minds go blank. Though our better knowledge may still tell us that this is somehow the wrong verdict, that it is at any rate not central, or not the diagnosis that we need, the force of it already ends the possibility of any genuine thinking. And it is the same if we want to know what we should aim for now, in what direction we should move. Then, too, the answer "towards greater freedom" does not tell us. Again that sound merely rises. Everyone joins in and, deafened, we still mouth that word, yet we all mean different things, and no intelligence or information is communicated.

It should be understood that it is not the intention of this writing to put a few grains of salt on the idea of freedom, nor is it to pull out of the hat yet another definition of what freedom "really" means. Rather, it is motivated by a strong suspicion that *the concept of freedom is not a fit instrument for thought.* The effort to come to a workable understanding of social matters is snared in the tangles of this notion. A guiding theory of society or of the state cannot be built upon the base of that idea. The point is therefore not to argue for or against the value of freedom. Instead we want to lead up to the recognition that this intellectual contest is badly posed, that it is a futile and tiresome rope-pulling. The goal, in short, is just the opposite from that of taking sides in the disputes involving freedom. It is rather to prepare for a way of thinking that does not stretch itself between the opposites that it marks out.

This does not mean that many of the things advocated, fought for and conceived under the idea of freedom were not good and great, and that likewise much that was conceptualized and understood as "oppression" was not really evil. It means rather that this idea serves no longer as a basis for evaluation and that we therefore need a new coordinating matrix in which things will receive their place. It means that the old reasons are no longer telling, and that what is Up and what is Down has to be rethought.

In the present situation most social thought lacks self-confidence. Most of us know in a numb and addled fashion that the foundations shift, that our feet keep sinking in, and we therefore struggle from one support that offers itself on the wayside to the next. There is very little independence, hardly any venturing out. No real structure that could carry its own weight let alone suggest new outlines (and lead up to and hold in place heavier conclusions) seems to take shape. The peculiar ambiguity of the idea of freedom has contributed to this debilitation, for it, on the one hand, postulated a goal and framework, while on the other hand it is such an altogether problematic notion that it gives neither guidance nor coherence. We don't advance beyond a casuistic game of blindman's buff. The idea of freedom has been like a hood that kept the falcon of thought on the leather glove. For it gives the illusion that we have a goal, that it is known, that there is a framework and that all is fairly understood—and so the major questions are not even asked.

2

A Theory of Freedom

WE NOW HAVE to shift gears. So far we have simply planted question-marks next to some commonly made root-assumptions and marked out ground that is debatable and problematic. From here on, however, we shall proceed in a more methodical and systematically progressive fashion, for now a Theory of Freedom is to be developed.

It should be clearly understood that the subject matter of our theory will in one sense not be freedom itself. The aim will be to explain the views that have been held concerning it. So far these lie about us in bewildering variety. The intention now is to move up one level in abstraction and to bring to light a logic and a lawfulness that governs the diversity of these interpretations, that orders their perplexing multiplicity. What we mean to propose is therefore in that sense a kind of meta-theory of freedom.

I shall start from an experience, partly to give the coming high abstractions a concrete reference point, but also for other reasons that will soon become apparent: there are moments in which we feel that our real life has not yet begun. The whole of our past seems like a long rehearsal. In different degrees it seems as if everything so far has been only "hypothetical," only one of many possibilities that we have considered, that it is not actual and final, and has not yet used up a part of our total time. Sometimes this feels as if we ourselves had not been the agents, had not been properly "inside" our life, but had observed it only, as spectators that saw it happen—impersonally, the evolution of an interplay of forces. It is as if a wooden counterfeit of ourselves went through the motions that are our past, and what we really are has all this time lain patiently ducked in a blind, waiting to make its move. Only a sudden entrance would at last bring the self—so far hidden

15

behind the scenes—on stage. And that would be our first real action, a kind of birth, the long-delayed beginning of our genuine life.

What would be required for the accomplishment of this is subject to quite opposite perceptions. Sometimes it seems as if it would be marvelously easy. We feel that everything could change between this breath and the next, that a new internal will would be sufficient, that one would only have to nod, say yes, and one would step as through the opening of a curtain. But much more often it seems discouragingly difficult. All ordinary measures seem inadequate. It is as if we had to make an absolutely new beginning that cannot happen here but only on some other side to which we must cross over; as if this new start had to be purified from every connection with the present since any continuity with our past would compromise it. Then we dream of utterly fantastic extrications, we want the life of a beachcomber, or of a hermit, or to join the Foreign Legion. Paradoxical and mad, it seems that only such a drastic cut, only something so wild and unheard of would finally be "real," as if only such a far-flung act would bring at last one's hidden self to the outside.

The anguish and the frenzied search for an impossible determination that come with this experience, gain plausibility if we concentrate on the manner in which the self is unavoidably conceptualized when it occurs. When the experience is intense we feel disconnected from everything we are. Not only our past, but even our present thoughts and feelings, seem somehow apart from us, strange, like things we observe. But when so much has been "split off" and made an "object," then hardly anything remains for the self that does the observing. If the self disassociates itself from its own constitutents, then it has reduced itself to something insubstantial, to nothing but a point— the point from which the rest is seen. The base from which I then experience, the domain that I genuinely feel to be my-"self" has then shrunk to almost nothing, and it is this that renders the sense of isolation and bereftness commensurately absolute.

As a first example we shall set a most unqualified and drastic view of freedom against the feel of this experience. It is this extremity which makes it theoretically instructive. One could think of it on the analogy to a limiting case in mathematics. The substance of this general conception occurs in many places but a particularly evocative expression of it can again be found in Dostoyevsky, this time in *Notes from Underground*.

In the first half of that work, in which the taunted, ever-pacing, little government official records his philosophy of spite, there is a passage in which Dostoyevsky brings that part of the novel to a concentrated, pitched summation. His clerk explains that only an act of sheer caprice, performed in total independence, in rebellion against every consideration of advantage or of reason, has a genuinely metaphysical dimension. He proclaims it as the *summum bonum*. Nothing else gives man true freedom. Only such an act breaks through the neutral shell of anonymity that holds man captive. In this way alone can man achieve uniqueness and establish his distinction. Without it the self has no more identity or definition than one egg has among a dozen.

This clerk has a friend of whom he says: "When he prepares for any undertaking, this gentleman immediately explains to you, elegantly and clearly, exactly how he must act in accordance with the laws of reason and truth. What is more, he will talk to you with excitement and passion of the true moral interests of man; with irony he will upbraid the shortsighted fools who do not understand their own interests, nor the true significance of virtue; and within a quarter of an hour, without any outside provocation, but simply through something inside him which is stronger than all his interests, he will go off on quite a different tack—that is, in direct opposition to the laws of reason, in opposition to his own advantage, in fact in opposition to everything."

In a frenzy of exasperation Dostoyevsky's clerk turns on all the "sages, statisticians, and lovers of humanity," on all the wise and calculating system-builders, and flings against their efforts his one, but to his mind, shattering objection. All their rationally founded, carefully constructed edifices fall to the ground, so he insists, for, in their enumeration of the ends and goods that man pursues, one aim and one desideratum has been invariably omitted. And it, ironically, is the most important; it is "the most advantageous advantage." This boon which is "more important and more advantageous than all other advantages" consists precisely in acting "in opposition to all laws; that is, in opposition to reason, honour, peace, prosperity—in fact in opposition to all those excellent and useful things," it consists in "one's own free unfettered choice, one's own caprice, however wild it may be, one's own fancy worked up at times to frenzy." "What man wants is not 'a virtuous,' 'normal,' or 'rationally advantageous' choice. What man wants is simply *independent* choice, whatever that independence may cost, and wherever it may lead."

That the representative expression of this idea of freedom did not occur in a classic philosophic text, but instead had to be taken from a novelist like Dostoyevsky should not be surprising. Even those philosophers who limit the capacities of reason are not apt to identify freedom only with those acts that offend against it. In works of literature, however, close variants of this idea are encountered fairly often (e.g., in Blake, or in Gide—the gratuitous act; or in D. H. Lawrence). What is more, if there is such a thing as a basic experiential meaning associated with the idea of freedom, then it is not far from the Undergroundman's view—and literature is of course more likely to preserve this raw sense than are more cautious philosophical definitions. The idea of being totally unbounded, of yielding to no authority whatever (not even to that of reason), of acting without any encumbrances—that image seems close to the root-experience of freedom, and captures some of its original appeal. And since a distant memory of this expectation still glows behind all talk of liberation, we have begun from it.

The import of this idea of freedom can be grasped more firmly if the several ways in which it represents an outer limit, a maximum, are specified in detail:

It is not only that in all his unfree actions man is like a puppet, pulled by the string of the laws—"the damnable laws"—of nature and of reason, so that he is a "piano key," indifferent, anonymous, dependent, while only the act of whim, the capricious act is different, it alone creating the possibility of uniqueness and self-definition—there is also the extreme insistence that freedom requires that rationality be violated. On this score this notion bears resemblance to the stance that a son might take when he struggles for independence from his father. To a son mere "independence," the fact of making his own decision, also might not seem sufficient. He experiences "real" freedom only when he moves in direct opposition to his father's wishes. It is as if nothing short of demonstrated freedom meets his standards. This is an essential facet of the Undergroundman's position, for without it the "system and the theories" would not be "shattered to atoms." This only happens because freedom for him consists precisely in actions "directly opposite" to reason, and because this freedom is the most "advantageous advantage."

This idea of freedom touches still another outer, not-to-be-transcended limit when he advocates this contrariety to reason not in the name of a spontaneity which too much rationality might damage, and also not for the sake of an emotion, or a sensibility, but as an absolute and final end.

To this one could still add that the transgression of rationality represents an unexceedable condition in yet another sense: one could see sheer reason as the last, and least burdensome of all "constraints"; to rear up *even* against it then represents a kind of measure. If the mere presence of a reason for it renders an act less than free, then what will count? Only an act that materializes out of nothing. It is as if there could be no context whatsoever, as if an action could be "free" in that sense only in the specious presence of creation—when God said: Let there be light.

This version of freedom obviously provokes numerous questions, but for the moment we shall not consider how this concept could possibly be justified against other rival claims concerning freedom, or whether anyone in seriousness could place such an extravagant value on the exercise of the blindest and most obstinate caprice. We shall instead concentrate on one single issue: What is the *experience* presupposed by this idea of freedom? What general relationship must a man have to "reason" if this concept is to be true for him? How, in other words, must he experience the thoughts that in a given case suggest to him the "sensible" or the "judicious" course, if the adoption of this course is then "unfree," is mere obedience and servility?

To pose this question is to know how it has to be answered. The affirmation of the Undergroundman that one must act contrary to reason to be free presupposes that he experiences his rationality as something other than himself. I do not mean that he literally believes his own thoughts to be someone else's (that would be insane), but if he submits to coercion when he obeys his thoughts then there must be a sense of distance, a sense that they are not intimately part of his own person. His reason can make him unfree only if it is not included in his own real self. There has to be a degree of disassociation. He must experience his rational thoughts as somehow "on another side"; as "objects" for a "subject," as "things" that he encounters and confronts.

And this is true of Dostoyevsky's humiliated, spiteful, ineffectual clerk. In all sorts of situations his reason gives him sensible advice: not to force his way into the dinner party of his friends, where he is not wanted, where he will be grotesquely out of place, where he is bound to cause embarrassment and be the butt of every joke; not to persist in his protracted search for vengeance against the officer who "moved him aside" in the pool hall. But it is always the same. He experiences this "reasonableness" as only yet another bridle out to tame him (in fact it is the most insidious hindrance, for it is the enemy inside his camp); and so he hears it out with fascination, but then runs on against it with all his gathered force, bursts through it, and does precisely the very thing against which he has been warned. In his perception these rational counsels ultimately do not speak for him. They pronounce the interest of society, or something even vaguer, the judgments of order and of lawfulness. Forces out to overwhelm him, to crush his individuality, speak to him in a voice disguised as his own. Thus they are dictates and constraining orders, not issued by him, but inflicted on him and imposed. To follow them is still to be led on a leash. His reason conveys to him at most the ways in which impersonal considerations affect and balance and outweigh each other. By acting in accord with it he would therefore but transmit their neutral and indifferent resolution. He would still remain but an anonymous passivity, an inertness submitting to a pressure.

It would be wrong to think of the Undergroundman's experience as bizarre and unheard of, and to imagine that anything so strange could only have small bearing on the normal and familiar. On the contrary; the point is very much that he exemplifies in a strong fashion a syndrome which in milder forms is known to all of us, and which is everyday and even humdrum. One very common situation, in which we, too, experience our thinking as an objective process that happens at a distance from us, occurs when we lie awake after a party or after an examination and cannot fall asleep because now, at 3 a.m., our mind comes up with all the clever repartee and superbly telling answers which earlier it withheld. If our thoughts, enamored with their productivity, get ever more excited and chatter, while the clock moves on to 4, then nothing is more natural than for us to turn on them, and to tell them to "shut up!" Soon they might as well come from a record that goes on and on beneath the bed, and as the babble grows more distant we at last might fall asleep.

During such a night we, too, experience our thoughts as events which we observe, which seem to happen at a distance from us and are not really thought by ourselves. And this is not unusual or odd. Something quite similar happens at every moment when we find it hard to concentrate. For our thoughts then also seem to go in their own directions, and not to be controlled by us.

But there are also more extreme and memorable cases: take the last few seconds when you for the first time get ready to parachute down from a plane. You have practiced every gesture many times, and resolved days ago not to pull back in the last moment, and all the likely psychological reactions were rehearsed in advance. If your mind, in the minutes of the last approach, predictably starts to flutter like a frantic bird, then you again might disassociate yourself from it. Perhaps you listen to it briefly with bemused detachment, but then you shut the door on its small cell, and place yourself into the hands of your body, so that its instructed reflexes can take command. You jump, feel yourself fall, and return to your mind only when you land with a thud.

Yet consider two additional illustrations: You are pushing your cart through a supermarket, weary after a hard day, and inexorably the jingle "It's the real thing" jangles in your head, till, drowsy, you suddenly find yourself before an opened cooler with your hand already on a Coke. Or, to make the point still clearer: Imagine that you had been hypnotized, and that awake now, you obey the order to drink six glasses of water in succession, and assume that you were not instructed to feel thirsty, but to merely have the thought that you must perform this action.

This should set the key connection into strong relief. In both of these situations you would experience your thoughts as not quite your own—just like the Undergroundman—and you would also realize—again just like the Undergroundman—that you would have to "go against them" in order to be free.

Still another parallel to the Undergroundman's extreme idea of freedom appears in a scene in the film made after the life of T. E. Lawrence. It occurs in the last third of the film when Lawrence is already in command of a small but formidable Arab army with a long string of brilliant exploits to its credit. After a temporary setback Lawrence is in the process of preparing a major and well-planned campaign that promises defeat to the Turks and glory and loot to his men. He needs troops, however, and the scene narrates his interview with a proud tribal leader. In its course Lawrence tries out reason after reason on the chieftain. "Your fame will spread far if you join me. There will be much money. This is your long-sought chance to get even with the

Turks. Together we will lead your people out of their servility. We will lift them up out of their obeisance. You can be the father of a new, proud nation." The Arab sits unmoved and distant. Disdainfully he shakes his massive head to each of these reasons. But he knows full well what force they have, and he feels it. His gesture is a refusal, a fending off; really the sign of his determination not to surrender to their power. Eventually Lawrence's arsenal is exhausted. He has given every reason and all have been parried by the same shaking of the head. So both men sit through a silence, till Lawrence is just at the point of rising and taking his curt leave. Then at last the chief speaks: "I will join you," he says, "but not for fame, nor for money; not even for my people. Not for any of the reasons you have offered. I will do it, but only because it is my whim." This man acts in fact not against but with reason. Yet he tries to shroud this, to present it as a mere coincidence. If the action were the result of reason, it would be forfeited. Then he would only be the servant who does what he must do. So he insists that it was gratuitous, a mere whim. In this way he attempts to isolate his action from all outside forces, to give it autonomy and the guise of having come from nothing. He sets it free and thereby makes it more his own.

The generic view of freedom just examined is obviously "late." Housed in deep subjectivity, its gloomy flamboyance and desperate extravagance is the final variation on a theme that recapitulates in brilliant willfulness once more the otherwise abated impulse. We turn now to the opposite point on this horizon and look to the beginning, to a very early, still rough, and therefore all the more revealing philosophic presentation of a view of freedom.

It was the most tantalizing, the most Socratic of Socrates' paradoxes that set the stage for Plato's engagement with the problem of "free" action. With splendid irony Socrates had cast his perhaps most upsetting doctrine into the formula of an apparent platitude: "No one errs voluntarily." What could be more innocent or less controversial? Who could possibly object to that? And yet, seen differently this seeming tautology articulates the essence of a view concerning man's relationship to evil that is anything but bland. Its implications make this very clear. If no one "errs voluntarily" then all evil (all wrong action) is the result of error or of a *force major*. So it in truth lays down the radical assumption that the "natural" impulse of all men is always in the direction of the good—for nothing less would guarantee that man acts badly only when he is deceived or forced.

Socrates' deceptively innocuous formula dispenses in reality a universal exculpation: none are truly guilty. All are victims of ignorance or of coercion. How very untautological this dictum in truth is becomes still more apparent if we compare it to Christian ideas, such as Calvin's "elect," or Luther's "not through works but through faith alone," which embody the very opposite assumption that man's "natural" impulse and even action is to no avail.

The essential benevolence and "charity" of his position was possibly not more important to Socrates than the subtle implication that knowledge, and particularly the knowledge he communicated, knowledge of the Good, is then of cardinal importance, since once man has this knowledge the good will be invariably done, unless there is coercion. This must have delighted Socrates' sense of the ironic.

That this idyllic vision, in which freedom and knowledge together suffice to make man good, accompanied the birth of freedom and of knowledge had portentous consequences for the later histories of both. But our concern is with the importance that Socrates' paradox had for Plato.

We know that Plato executed his philosophic enterprise amid a great shifting of values. The ethic that for us is still exemplified in Homer's poems, a structure of virtues appropriate for a warlike feudal people, who are not yet comfortably settled, no longer fitted the Athenian city-state. Its plausibility had faded and new requirements were making themselves felt. Prowess, incontrovertible success, no matter how it was achieved, had been indispensable for the survival of the older agrarian society, which was more susceptible to external threats, and these qualities therefore had been elevated to the rank of virtues. In the old ethic the estimation of one's peers, and reputation generally, had counted for much: it represented the gratitude bestowed by this society on those who visibly excelled on its behalf; it inspired feats of daring and magnificence. But now, in the polis, other virtues were required. Order, dependability and internal cohesion had to be enhanced, and the emphasis turned to the "quiet virtues," pre-eminent among them Justice.

Two circumstances attendant on this change require particular attention. There is, first, the fact that the more ancient values of warlike excellence and visible success carry "their own reward" quite obviously with them. They still do this for us, if somewhat less conspicuously than they did for the Greeks. The desire for the goals that they extoll is indeed so "natural" that no further elaborate justification seems required, more particularly not, if they have the support of long and colorful traditions. With respect to these values one could truly say that "no one errs voluntarily." No one would *on purpose* aim at weakness, or incompetence, or degradation, and voluntarily prefer failure to success—that indeed could pass for an innocuous or tautological assertion. But with the newer values of the polis, it is at least not obvious that orderly behavior, honesty and justice are always "naturally" satisfying, especially not when they require sacrifices. It is not at all evident that no one falls short of these new values voluntarily. These values require, therefore, a justification in a sense in which the earlier values did not.

The second difference concerns the matter of "visibility." The older values of excellence and success required actions that were in essence public, that displayed themselves to spectators and glittered in the sun. Not so the newer ethics of the polis. Justice and honesty demand adherence even when they are not seen, when no one else is present. They must dispense with the enticements of "reputation," and this makes their justification at once more necessary and more difficult. (Hence Gyges' ring in *The Republic*.)

The complexity of Plato's involvement with the Socratic paradox and with the notion of freedom implied by it should now take shape. In essence Plato made this paradox the one main premise of his superb attempt to construct the sorely needed philosophic justification of the newer, quiet virtues. His strategy was natural, perhaps the only one available to him. His principal design was simply to bridge the gap between the old and new, to show that the same rationale that had patently applied to the old values, was still true for the new—though in a subtler way. It became his aim to demonstrate that justice and the quiet virtues were in the end as "naturally" desired as were success and excellence, that considered deeply they too "were their own reward," that rightly understood one would no more "voluntarily" fall short of them than one would "freely" seek disgrace and failure. The Socratic dictum was thus the Archimedean fixed point around which the whole undertaking of justifying the new values was to turn.

Thus Plato in essence substituted the new for the old values in the

Socratic paradox. He shifted its meaning from the idea that men freely pursue honor and magnificence to the quite different notion that they freely follow justice. In this way he created the appearance that the new morality was not a requirement exacted by society but represented only what men "really" want. In the process he in effect imposed a false psychology. He sacrificed an accurate perception of man's actual desires to provide the new values with an air of being natural and justified—and the results of this are still around us.

This stratagem laid the base for the single idea of freedom which had more influence than all the rest, for now freedom was linked to the good, and only one small further step was needed to reach the notion that man is free when he acts in harmony with reason and unfree when he violates it. For Plato this was perhaps no step at all, since virtue and rationality were for him most closely linked. ("Virtue is a species of knowledge.") In any case, the idea that one is free in following reason often underlies even the details of Plato's exposition. To give one example, in *The Republic* (Book IX) Socrates poses the question "To begin with the state, is it free under a despot or enslaved?" and receives the answer that under a despot a state is of course enslaved. Then he continues "If the individual then is analogous to the state, we shall find the same order of things in him: a soul laboring under the meanest servitude, the best elements in it being enslaved, while a small part, which is the most frenzied and corrupt plays the master. And just as a state enslaved by a tyrant cannot do what it really wishes, so neither can a soul under a similar tyranny do what it wishes as a whole. Goaded on against its will by a strong desire, it will be filled with confusion and remorse. Like the corresponding state, it must always be poverty-stricken, unsatisfied and haunted by fear. Nowhere else will there be so much lamentation and groaning and anguish as in a country under despotism, and in the soul maddened by the tyranny of passion and lust." The point here is that a soul dominated by a passion or lust is as tyrannized and enslaved (as unfree) as a state is under despotism. That a soul governed by reason is in contrast free is clearly the intended other side of the same coin. (And it is easy to cross again from this side of the analogy back to the state and to conclude that the state, too, is free when reason—the philosopher-king—governs it.)

Customarily the idea that freedom is obedience to reason is attributed to Hegel and this makes it easy to treat it as the sophistry of a "metaphysician" who was supposedly "conservative." But this thought is not so easily exorcised (nor for that matter is Hegel). For one thing the same idea occurred previously in Plato, and also in a host of other thinkers including Rousseau (dearer to liberal hearts than either Plato or Hegel), who in the *Social Contract* says quite flatly: "For to be subject to appetite is to be a slave. while to obey the laws laid down by society is to be free." But more importantly, this connection between freedom and rationality with its built-in guarantee that the exercise of the irrational and unacceptable will from the start not count as free, is basic to the force and history of the idea of freedom. That presumption, together with its counterpart that freedom only means the freedom to be reasonable, gave much of its power and persuasiveness to that idea. Without that tacit understanding it would have been much harder for a subject to make his claim to freedom legitimate, and were it not for that guarantee rulers would have been even more reluctant to grant it or furnish it.

The degree to which this conception is still central to our view of freedom can be gauged from the ease with which we say that freedom is of course not license, and that its counterpart is patently responsibility. These and other similar clichés would be without foundation on anything like the first paradigm of freedom we examined. If freedom is "caprice" then it most definitely does not end where "license" starts, and responsibility on that earlier view is not the condition but the death of freedom. These assurances hold only if something like the present view of freedom is presupposed. And that is some indication of just how pervasive and extended this view is.

Yet the roots of this view go even further down. It is implicit in many everyday experiences and also in much common language. If a man struggles against a temptation and loses (say, he does not want to drink, but ends up drinking), we quite naturally think of him as under a coercion. We might say: he did not want to drink, but his thirst was stronger, and it made him do it. This is so much the normal way of talking that it slips by us and arouses no attention. But it should, for it is really very curious. When we say "He did not want to drink, his thirst overcame him," we nonchalantly split one thing in two. We speak of the man and of his thirst as if the thirst were a separate thing. In a sense we do even more: there is one person who has made a resolution and who is also thirsty. These two attributes have equal status. But we arbitrarily end this equilibrium. We transfigure the resolution into *him*. He is nothing but this good intention and for it he receives full credit. The thirst, on the other hand, is sent to limbo. It is a bad, independent thing that he encounters and fights, like St. George the dragon. There could be no question of his "defeat" or of his suffering "coercion" if something like this were not envisioned.

Plato's view has its base in this sort of experience—and it is a matter of experience and not just of language, for we experience the thirst as something against which we struggle. One could conceive of Plato's principle as a generalization, as an inductive inference that moves from these experiences to the whole sphere of passion and of reason. In all probability there also occurred some interaction: this way of experiencing temptations very likely exercised some influence on Plato, but his authority in turn reinforced and spread the custom of this kind of thinking. Plato helped to make it "normal."

And the same holds for morality. We as a matter of course hold a man more responsible for premeditated crimes than for "crimes of passion" and we accordingly punish the former more severely than the latter. Again we say: "He was not responsible, his passion got the better of him" and this too sounds entirely natural and normal. Yet it again is actually very curious for on either of the two most current theories of punishment, those of deterrence and reform, one could argue that our practice should be precisely the reverse. Surveys might show that punishments for crimes committed after long and careful thinking are not nearly as effective as penalties for acts done in a fit of passion. Punishments might change people's passions more than their thinking—especially if the punishments come quickly. If this were so, we should be held more responsible and punished more severely for crimes of passion than for premeditated felonies. In terms of reform or deterrence this would only be consistent. But we refuse to do this, and to reverse the relative severity of punishments in this way would be morally repulsive to us. Yet why am I more responsible for premeditated acts and less responsible for acts of passion? Why is an act more mine when I have thought about it and less mine when I do it in anger? The anger is me too—it may be more me than is my thinking. The answer is that we here, too, assume something similar to Plato's notion; and in this case again some interaction probably took place: this manner of holding men responsible in all likelihood exercised some influence on Plato, but he in turn lent his authority to it and thereby reinforced this "habit."

This element in everyday experience and morality represents the bedrock—maybe the sandstone—on which this second view of freedom ultimately rests. All of its variously shaded formulations are supported by this common ground. Without it Plato never could have shifted the Socratic paradox to its new meaning, and if that base had not been there, freedom and rationality could not have been linked together.

Now that we have a crude sketch of a second, very different "theory" of freedom we can address to it the same single question that we earlier put to our first example. Then we faced the extreme insistence that an act is only free if it is "completely independent," and we selected one element from this sweeping notion, the part which requires that a free act must be contrary to reason, and asked how a person would have to *experience* his own reason for this to be true. Now we have before us the exact denial of this proposition. An act, according to the present, philosophically far more prestigious notion, is free only when it is rational (even though it "obeys" reason), and we are unfree precisely when rationality is violated, we are "enslaved" when a passion or an appetite leads us to irrational behavior.

The simple-sounding, yet crucial, question now is again: What experience is presupposed by this position? Under what conditions would this double-claim (if rational then free, if contrary to reason then coerced) be not only plausible but true? How, in short, would a person have to experience his own reasoning if he is to be always free when he acts according to it, and always unfree when he goes against it? And further, what experience of all else that can prompt actions (e.g., of motives, passions and desires) must someone have if he is always unfree when these other forces sway him against reason?

Let me quickly interject before we answer this that the claims involved are of course far from obviously true. Why should an act be "free" just because it is in congruence with reason? Or "coerced" because it is irrational? It is not at all apparent why there should be any such connection, why one should in any way affect the other. More particularly, why should it be impossible for the dictates of reason ever to oppress us? For it is an essential part of this view of freedom that this cannot happen, that reason can govern the passions, the will and the conduct of the whole person, without any risk that it will ever tyrannize us.

How extraordinary this contention actually is becomes more evident if we recall that Hegel (in his early writings on Christianity, and in the *Phenomenology*), and also the German playwright and essayist Schiller, conducted a polemic against Kant's ethic for the very reason that Kant had insisted on resolute conformity to the imperatives of "practical reason"—very much with the understanding that in obeying reason one was of course free. Both Hegel and Schiller argued that Kant had invested reason with tyrannical powers; that he had split man in two, and had sold the larger part of man into slavery under the lordship of reason. They went on to say that this form of slavery was uniquely vicious since it divided man against himself and degraded him completely, making one half tyrant and the other slave.

But back to our question: What experience of reason would render all my rational acts free? The answer again is hard to miss. Clearly there is only one condition which would make this the case: I would have to experience my own rationality (or, if this is clearer, the dictates of rationality when I apply them to myself) in a fashion that is the exact reversal of the Undergroundman's—therefore, not as an impersonal voice that imposes alien commands on me, but precisely as that which speaks most truly and authentically for me. I will be free in following the requirements of reason, no matter what they are, *only* if reason and I are one and the same. Then it is obviously impossible for it to oppress me.

On the other side, all my deviations from the rational course will be coercions suffered by me only on the condition that whatever prompts them is experienced as somehow other than me. Everything that is dissonant from reason, that inveighs against it, must be disassociated from me, must be something that I encounter and confront. Then I will be the victim in every case where anything other than reason prevails.

The mutual dependency between this concept of freedom and this structural division of experience is a simple logical connection. It would hold even if no one had actually ever advocated this idea of freedom. And it alone is crucial to our enterprise. The fact that all kinds of variations on this view have played their roles in the history of philosophy (and one could mention others besides Plato, Rousseau, Kant or Hegel), and moreover that it corresponds to one sense of freedom that frequently crops up in everyday experience and language adds enormously to the interest of this example. But the main evolving argument does not hinge on this. It is concerned only with this view as a general type. In the various historical philosophies this view naturally does not appear in its simple, clear-cut essence. But the details of just how Plato or Rousseau (the General Will) or Hegel shaped and qualified the straight lines of this "model," or of how on its chessboard pattern the controversies of "positive" versus "negative" freedom, or of freedom versus license were played out will be discussed when we are ready for them. For now I will only mention one example to give some idea of the explanatory power of this postulated pattern.

Consider Plato's well-known hierarchy of the human faculties in which reason is assigned the highest place, since reason raises man above the rest of nature and only its full exercise renders a man truly human. Here reason is the quintessence of the human; the emotions and the body belong distinctly to a lower order. This attitude towards reason clearly matches the presupposition which we discovered independently behind the general view of freedom implicit in Socrates' paradox. On the one hand this could be regarded as a kind of confirmation. We argued that a certain view of freedom presupposed a certain experience of reason, and it now turns out that Plato, who held this view of freedom, also maintained the corresponding view concerning reason. It is a little as if we had made a prediction that now has come true. But we could also regard it as an explanation, as affording us a deeper insight into Plato. We can now see how two seemingly separate parts of his thinking fit together. The placement of reason at the apex of the hierarchically arranged parts of man is now connected to the tenet that man is never free when he knowingly commits an evil or irrational act. These two contentions can now be regarded as expressions of a single underlying view.

To stress and fix more firmly the single major point at issue we might have recourse to a simple diagram. The heart of the argument so far has been the proposition that reason must be experienced as one's most intimate and truest self if all rational acts are to be free, and that conversely, all other parts of a person, such as the desires, the body and the passions, must be experienced as "once removed" if all actions prompted by them are to be coerced.

We can represent this in terms of two concentrically drawn circles (diagram below). For the moment we could say that this pictures the self-image, or better, the *identification* which this view of freedom, traced back by us to Plato, presupposes.

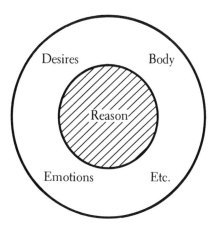

 Area of identification; locus of "true self"; origin of free actions

But a third conception of freedom waits for us. This one has a plain and homespun quality. Without subtle iridescence, it is made of un-deceptive cloth, meant for hard use. Like the other two it is a generic type that appears in a multitude of species-variations which qualify the outlines of this prototype. Most fundamentally it draws the line be-tween the free and the coerced in what appears to be the crudely obvious place: you are coerced if forces literally external to your person compel your action; you are free if this is not the case, if what you do is controlled or prompted by yourself. This rough-hewn idea of freedom of course again crops up in countless places. Its cleaver cuts the joints of practical, everyday decisions, its guidelines are invoked in court to govern legal determinations of innocence and guilt, and one could naturally cite no end of literary and of philosophic places in which it has been discussed. But one of the first and also most revealing treat-ments of it occurs in Aristotle.

In the *Nicomachean Ethics,* in the second paragraph of Book III, Aristotle defines "the compulsory" as "that of which the moving prin-ciple is outside, being a principle in which nothing is contributed by the person who is acting or is feeling the passion." And he reiterates this a page later: "What sort of acts should be called compulsory? We answer that without qualification, actions are so, when the cause is in the external circumstances and the agent contributes nothing." We, in other words, are coerced only when "the moving principle" of an action is physically or literally outside us, and we are free if that moving principle has been contributed by us.

Compare this to the other two ideas of freedom. On the first version the freedom of an act was already spoiled if it was conditioned by anything at all. Its claim was most demanding and therefore also most easily transgressed. To be truly gratuitous an act had to materialize as if from nothing; even mere rationality disqualified it and therefore even reason needed to be crossed. The "Platonic" conception was one step less extreme. If a desire or a passion or any other force controlled one's action, then it was "tyranny." Only reason was exempted and we found that this was possible only because reason was thought to be the most authentic self. Our third example, the "Aristotelian" view (I only use this designation for easy reference; it is not the only view that can be found in Aristotle, any more than the just-discussed position was always held by Plato), is once more, less restrictive, but now by several degrees. On its interpretation the "moving principle" of an action can be not only reason but anything belonging to the agent, and as long as this is true the act will still be free. It does not become "coerced" until the moving principle lies literally outside the person of the agent.

If we now ask for the third time our peculiar question about the *experience* on which this latest meaning of freedom seems to be predicated, then the answer is once again as patent as before. If the Undergroundman could secure freedom only by transgressing reason, and if this was so because he experienced reason as something that society imposed upon him, so that even his own rational thinking was not truly part of him but measured only the depth to which he had been invaded; and if on the "Platonic" view rationality becomes the very opposite, the guarantee of freedom because rational thought is now experienced as the only faculty that is truly *self*, then the "Aristotelian" view clearly presupposes that no parts of the acting subject are experienced as "alien," as belonging to the self in some lesser sense, part of it but still at one remove from what one "truly" is. Only if all parts of oneself are equally accepted as one's own can all the actions that flow from one's whole person be free, and only those actions whose moving principle is outside be coerced.

And once more we find that Aristotle himself in fact held this view. In the first section of Book III of the *Nicomachean Ethics* he says, "The irrational passions are thought not less human than reason is, and the actions which proceed from anger or appetite are therefore the man's actions."

This statement flatly denies Plato's disparagement of the irrational passions, emotions and appetites. It attacks Plato's hierarchy of the human faculties which gave primacy to reason and relegated the passions to an inferior state. In fact it almost sounds like a direct response to Plato. It is as if Aristotle had marked out a major difference that distinguishes his own position from that of his teacher. To say that "the irrational passions are not less human than reason"creates an equality that to ears that had heard Plato must have been blasphemy. For Plato had dubbed reason "divine" and to pronounce even the irrational passions as on a par with reason meant that hogs now fraternized with gods.

This again constitutes a kind of confirmation. As in the case of Plato, we decided independently that a certain theory of freedom presupposes a conception, or a manner of experiencing the self, and now we find that Aristotle did indeed hold the corresponding view. We argued that his view of freedom required the equal acceptance of all elements in a person, and it now turns out that this was indeed the attitude he advocated. But the important point is once more that this illustrates a logical connection which would exist even if Aristotle had failed to observe it. The idea that we can be coerced only by external forces but are free if the moving principle is inside us inherently requires that the passions and the appetites are not banished to some outer sphere from which they invade us. Why should they always play the part of the opposing forces, and why should we (*we* being suddenly nothing but a pure intention and a high resolve) be only the innocent victims of their alien power? This view in the same way necessitates that reason be demoted, that the claim to its hegemony be discounted as a snobbish prejudice. Only one attitude is consistent with this idea of freedom: namely that everything about us is equally human. We are not only our reason but all the rest is part of us as well, and has equal status. We are all of our elements and none of these is less *us* than others. There are no gradations. It is reminiscent of Sartre's "You are the totality of your actions," except that this attitude goes further. Why single out actions? You are just as much your deceptions, fears, hopes, hesitations, feelings and your body. None can be written off.

This way of relating to oneself seems so natural and so attractive and somehow so right ("we are obviously our total self, it is simply self-deception, or neurosis to think otherwise") that one is tempted to conclude with premature relief that this is the "correct" relationship to one's experience, and that the corresponding view of freedom is therefore "true," that it tells us what freedom "really" means.

Only to indicate how very far we are from this (we still have to climb up a whole level of abstraction) we should look at the other side. For this view actually runs into sharp conflict precisely with common sense. In effect it denies the phenomenon of compulsion, and not just in a technical, say Freudian, sense, but even in the very ordinary and old-fashioned meaning. On this position the excuse "I could not help it" can never be invoked when an act "originated from within the person." The other side of what at first seems to be no more than the welcome democratization of the parts of man is that we now have only one and the same relationship to all of our actions, that we are equally responsible for all of them. And this increase in guilt is at least a disadvantage or a difficulty that all those attracted to this view must face, and it in turn illuminates the motives that underlie the alternative contentions.

In the particular case of Aristotle one could conjecture that this implication was most unwelcome to him. Conceivably he thought of the equality among the parts of man as a most basic and important doctrine and regarded this consequence simply as a kind of price that needed to be paid for it. But that would have been an easy and uncharacteristic stance. Instead one might (but this is emphatically only a suggestion) read the *Nicomachean Ethics* with a view to this dilemma. This could throw light on the complex qualifications and restrictions which Aristotle introduced; some were designed to keep the totality of man together and preserve the equality among all parts, yet also diminish the weight of this unwelcome implication.

The single most important claim concerning this view of freedom can again be pictured through a diagram (below). This time the darkened area (the area of identification, or the locus of the "true self") will be larger and will in fact coincide with the whole person. Our contention is again that this represents the self-image or the identification presupposed by this Aristotelian view of freedom.

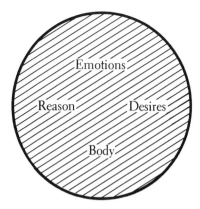

  Area of identification; locus of "true self"; origin of free actions

Let us now return to our first example, that of Dostoyevsky's Undergroundman. Earlier we said that in his case an act is not free unless it contravenes reason and that this presupposes a non-identification with his rationality. But this is only one part of his idea of freedom. To be free an act also had to be contrary to considerations of advantage or of value, contrary to his habits and emotions and desires; in fact, it had to be "in opposition to everything and completely independent." We are again primarily interested in this as a type. It is for us one possible expression of the paradigm which insists that freedom is not freedom unless it is *complete*. What experience of the self, or what identification stands behind this view of freedom?

Clearly it would not be sufficient if the Undergroundman disassociated himself from the cerebral and the foresightful, but identified with his dark and mad passions. This would be more nearly the self-image of a Romantic. The Undergroundman is not free when he acts out of an emotion, but he experiences his feelings too, just as his reason, as a noxious, irritating pressure, which often breaks in upon him when he least expects it and then whirls him into a "vile" and "shameful" action.

He is free only when he flouts not only reason but also everything else that could have prompted or motivated or excused the action. The act must have no basis whatsoever. It must arise suddenly as if from nothing and from nowhere, a spark with neither purpose nor direction. It is as if a deed becomes truly his own only through complete elimination. Anything at all that surrounds or attaches to one of his actions takes it from him and is enough to relegate him to the role of an ineffectual observer. The act must be sheathed in pristine isolation. Only then does it return him the assurance that it was his act, that for once he had not been the victim of manipulation.

There can be only one self-image behind this rarified and over-wrought sense of freedom. He must not identify with any of his natural components. He experiences everything that he actually is as once removed from his "true" self. All his thoughts and acts and feelings happen like events that he observes as from a distance; they move like placards on the far shore of a river. His mode of experience gives a precise sense to the vague idea of being in self-alienation. Everything is for him an object. He himself is nothing but the point on the horizon from which everything is seen, he is only a pure incessant glance. It is as if the everyday experience of being too self-conscious, the incapacity simply to be or to do, and to end the division into spectator and actor in him had frozen into solid shape.

The key claim can again be pictured in a diagram (below). Only if all the actual components of a person are relegated to an outer sphere so that the "true self" becomes an unreal postulation—a point—do all existing forces spell coercion, while an act of pure caprice alone is free. Only if all of one's desires and passion, and also one's own body and even reason are somehow not one's own "true self" is one coerced and rendered unfree even by them. But if one is so disassociated from them, then one is bound to suffer oppression from them, and those so constrained are free only in the moments in which they contravene even every part of their own person.

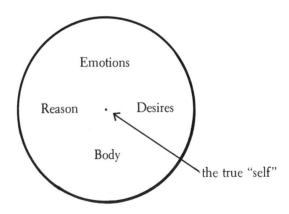

If we now set these three concepts of freedom side by side, then it becomes apparent that they all point in the same direction for they exhibit a straightforward correlation. Each of the three views draws the line between the free and the coerced in a different place, but each also assumes a different identification. And in all three cases the line dividing the free from the coerced and the line separating the area of identification from the disassociated coincide. On the "Platonic" view only rational acts are free, but reason is also the only truly human part, it alone is the "true self." The "Aristotelian" position includes more in the circle of free actions—it holds that all actions originating from any part of the whole person are free, but it also, at the same time, enlarges the area of identification, and considers all parts of the whole person "equally human." The Undergroundman's version reduces the class of free actions to a limit—only acts that are "completely independent" count as free. But the identification, or the "true self" is again correspondingly diminished, for all actually existing parts of the person lie outside it. A shift in the area of identification is thus always matched by the same shift of the distinction between the free and the coerced. All three ideas of freedom thus have the following in common: in all three, acts originating from the area of identification, from the "true self," are free, while acts originating from elements that are disassociated are coerced.

On this basis we can now advance a kind of definition: *an act is free if the agent identifies with the elements from which it flows; it is coerced if the agent disassociates himself from the element which generates or prompts the action.* This means that identification is logically prior to freedom, and that freedom is not a primary but a derivative notion. Freedom is a function of identification and stands in a relationship of dependency to that with which a man identifies. If an identification is present, the corresponding freedom appears. The primary condition of freedom is the possession of an identity, or of a self—freedom is the acting out of that identity. Tell me a man's identity and I will tell you his freedom, tell me its limits and I will tell you when he is coerced.

This definition is not a neatly packaged final product. It is only a tool that will be used as we advance with this discussion. And for a beginning a few of its grosser implications should be seen.

It should be very plain that this definition is not intended to be one more addition to an already overcrowded field. It by design is framed one level higher in abstraction, and in a sense is really a theory about other *theories* of freedom: its proper subject matter is more the already existing philosophical concepts of freedom than freedom itself. In the simplest terms, it is intended to display a logic, a kind of order, that is really there but hidden in the bewildering variety of meanings which freedom has been given. It is as if beads so far strewn randomly on the floor are now gathered on a thread. Or, in a different analogy, we now have something that stands to theories of freedom as an equation stands to the values that its variables can assume. Most of the historically developed interpretations of freedom represent the advocacy of one particular identification, and other meanings assigned to freedom differ from the given one in a now quite transparent way: the general logic is the same, but the identification that is being advocated has been changed.

To realize that the presentation of one preferred concept of freedom in effect amounts to an invitation to adopt a certain identification and to act from it, helps not just in the taxonomy of the genus and the species of freedom. It also should be like seeing a play—or a magician's trick—not from the front, but from backstage. To give just one example of this: Rousseau's famous formulation that "Freedom is obedience to the General Will" loses the aura of paradox that in part protects it. On our interpretation Rousseau here advocates an identification with the General Will, and enunciates that freedom is action from, or in harmony with, the General Will. And we now can see much more clearly what this actually involves: a proper citizen according to Rousseau (if we were to take this single sentence *out of context!*) identifies with the General Will; i.e., far from pursuing his own private, selfish good, he regards the general good as his very own. (One could almost imagine him as the political equivalent of a religious saint.) Such a citizen would of course be "free" if he "obeyed" the General Will, simply because the General Will is, so to speak, his very own. But some of the irony implicit in this dictum now also starts to show: for this citizen of course would not have to be "coerced"—but only because all coercion has already been pre-empted: with that identification he would "freely" do far more than society normally expects. He would act only for the public good, and to grant him this freedom is of course a concession that society can well afford. Society loses nothing, and gets everything in return, for this citizen gives to society the maximum that it could possibly demand.

Seen in a different perspective, this definition represents a shift in focus from the outside to the inside of the person. Rearranging the external circumstances in the end is not enough. One can remove obstacles one by one, but this produces only level ground, or worse, the absence of all resistance, a kind of vacuum, and that is not freedom. The elimination of barriers and of risks misses perhaps the deeper problem. At some point most of us have done some hard and maybe costly thing, but we were liberated in the act, and maybe even for the first time really free—not because all hindrances had been removed, but because we at last had manifested what we theretofore had only darkly sensed ourselves to be. This is one point at which this way of thinking about freedom touches ground. The primary prerequisite of freedom is an impulse, is a *self* possessed of something that wants to be acted out.

But if the formation of identifications really is the precondition for the possibility of freedom, then there also arises the possibility of a strange cross-purposedness. One easily could imagine a society in which two forces work against each other. On one side, large efforts may be expended and sacrifices made to create the framework for the exercise of freedom. Institutions that allow for choices and for participation may be established, and hosts of similar arrangements may be made. Yet if other forces in the culture at the same time undermine the growth of identifications, if they diminish what would be the self, then the efforts given to these institutional arrangements are completely wasted. For in such a society there would be no freedom in spite of the elaborate preparations. If the first condition of freedom is a genuine self, then a society precludes the very possibility of freedom when it erodes the self.

One of the strengths of this view of freedom is that it brings this priority of the self to light. For this two-sidedness, this possibility of cancelling with one set of forces the very hope that another set of forces raised, and the dreadful waste involved—the picture of a splendidly designed machine going to rust because the one gear that alone can drive it fails to engage, and spins in the air—comes close to home. Even with dim eyes one cannot fail to see that something very like this is happening in our own society: we have often with great sacrifices, devised a set of institutions the purpose of which has been to realize liberty. Yet we have also evolved a society in which the self is stunted, a society which makes it very hard to find objects with which one can identify, so that a self could form.

And this carries forward two plain implications. For one, we now begin to have a better understanding of an experience which many of us have had. It is a sense of disappointment, or a feeling that one has been deceived. It vents itself in bursts of anger, and in a blindly flailing search for the "more" that one expected. Of this experience we now have the outlines of an explanation: we have the institutions that were presumed to give us freedom, and yet we do not experience it; in our actual lives freedom eludes us, as the cup did Tantalus. And if even we, who are the privileged, who cannot point to deprivations, or inequalities to explain to ourselves what we still lack—if even we still feel bereaved, then it may be because we lack that other side: a self which could fill the mold of these institutions, a self that in and through its actions can alone make freedom real.

The other inference leads us to the recognition that further alterations and still more refined elaborations of the same institutions may not help. The flaw, or failure may not lie with them; the lack may not have its origin in their imperfection, but may stem from a quite different source. If the prerequisite of freedom is a self with a firm identity, then the customary medicines are prescribed through a faulty diagnosis—we may have stretched the shoe that did not pinch. An altogether different problem may have to be addressed if we want to create a society that gives us freedom. It would have to be a society so constituted that a self could find within it objects with which to identify, and one minimum that this may in the end require is a society of which the self is not ashamed.

3

Freedom and Absolute Independence

THE MAIN CATEGORIES we have so far introduced—those of identity versus disassociation—are intended to have the most laconic meaning. For the moment we want to strip these notions of their rich associations, to employ them simply to differentiate elements which are accepted as part of the self from those which are not, and we think of this division as a very modest and uncomplicated fact. However, with each of the different identities goes a different way of structuring the totality of experience.

One could study all of the various patterns into which the diverse identifications organize experience, but we shall concentrate mainly on the implication of the structure which we associated with the Undergroundman, where no parts of the self are accepted, and the identity is analogous to a mere point.

Among the reasons for this choice is the possibility already suggested, that our own culture fosters the crystallization of this type. But there is also the fact that any attempt to capture the real quality of freedom is always haunted by the question: But is this sufficient? Would the occurrence of these conditions be enough to set a man "really" free? The advantage of studying this type is that in the case of a full-scale disassociation the demand for an unconditional and total freedom becomes explicit and takes shape. It, therefore, might hold clues as to what being "really free" and "absolutely independent" might involve.

What then is the psychology of this minimal identification? One feature clearly must be fundamental to this type: there would have to be an ineluctable and almost constant sense that all one's qualities and actions represent only an adopted surface, that they do not grow out of a deeply structured firm necessity but are somehow arbitrary. One easily could be an entirely different person, one only has fallen into this rather than some other role because of a few chance circumstances.

In the Undergroundman this sense of inauthenticity takes the form of his complaint that he "has no qualities," which brings him to the thought that it would be ever so comforting and reassuring to be a sluggard, or at least to have a red nose. Being a sluggard would give definition and solidity to one's whole existence—it would be like having a profession. This sense of not having qualities, or of experiencing them as detached, so that they leave the self unqualified, and literally nondescript and empty, is almost a restatement, an amplified description, of what we have called non-identification.

But this seemingly simple feature could easily have a great variety of consequences. Take, for instance, the spitefulness which Dostoyevsky ascribes to his Undergroundman, which goes hand in hand with the resentment he feels for all others, and with the hatred he feels for himself. One could derive these characteristics immediately from the experience of freedom generated by his identity. For this type feels genuinely free only when he performs an utterly capricious act, when the act is prompted neither by a rational consideration, nor by anything else that is either within or without him. The converse of this already gives us an inkling of what feeds his self-hatred. If he feels free only in these actions, then he must live with an almost constant sense of being victimized and managed. No man can perform very many capricious actions; they unavoidably are fairly rare. Most of the time he will respond to some impulse, or obey a rational consideration. He must cross streets, and has to fill his stomach. And if he experiences all this as an insidious coercion, as something that is forced upon him, something that he does only because he lacks the strength to resist it, then he must inevitably feel a sustained exasperation. Most people grow irritable when even only some small elements in their experience blur the difference between what they want, and what is clearly an external pressure—when they no longer know to what extent they follow their own or someone else's will. Yet this confusion would pervade the whole of this man's experience. If a situation made upon him the most humdrum, natural demands, or if he satisfied one of his common everyday desires, he could never say: "Yes, this is what I wanted." The repose and calm of this finality would be inaccessible to him. His world would be full of hidden, mocking forces.

This would make the resentment he feels for all others natural, and would explain why he vents his spleen and his caprice on everyone who comes within his reach. He continuously feels imposed upon. He experiences even an exchange of the usual affabilities as the working of a stratagem, where some part of himself has been activated by the acquaintance he is greeting, which now forces the little pleasantry through his resistance. If this is how the minutiae of social intercourse appear to him, then God help him in more complicated situations. What a quantity of rage and anger, fed by an incessant stream of humiliations, he would accumulate. In his eyes everyone else would possess a daemonic knowledge of his inner springs, so that they could always make him do their will. How could they fail? No matter what reaction they produce, it never can be what *he* wants, for any influence, or cause, or reason infringes on him. Like the Undergroundman, he might spend his whole life lying in wait behind his desk, ready to ambush a petitioner. "For once to force *my* will on someone"—that might be his only dream. He would force himself on the haughty, snobbish mates from his boyhood school, though he knows that they despise him; and he would do it precisely because he was not invited, and very especially because they celebrate a farewell dinner at which he will be grotesquely out of place. He will do anything to calm the knowledge that he is always led by hooks that someone else planted in his soul.

If this could cause his isolating hatred toward others, then it could also be a source of the venom he feels for himself. That, too, could be explained from the locus which he assigns to his "true self." If he hates others because they in all situations tyrannize him, then he hates himself for allowing this to happen, for his incapacity to offer more resistance, in short, for what must appear to him as his insufferable weakness. The extent of the weakness he sees in himself can be measured by the fact that even his own thoughts are experienced by him as objective forces. They are not *his* thoughts. From his point of view there is an other which relentlessly fires thoughts in his direction, and their upshot is not subject to the exercise of his volition. To give one quick example: near the end of the second section of Part II of the novel, the Undergroundman describes the moments that immediately preceded his intrusion on the schoolmates whom he hates, and has not seen for almost a year. "Climbing up to his fourth story, I was thinking that the man disliked me, and that it was a mistake to go and see him. But as it always happened that such reflections impelled me, as though purposely to put myself into a false position, I went in." Here he is coerced by a reflection.

One might say that this type is the inversion of a Stoic. The Stoics tried to parry the vicissitudes of actual existence, and sought to bring at least their own reactions to them under their control. Each man's mind became each man's own kingdom. But there is no place which this self-disassociated man could call his own and over which he would have power.

This throws light on the peculiar "passivity" of which those with this identity complain. The Undergroundman describes at great length his "inability to take action." Allegedly he can see too many sides of every question. Every motive is examined till it suffers chemical disintegration. Every doubt is caressed so that his mind never finds the equilibrium, the stability to initiate a real action. But is acute self-awareness so debilitating, and is he all that "passive" in the first place? Is he not on the contrary in a constant frenzy of perpetual action? And isn't therefore, the real question: What is it that gives this man the illusion that he is unable to perform a single action? His true complaint is not that he cannot act: it is rather that none of his actions are quite his; he never feels that it is he who performs them. They flare up around him, they happen, they leave him behind, and he then pursues them. His sense of passivity thus could be directly derived from the "transcendence" which he gives to his "true self." One might say that he asks for the impossible. He has objectified, has disassociated from himself all the forces that could conceivably generate an action. He is the pure spectator, the astral, unbodied observer. Thus everything that could generate an action he does not consider truly his, and what is truly his could not generate an action. He has to feel passive. But the reason for this is not his excessive self-awareness. The reason is at once deeper and more stringent: given his self-image it becomes inevitable. It follows by a straightforward logic of elimination.

To say that he experiences no actions at all as his own would of course be a slight overstatement. There are exceptions, namely the capricious actions. These, however, he regards as his precisely because they seem to him without foundation. (Objectively they of course may have their causes, but we are now concerned with his experience.) This shows his self-hatred in yet a different perspective. Consider that he lays claim only to his capricious actions and disavows all those with genuine motives. This means that he never gives himself full credit for reasonable deeds, but takes responsibility only for the mad, gratuitous acts. If one selects the actions which one shoulders in this fashion, then the burden must grow crushing.

But his self-perception is still more complex and more instructive. It is fundamentally ambiguous or, more precisely, it tilts from one extreme to the other. And this part of the syndrome, too, could be explained from the place where the line between the accepted and the disassociated is now drawn. A fuller description of the more elaborate structure that underlies his episodes of self-denigration would have to start from the paradox of his monstrously elevated self-opinion. Karen Horney once said that the neurotic thinks of himself as God, and something analogous has to occur if the self is identified with the Subject that observes all of experience. For if the "true self" is only the elusive, postulated point from which experience is viewed, then none of the shortcomings or failings of one's actual behavior ever qualify, or taint this self. Nothing could ever force it to step down from its heights and it therefore remains godlike and immune. The totality of one's concrete, unresolved existence is not assimilated to the pristine essence of one's being. That is dismissed as an uncouth and deceptive shell, while one's core remains innocent and without taint. Yet this very immaculateness unavoidably faces him also as an exorbitant and hopelessly high standard. Since his experience never mitigates his real self, its demands continue to be absolute, and this results in the disgust he feels for himself. In the hours in which he cannot demean himself enough, he measures the reality of his day-to-day existence against this inhuman standard, and then he naturally finds himself so wanting that he appears to himself as a "mouse" or a mere "vermin." The moments when the pendulum swings back to the other side, when he looks down on all others from the mad heights of his arrogance, represent on this interpretation only the other half of this same pattern: this happens when he compares not himself but others to his unqualified and sacrosanct "real" self.

Though other features could easily be added, these should give some indication of the general pattern that this touch-me-not identity engenders. At stake is the logical coherence of the type and not any one particular example. That there is some correspondence to Dostoyevsky's Undergroundman is naturally a welcome confirmation, but nothing could be further from our mind than the notion that Dostoyevsky wrote the case history of a non-identifying subject. The connections we have traced are intended to represent an ideal type in Max Weber's sense: they should illuminate empirical examples, but it is understood that all reality—and all of literature—is more than an embodiment of abstract patterns.

Corresponding structures could be developed for all the other possible identifications. In the case of an identification with reason one could again elaborate on the selection of actions for which responsibility is taken. If that identity is present, full credit is taken for all the reasonable, thoughtfully executed actions, while the less flattering are disavowed. The dynamic operates, therefore, in just the opposite direction: we saw that the point-subject identification forces one's self-estimation either down, or into an ever widening split. If one believed, however, that all one's evil or irrational actions are not quite one's own, then the propulsion clearly would be upwards. The beneficial effects of this would extend to the social organism, for from a cultural point of view "reasonable" actions now receive the additional encomium of being "free," and of bringing the real self into action, which would naturally operate as an inducement. Most significantly, the fundamental posture that goes with this identity would be radically different; one could compare it to that of a knight who defends the castle of his rationality against all attacks from the outside. The world is no longer the cabinet of magic mirrors into which those with a point-identity are locked. It is now brightly illumined and furnished with things that are what they are. If everything is not completely understood, still nothing is finally mysterious: nothing hides in the darkness that more light could not reveal. It is a martial world in which the battle lines are clearly drawn: the knight can be guilty only of one failing—he can be too weak, and see his reason fall. One could say the identification with the hidden subject creates the world of dread and ambiguity and the other "existential" categories; the identification of the "true self" with reason generates the world of a Lessing, or of a Voltaire.

The larger pattern implicit in the acceptance of one's total person could again be unfolded along similar lines. Now the whole weight of *every* act clings to the actor. Credit or blame, glory or disgrace fall to him not only for what his reason chose, but that the deed has issued from any part of him is enough. That he did not know, did not intend, was tricked, was forced—none of this counts as a real excuse. A first suggestion of the configuration engendered by the "Aristotelian" identification thus might come from a comparison to Oedipus. Those who accept their total self would have a concept of "responsibility" similar to his, for Oedipus kills his father without knowing him, and marries his mother thinking her a foreign queen, and makes every effort to evade his fate—and yet blinds himself in self-punishment for committing deeds that had been preordained.

One could speculate whether the presence of this identification constitutes, perhaps, a precondition of the tragic. Maybe the spirit of tragedy requires submission to a paradox: that one accepts deeds that one did not choose as, nonetheless, fully one's own acts. If so, one could imagine that the introduction of a much more cautious and restrictive idea of "responsibility"—where an act must have been intended, and the consequences known, and where far from it being preordained one must have had a choice to be "responsible" for it—worked a broad and fundamental change, one which among many other consequences made the writing of tragedies more difficult.

One general feature all of the various identifications have in common: their dynamic is cyclical or self-reinforcing. The present moment of experience is so restructured by each of them that the identification responsible for this way of viewing things is itself continuously reproduced and solidified by it.

The sense of "passivity" that characteristically accompanies nonidentification illustrates this particularly well. Once the subject structures his experience in a certain way, he *has* to feel passive, but the sense of passivity in turn reinforces the non-identification: the self that is overwhelmed at every moment withdraws still further.

On one side this affects the manner in which these identifications operate as explanations. The causes of a syndrome like that of the Undergroundman need not be sought primarily in his early childhood. The original impetus might have been no more than a minute displacement, but this initially small shift triggered a progressively enlarging process that was carried forward by its own momentum. The original cause thus may be quite irrelevant to the present situation, for the force which maintains the nonidentification in existence is not due to long past events, but derives immediately from the interpretation of the present.

This line of thought could be pursued: a neurosis, in this perspective, would be a radically self-perpetuating pattern; and the contrast between the emphasis on the past, versus the concern with the immediate present is clearly germane to the difference between classical Freudian therapy, and the modes of therapy associated with, for example, Perls and Laing. But other aspects bear more on our topic.

To grasp the internal coherence of these patterns—and the fact that they are self-reproductive is only the most manifest expression of their systemic integration—is crucial for any understanding of what freedom more concretely means within the context of any one of them. The Undergroundman's spite, his self-hatred, his peculiar relationship to others, and the remaining facets of his non-identification, are all inseparable from the character that freedom has for him. Moreover, all of these together constitute more nearly one phenomenon than our usual language—which splits them into separate entities and draws divisions where no seams can be found—suggests. (The erasure of this misconceived separation, and the verbal reflection of a greater unity is one conceptual advantage of the framework of identifications.)

For those without identity freedom is indeed "absolute independence." They, it is true, must "go against everything" in order to be free. But this is not the case for all those who do not share in this extreme condition. The greater the extent to which they do identify with something, the less is this complete isolation perquisite to their being free. To put the point paradoxically: "dependency" on something does not in any way diminish one's degree of freedom as long as one truly identifies with the thing on which one is "dependent." If I am in harmony with something—if in fact it is me—(and that is the point of talking about "identification")—then I need not be isolated from it, and need not be protected from it, to be "free." The demand for freedom takes the form of an insistence on total independence only for those who lack identity. For all others the claim is not compelled to this extreme—and yet, in terms of freedom, they have not compromised and do not receive less.

To speak of "spite," of "hatred for the self, and for all others" therefore describes the other side of the coin of "complete freedom." For if only the completely disassociated self requires "absolute independence," then that absolute independence requires also a completely disassociated self.

And the point now is not that the demand for total independence is "irresponsible," or that "too much" is being asked, and that the expectation should become more "realistic." At stake rather is the recognition that this is the actual shape which the upper limit (of at least this form of driving freedom to its extreme) is bound to assume. The image of total freedom thus resembles a mirage: we see a vision of open and unbounded space, but if we walked out in that direction then what we would find is only the desert of self-disassociation.

Caligula, in Camus' play, wants to affront the world with the example of his own pursuit of freedom. That he orders executions to satisfy a whim, and cuts every tie that binds him to any other human being, and finally wants the impossible—the moon—these are still understated metaphors for the conditions along the outer bounds of freedom. They do not reflect (and perhaps no image can) what freedom, also from the inner self, would actually be like. In a state of non-identification there would be nothing, even in oneself, that one would not encounter as a hostile object. One's solitude would be a metaphysical condition. There would be no other subject in one's world, and even one's own subjectivity would be an emptiness, continually threatened by the density of the surrounding world. Any movement would be an invasion. Shell after shell would be cast off as hindering encumbrances, till one would be diminished to a point in space.

To have made this extreme possibility explicit should give us a different understanding of the strange fact we mentioned close to the beginning: that freedom is not only glorified but also dreaded and avoided. This is not merely because some are more robust and others are more fragile. The two reactions often do not respond to one and the same thing. Freedom for those at all close to the condition we have just considered differs radically from what freedom means for others. If nothing short of a mad, gratuitous action counts as free, and if freedom requires total solitude, then it *is* dreadful and to escape from it is natural. If it is action in conformity to one's own reason, this is much less true. Certainly not all who have avoided freedom did it with such excellent excuse. But some of the writers in whose account of freedom anguish plays an important role had perhaps that kind of freedom in their minds. Freedom in that form does not even carry with it the reward of acting out some portion of oneself; it then becomes a flight from everything; it *requires* that the self collapse, that it shrink to a point. Only a self so totally diminished could be "really" and absolutely free.

Our understanding of the desire for "absolute independence" can now illumine one critique of our own society. The charge has been brought that our technologically advanced culture, especially because of its sophisticated use of the means of mass communication, represents a more insidious and more cunning form of tyranny than earlier, bloodier systems of oppression. On this view—expressed, perhaps, most prominently by Marcuse—the less refined, old-fashioned forms of subjugation permitted the desires and the needs of men to grow in natural wildness. They only interfered "after" the aims and inclinations of men had taken shape, and coming so late their measures needed to be brutal: with the desires fully grown it was hard to stop the action; when the individual's determination conflicted with his master's will, only harsh, repressive force could still assure obedience.

Under the present dispensation, so these critics claim, even our earliest and subtlest impulses right down to our dreams are molded, and the need for overt repression is thus eliminated with one smooth stroke. Conflict cannot possibly arise. Why cut off a grown man's legs when you can stunt the child so it will fit the bed? To force men to conform is inefficient, when one can make sure that everybody will agree. Denying needs gives some offense, which can be avoided if only the preordained and cheaply granted will be asked. The old tyranny was grim; under the new version the subjects never have a wish that is not fulfilled. That makes the slave's condition truly hopeless, for now his will no longer runs against external walls, and therefore nothing even informs him of his own oppression, nothing can still serve him as a gauge; his subjection now is absolute. The prognosis says: this time the slaves will clap for more.

There is, of course, truth in this story. The instruments of influence have multiplied, and their efficiency has been refined and studied. I am not sure that they have become more powerful—think of the Church, or of the uniformity of early cultures—but they have been isolated and detached, and made into specific tools, suited to exactly calculated ends. Above all, they are more available and can be bought, prepackaged, by the highest bidder. Manufacturers of clothes and furniture decide three years in advance on an exact shade of green, and then prepare the public so that it will accept that shade as "in" when the goods with that color hit the market. Elections are swung by a dose of this or that "image," for sale at certain stores. Subliminal suggestions tease our sexual drives. But the development of these techniques only exacerbated the deceptions performed behind the screen of freedom. To pretend that a choice was autonomously reached by the individual alone, to still speak of "free elections" with no trace of scepticism, requires by now something like cold blood. Unquestionably, major historic changes have occurred, and the tension between the mystic ideology of freedom and patent social facts has so increased that this string now has to snap.

But—the difference is nonetheless grossly overdrawn. No culture gives free reign to the inner man, and interdicts only external actions. No society ever was like Marcuse's old system: none stood back and waited till the needs or desires were completely formed. All began to shape man as soon as he was born. The new system of oppression, therefore, is not radically new: the imperceptible and yet relentless bending to make man fit his social bed, and the cunning trick of magic, where one first instills desires and then says: "See, we gave you what you yourself have asked for—what *you* chose"—all societies have always done this, and it is utterly impossible for them to avoid it.

If the idea of freedom has this double-bottom, it is not peculiar to our technically accomplished age but lies deeper: fundamentally this has been true from the beginning. The difference is only a difference of degree. And here rests the main mistake of the approach which contrasts the two modes of control: the real trouble is not that freedom has eluded us once more, that we imagined ourselves closer to it, when we in truth were further from it. The actual situation is quite different: the real flaw lies in this mode of thinking. The image of autonomy and independence which it projects was an illusion all along. Yes, the methods with which we are now influenced are more blatant, but this means also that a deception which previously could be sustained, can now no longer be palmed off. What we have reached, therefore, is not so much the point where the reality of freedom has been finally eclipsed; but more the point where the bankruptcy of that idea of it can no longer be concealed.

And this is the conclusion that those who make the charge of the newer, more insidious tyranny refuse to draw. Their opposition still posits the idea of freedom as the negation of all influence. They do not realize that the standard they apply is not too high or distant, but that it is a phantom shimmering in the sun: that even if we reached it there would be only sand.

It is the deceptiveness of their envisioned goal that also produces their general despondency. For once one accepts the image that our actions and social influence spin in a cycle, and one wants to be "free" of this, there can be no escape. The more one tries the quicker one will turn around its vortex. And in this lies the viciousness of this one form of the idea of freedom, for not only do all parts of every social order become uniformly and monotonously black, if every form of influence is seen as equally oppressive; there also must occur a literal and systematic self-destruction. For if every layer of oneself, that is merely influenced, represents the Other and signifies confinement so that one will have to withdraw it, then layer after layer will have to be shed until no self remains.

And yet—this cobweb of wires can be cut. Freedom is not the absence of influence; and to be exposed to influence is not to be enslaved. Freedom and influence negate each other only in one very special, and moreover pathologic case. Only if one in advance opposes "everything" will every influence be tantamount to an oppression, and only then will one be free in the absence of all influence. So this way of "defining" freedom cannot merely be rejected in favor of other, more viable conceptualizations: this view can be *subsumed*. It can be explained as the extreme case for which our "theory" provides: only if one refuses to identify with anything will the idea of freedom assume this extreme meaning, but then it must. Or, differently expressed, "freedom from influence" is not another "sense" of freedom, it is an instance of our own earlier account: we can say more than just that this is not what we mean by freedom; we can say: this is what *only* Undergroundmen meant by it.

Still more concisely: (1) Only Undergroundmen must be uninfluenced in order to be free. Influence denies only the peculiar idea of freedom which corresponds to a self with only "one dimension"—to a self that is a point. (2) For all other identifications freedom does not require the absence of all influence. (3) I thus need not be independent from everything in order to be free. The exception is whatever constitutes my own authentic self. Freedom does not require that I am independent from even myself—it demands the opposite: that I achieve a harmony with what I truly am.

4

Freedom and Choice

IN THE THOUGHT AND LANGUAGE of our culture, choice and freedom*
are so intertwined that the making of one is the exercising of the other.
To bring the actual connection between the two into our view requires
something like the detaching of a nerve from our eye so as to look at it.

We might start once more from the example of a total non-identity.
The very fact that this is a limiting and in a sense only theoretically
conceived condition makes it instructive and revealing. The context
that we should now imagine is, however, not that of a gratuitous
action. Such actions are best understood as a hyperbolic variation on
the theme of spontaneity. They exemplify—if they are ever more than
an idea—a complete absence of all motivation, and are therefore best
conceived under the image of a bizarre and sudden swerve from anything that might have been expected. And that is not the prototype
associated with a choice.

While a gratuitous act typically can be performed anywhere and
anytime—while walking on a beach, for instance—a choice characteristically presupposes a firmly delineated setting. In the simplest case
there are two sharply defined alternatives (A and B) and reasons for
doing one or the other, including expected consequences, pressures and
the like. How is a choice experienced by someone whose self is radically
disassociated, i.e., by the type resembling the Undergroundman?

Basically, he would see in front of him the same kind of forking of
two paths that we all experience. The passage of time would gradually
reduce his distance from it, and there would be a sense of being
pushed, of floating on a raft inescapably down a fast river towards a
bifurcation. Maybe he would perceive the possible calamities that

*The relationship between freedom and determinism is discussed sepa-
rately in the Appendix.

might ensue, the pressures loosed on him, the scorn or the derision already waiting in the face of others with quicker eyes—but mainly this is not different from what all of us have felt.

One aspect, however, would vary markedly: his own hopes and desires, and even the unexpected and healing breeze of a great longing, but just as much the agile shuttle of the calculations that shift pros and cons from side to side: all of that is for him also part of the observed and independently evolving situation. He sees these as not categorically different from the myriad of other sharp-edged factors that enclose him. He witnesses the transfiguration of his thoughts—the game of tag they play, the flareup of a quarrel on the side, the droning circular procession going on and on, as someone, fascinated, might observe a hive of bees. He watches the recurrent patterns and searches for their esoteric meaning; he notices how small, chance events seem now to carry a private message just for him (rain in the morning—was I meant to stay?); he finds that he has begun to tilt between extremes: that in one moment every doubt or disadvantage attached to one course has dissolved, that adopting it now seems shiningly and luminously right, while, five minutes later, the same act scowls at him like a monster. All this—and the details do not matter, they could take all kinds of forms—he merely sees—it is a spectacle that he observes.

This might be the picture, without any change, right up to the crucial moment. And there would be no gap, no pause, no period of silence, but all at once he is at the forking place, and in the next second it is already passed and begins to fall behind him.

We may, since so much seems to hinge on it, distinguish two main possibilities: in the first of these his mind goes through something like the process just described, and some event external to him (anything, the falling of a rock, another person's action) exercises the decisive influence. In the second alternative, everything would be the same, except that it is now a thought, or an emotion, or *ex hypothesis* anything at all that is internal to him, that makes the final difference. And we need not assume that his mind is agitated. The logic of the argument would be the same even if his mind were lethargic to the point of immobility.

Whichever of these alternatives in fact occurs, he himself in either case would not come into play. From his point of view the two come to the same thing: there were two distinct courses of action, both were possible, and then some force that he observed, but that was not under his control, nor anything that he accepts as his own self, sent him down one alternative and not the other. So that in his case there could be two alternatives and more than that, a thought observed by him could even make the difference between them—and yet this thought would only be another fact that clicks into place in the great machine of all events, and thus he still would not have even acted, let alone have done it with freedom. And this would still be true even if his last thought before the crucial moment had been something like: "All right, let it be A." As long as that thought is only one additional event, that occurs like all his other feelings and reflections, which in his case are not really different from the strung-together happenings in the external world, no basis and no reason for any talk of freedom has been given. The whole is one compact mechanism that somehow managed to include even his own thoughts into its cleverly designed revolving gears. That his thoughts did play this role and were part of this process, if anything, enlarges the measure of his servitude.

The movement towards an open alternative, thus, does not ameliorate this man's condition. Choices present him only with additional demands; they are only one more thing with which he is forced to deal. He is harassed and mocked by them. And clearly this does not change if one deliberately, and perhaps with the most magnanimous of intentions, multiplies the choices that he will be "allowed" to make. If one arranges for him a world that crackles with live options, one only makes his situation worse.

But he is, admittedly, a special case. Still, there is a different, very blatant fact, which stands quite apart from the elusive phenomenon of identification, but raises another preliminary question: the fact that choices, normally and for anyone, occur in a context that is determinate and fixed. To put it a little harshly: to have "had a choice" may only mean that there was one other thing one could have done—where that one thing, however, may have been even more of a disaster than the still awful alternative which one in fact adopted. That one "had a choice," in other words, says nothing about the whole nexus of constraints operating in a situation, or about the totality of factors that were not under one's control.

This puts the countless situations in which some hapless soul is told that "he had a choice" into a quite different light. The presumption often seems to be that if he did then he was "free"—and from that a weighty chain of consequences is easily derived: if free, then the responsibility was his, then he can be blamed, and more, he can be punished. But, conversely, if he was free, then his freedom was a gift of incommensurate value; and for that he can now be asked to make a recompense—and the bill delivered in this fashion can be rather steep; it can run to obedience and loyalty to the state, to joining the armed forces, and to permitting oneself to be killed.

The crude fact that choices are made in a context is meant to raise the simple question whether the size of the privilege that has been granted is in any way commensurate to the high price that is now exacted for it. Or, differently expressed, how much freedom did a choice—if we look at the context in which it was made—actually provide? And how much can, therefore, be reasonably asked in return? Is it not in some cases, where the alternatives were few and perhaps calamitous, misleading and even a trap to speak of freedom at all? Certainly I may have had a choice—there was an alternative—but if that alternative meant starvation (for example because I would have had to leave the country, and my profession requires a license which is not valid in other countries), then how much irony is there in telling me that I was free, and how entitled is anyone to say to me: you "freely" chose this state, and therefore you now owe it a Shylock's debt?

The question—how much freedom did I receive, and what is an appropriate return—given the nature of the context, for what can I be held responsible, still omits a string of other questions: Who "gave" this freedom to me? And which of all the other things that I received in my entire life were given to me by "the state," or by "the nation"? Did the state give me my life, or had my parents more to do with it and, if so, can the state ask for my life? To whom do I owe for what? And what exactly did I receive from the particular men who now ask me to risk my life? What entitles them to gather up the sum total of what I owe to "society" into their own hands? Surely, in the course of my whole life, I did receive an incalculable sum, but much of this came from those very close to me, and a great deal came from sources far beyond the state, some from thinkers and poets who died ages ago in another corner of the world, some from a peasant who now tills his rice-field in Japan. And, in any case I did not receive, I also gave. So what allows either these particular men, or even "the state" now to collect for everything, as if my life, but for "the state" would have been that of an animal, alone, lost in some forest?

These questions aim at some of the foundations on which our key political theories were built. But the same crude fact, that choices are always made in a specific context, which may mean that I was very "unfree" even though I had a choice, also bears on quite unlofty contexts and raises the same questions in very ordinary situations: in high schools and in universities, for instance.

To multiply the choices that a student is allowed to make does not mean that he was given any genuine freedom. In the actual context of his life the significance of such a choice may only be that he can now enroll in a course which dims and darkens his mind more slowly than other courses might have done. And the problem of the disproportion is here essentially the same. Precisely the expectation that the large gift of freedom be properly acknowledged, that the student should now be satisfied and indeed make some return for such a transcendental boon, may well provoke a new exasperation: for the student may not feel that he was given freedom, and he may be right.

Still in the same spirit, one could consider an example from a quite different sphere. That the making of choices (whatever the precise connection finally may be) in any case is not equivalent to freedom, should be evident from the working life of most executives. More or less correctly we think of them as men who make decisions, and who make them constantly, and often even with more power than those whose offices have thinner carpets. Now if freedom really were a matter of making choices—if that were its definition—then these men's lives would have to be exceptionally free. But if we look at all closely, and with any sympathy, at their day-to-day existence, this seems cruelly false. They are more nearly harassed by choices as by a swarm of gnats, and the off-handed idiom in which we say, "they are forced to make choices" seems more perceptive than some philosophic theories.

This idea, that the presence of choices is no guarantee of freedom, could be threaded through a long line of further illustrations. Questions about how much freedom is actually offered by the choice among 500 models of cars, which differ only in the tinfoil of their styling, or by the selection among as many different kinds of homes, none of which is built with more imagination than it takes to boil an egg, could be raised. But here the ideological fig leaves are so dry and wilted that we already know the sores that they are meant to cover.

We instead can turn this table, and ask whether at least a kind of freedom is not possible even when we, in a rather strong sense, do not choose our eventual course of action. One illustration of this reversal occurred in my own life, and with apologies for the intrusion, I will mention it only because it happens to be quite clear-cut.

For a long time I strongly resisted becoming a teacher of philosophy. One compelling—although in retrospect embarrassing—reason for this was that my image of professors in general, and more that of professors of philosophy, was very uninviting. I must have seen them somehow as spun into white cocoons, secreted by their thinking, through which they only rarely gave a sign of life. So I chose a series of quite different professions, but was forced again and again—of course by something in me, but by something that opposed my will—to return to philosophic thinking. After exhausting myself like a hooked fish, I finally reached the point of saying "Other men have to live with even worse defects," and began to teach. So there is certainly a sense in which I did not choose philosophy. And yet nothing was as liberating to me as this resignation. There is now more exhilaration in this aspect of my life than in any other, and a part of me surely was set free through this capitulation.

In discussions of determinism students often speak of the not-chosen with a sense of degradation. In their abstract thought the verdict "if so, you really did not choose it" expresses categorical dismay; it articulates the forfeiture of dignity, and signals the betrayal of the human to a wooden puppet world. It seems a loss to which the only possible response seems shame, or an inwardly felt anger.

Simply the inclusion of all this into a more far-flung context may be of some help. The perspective changes if one recalls that in some cultures and religions, surrender and acceptance open up the door to wisdom, and that this attitude may be spread far more widely than its opposite, which may even be peculiarly "Western." Our predisposition is thus not simply the conclusion to which a pure and culturally untinged reason leads. The surrender of the insistence on the privilege of one's own choice can be seen as a step bringing one closer to what is really home, and not only as the moment in which one's manhood is cut off.

Such a comparison, like litmus paper, gives away the substance from which the attitude that seems natural to us is made. One idea that seems to underlie our habitual reaction is an imagined opposition drawn with willful sharpness, so that an unwarranted either/or results:

either I chose the action, or I was coerced. And more than just a conflict is implied in this perception: the self, the ego, is isolated from the rest of nature, but the ego is also in the process elevated, while the rest of nature is correspondingly demoted—it becomes the grey dominion of lifeless, mechanistic forces. (One could reflect on this opposition and wonder how far its roots go down into the history of the West. Could there be an analogy to the position that man is given in the Book of Genesis when nature is put at man's disposal, and he is given the prerogative to "name every living creature." And are, for example, Chinese landscape paintings in which the human figures can be barely seen, since they are so fitted into the whole setting, and so insignificant in size, an expression of a view on which obedience to nature would be less degrading?) Some such schematization seems to be presupposed. For only if the conflict is given this complexion are the stakes in the assertion of the self so high. Only then does not having one's way against nature become a true defeat suffered at the hands of an inferior enemy.

The kind of thinking we have so far encountered as a symptom in the pathology of total disassociation reappears here, and this time our philosophic thinking seems affected by the same disease. For if one does not accept the premise of a hostile confrontation that opposes the choosing self to the whole of nature, then one is not defeated, or dehumanized, or unfree as soon as one's own choice does not have its way. And there are contexts, much closer to us than that of non-Western religions, in which the claim that we have been advancing would not open a single sleepy eye. In the framework of psychoanalytic discussions the idea that the will leads into barren country, and that life nourishes us only if we listen and receive, rather than dictate and impose, is a thin platitude. Strange thus is only the dividedness of our minds, which in one context allows us to protest that without choice there would be no freedom, and yet allows us in other contexts to understand that the influence of forces outside the ego can be liberating.

The actual relationship between choice and freedom, as we perceive it, can be organized around two contentions. The first of these maintains that the presence of a choice does not guarantee the possibility of freedom—it is not a condition that suffices. The claim is that this is true even for the strongest sense of choice, where I in fact do go through a process of deliberation, reach a conclusion, and in acting on it am able to realize A instead of B.

We already described an example (that of the Undergroundman) which illustrates this possibility, but this proposition can also be supported with general arguments. We could start from any of the circumstances in which one of several outcomes may occur, i.e., in which I do confront a "forking" of two or three alternatives. Presumably we would agree that the mere existence of these alternatives gives me no freedom if either another person or some outside event makes the decision between them. If, for example, either of two classes could equally well be taught in my philosophy department, but if the chairman (without my having any influence on him) decides which of these two I am to teach, then the fact that two alternatives "existed" obviously does not magnify my freedom. Similarly, for the case in which I could for one day fly either to New York or San Francisco: if, on the day in question, all flights to San Francisco happen to be cancelled, and that outside event eliminates one of the alternatives, then this clearly does not constitute an exercise of my freedom. The existence of open alternatives in short does not affect my freedom, if it is something other than myself that closes them. And this would be true no matter how numerous such open alternatives might be. Even if we lived in a world in which all manner of things were "possible," this still would not provide *me* with freedom if it were not *I* who selected among these options.

If this much is granted, the crucial question becomes whether the cases in which a thought occurring in my consciousness (i.e., my decision) tips the balance are always sufficiently different from cases like that of the two classes, or of the two flights, to warrant the position that in them I am indeed free?

Once the question is so formulated there can be no doubt that under certain circumstances the contrast may not be categorical enough. If we are agreed that the closing of two open alternatives by some external event does not give me freedom, then why should freedom always be realized merely because the decisive event happens to be a thought occurring in my consciousness? From the point of view of freedom these two may still come to the same thing: in either of these cases it may not have been really me who acted to make the decisive difference.

In some contexts we imagine that "we can think anything"—that at least in the world of our thoughts no rope suddenly pulls taut—and perhaps this gives us the idea that we are free if an outcome depends only on our thoughts. But what we are capable of thinking is actually, of course, limited in a thousand ways. It is also, obviously, subject to all kinds of influences. And more than that, my thoughts are not peculiarly under my control. Far from it. Even very normal and ordinary people—and not just Undergroundmen—have, for example, trouble concentrating (i.e., they find it hard to keep their thoughts even just within the range of a whole topic), and when we have to solve an intellectual problem we often have to wait for a thought that seems as touchy as an ill-humored child. (Nietzsche expressed this independence, this separateness of our thoughts that allows them to follow their own course, by saying: "It is not I, but *it* that thinks.") Again, if we observe ourselves in a trivial situation—say we focus on the last few seconds before I either take, or do not take a shower—then my thoughts do seem to sway as if on a teeter-totter, but they seem to come to rest on one side on their own. And such examples and considerations again point only to the palest understatement of what in a Freudian context would be regarded as a dusty, old, home truth. So once more only the compartmentalization we perform is strange, for on one side we believe that our conscious thoughts are only the distorted shadows cast by a concealed reality, and yet, at the same time, we imagine that an open alternative closed by a consciously reached decision is always radically different from one closed by external agencies.

These considerations seem so patent that one could easily slip into the opposite extreme: one might begin to think that closing an open alternative through my thought, or my decision, is *never* different from seeing it closed by an external agency; i.e., one might deny that we are ever free. Yet a far more acceptable middle course can be found. In fact the general view of freedom which we developed earlier points to one as soon as it is applied. For it is of course a fact that I can identify with my deliberations, and with the acts to which they lead, in spite of their being influenced, and their not being under my complete control, just as I can disassociate myself from them. And this would lead to the plain and understandable position that choices are free if I identify with them (i.e., with the deliberations involved and with the later action) and unfree if I do not.

We hope that this position represents indeed a partial truth, yet we must first clarify how it is intended, and in what perspective it wants to be understood, for otherwise someone could suspect that we only stubbornly insist on the adequacy of our earlier formulation.

To begin with, this tenet should be regarded as a first portion of the whole "converse side" of our earlier general view. The substance of this "under-side" can be compressed into the contention that freedom is no more than action from (or with) identification—that this is all that freedom is. This means we believe not just in regard to choice, but with respect to the whole issue of freedom in general, that it is false to maintain that freedom is simply an illusion, that it does not "exist," or can be "disproved." But we also, on the other side, do not believe that freedom is the grandiose and glittering wonder which it often has been claimed to be. We do not think that it signifies anything like independence from all influence, or "autonomy"—when that idea isolates the individual from the world. More roundly, the association between freedom and a kind of empty, open space has to be cut. That openness in any case does not occur, and it would be dreadful if it did—it would be the vacuum that nature has always been thought to abhor. In essence, freedom is a simpler and far less mysterious thing: it is gross and crass and down to earth; at its heart lies the capacity to act.

It is one of the principal concerns of this essay to fend off the errors that rush to various extremes from this more central ground: freedom is neither more nor less than this. We want to reject at the same time the fluffy expectations that are sometimes aroused by it, the delusions of self-sufficiency, or self-generation and of being godlike that have been attached to it, and yet insist that nothing less than an act committed by my own self can count as free. And this last requirement is high, and not easily attained. One way of getting a more concrete idea of the whole range of ways in which one can fall short of it, and also of the odyssey that has to be endured before this seemingly basic goal is reached, can be gathered from reading Bettelheim's account of children whose terror of it is so great that they seek refuge in an "Empty Fortress" rather than become a self.

Interpreted in terms of this general setting, our first proposition thus comes basically to this: the meaning of freedom that we have proposed throughout this essay is more "down to earth" than other, more traditional interpretations. (One could think of it on the analogy to a "lower standard" which, just because it is lower, also can be reached.) Now we are saying that choice can fall short even of this more modest claim: even an act chosen in the strongest sense (I consciously deliberated, etc.) can nonetheless still not be free, even in this "lowered" sense of freedom. The critical requirement is still that of identification: only if I identify with the making of a choice is it free; if I do not identify with it, then it is not.

We have already illustrated our second proposition with several examples and, unlike our first, it should no longer require the support of abstract arguments. If it is now understood that the making of a choice gives rise to freedom only if I identify with the agency that does the choosing (i.e., if I regard the thought-process that makes the decision as truly mine, despite its being conditioned, or influenced, or so forth), then it should be clear that freedom can also result from my identifying with an agency other than those processes of thought—and this means that I may be free even if the decisive difference between two alternatives was not made by my choice, as long as I identify with (i.e., regard as *myself*) the agency that did tip the scales. In sum, choice is neither a sufficient nor a necessary condition for freedom.

If the essence of freedom consists in the fact that it was I who acted, then two possibilities can be distinguished; the first is, that a process of rational adjudication did occur, but the subject disassociated himself from this process—that possibility corresponds to our first proposition. The second possibility has been fulfilled as soon as, regardless of the absence or presence of deliberation, I do act—and this corresponds to our second proposition. The instances exemplifying this possibility are, therefore, not at all rare, as the anecdote about how I came to teach philosophy may have suggested. On the contrary, the absence of a conscious process of deliberation and action on it obviates my freedom only if I also make a particular identification (namely with my rational thinking, and with that alone). If I do not make that one particularly narrow identification, but accept other parts as genuinely belonging to myself, then an act can be free, even if it was not the result of a consciously executed choice, as long as I identify with that which prompts the action.

In the last few pages we merely performed a straightforward application of our definition (or of our "theory") of freedom. We took the meaning we had assigned to freedom and developed some of its main implications for the perplexities surrounding the freedom of a choice.

The results were uninvolved and definite enough, yet all the same a great deal remains to be done, and therefore we shall take a new approach. To clarify the issues further we will move away from our general definition and become much more concrete. We shall consider several examples, beginning with the classic democratic freedoms.

Nothing in our recent argument is plainer than the observation that we make all decisions in a setting, that we always swim in the great river of events, that every determination has to take stock of the drift and current of all sorts of forces, and is made in the anticipation of consequences that spread away from it like waves. Still, if we bear down on even just this platitude, some clarity can be attained. Some of the mist that envelops the classic democratic freedoms—Freedom of Speech, Freedom of Assembly, Freedom of the Press—can be dispelled, so that the actualities behind these ringing phrases are seen in a truer light.

The crude first expectation raised by the promise that speech will be free has to do with the concession that some bounds and proscriptions may have to be placed around our other actions, but that at least the utterance of words, our merely saying something, will be left unhindered. This presumption underlies the stock classroom example of someone shouting "Fire!" in a crowded theater, which is meant to lower this high hope by some degrees, when it initiates the patient process in which the exceptions to this general rule of freedom are then listed. But this procedure starts from the wrong end. Anything that I can ever say is tied into a net of circumstances. Every word I utter has unending consequences. It may offend or bore you; if what I say is stupid you will decide that I am a fool. No government, or any other social institution could possibly protect me against the countless subtle risks which every sentence spoken by me has to run. And any institution mad enough to try would only rob my speech of what little weight or import it may have, and bring us closer to the ice-age of indifference that is perhaps already on its way. To imagine that free speech grants a full immunity is, therefore, a pathetic fancy, or worse, an ominous over-estimation of the power that the political as such can wield. For the most this freedom could conceivably deliver is vastly less. Realistically perceived, this arrangement offers only the assurance that some particular, institutionalized costs will not be still added to the prices which unavoidably will be extracted, and which no government has either any business or any power to prevent. At best, I receive a guarantee that the burden of being sent to prison, or of being fired from my job will not still increase the weight of the innumerable other consequences that my merely saying something in any case brings on.

In all sorts of contexts we summarily call a society "free" because institutions like Freedom of Speech or Freedom of Assembly are respected in it, and we extend this to the citizens within it; and say that they now enjoy the benefits of freedom. And I emphatically am not proposing, in schoolmaster fashion, that we ought to improve the manners of our ordinary speech, that some other words would be far tidier, and would splash less of the mud of meaning on our freshly laundered clothes. The ruling out of a few words or phrases, even if it could succeed, seems to me in any case to pull in the wrong direction. Our language, as it is, falls short of what we want to express, and needs enrichment more than being rationed. The devising of a more artful choreography for our common talk seems also futile, for to understand what we really mean and think—what the realities at stake actually are—seems far more important than the observation of an Emily Post in the catch-as-catch-can of everyday communication.

So my point is not that these freedoms should be given some other and less shimmering name. But we should understand that the actualities involved can be expressed without the use of that bewildering word, and that our expectations would be far less misled if we conceptualized them in more restrained and simple terms. It should be very clear that in a sharp and literal sense, no government has the power to bestow "freedom" on me; that my actions always occur in a complex context, and that a government in essence can only refrain from the imposition of a particular increase in the risk or in the cost of some very few of them.

The fact that the classic democratic freedoms can be so reunderstood has one major implication for the general structure of the argument that this essay as a whole is trying to advance. When we first introduced our definition of freedom, we emphasized that it should not be regarded as a formula that would enable one to substitute mechanically some other phrases for every occurrence of the word "free," but, instead, that it was intended to be a kind of tool which with intelligent and careful use might help one when the idea of freedom casts its disorienting spell. We meant by this not just that it would not "translate" the freedom involved in "free tickets" or in a "free fall."

The point was more nearly that the one central and most baffling sense of freedom is indeed clarified through our analysis in terms of the various identifications. It is of course true that the word freedom has many other meanings. But these other senses can be rendered intelligible with much greater ease once the most mysterious core significance of freedom has been understood.

One could express this also in terms of an envisioned possible procedure: in many instances the word "freedom" is not indispensable. What is at stake can be expressed in plainer, more straightforward language. One could imagine oneself doing this not just for silly cases like "free tickets," but also for more serious ones, i.e., one could clarify cases like Freedom of Speech and Freedom of the Press in the manner which we have just indicated. One thus could distinguish two separate stages: one could "translate" the word freedom, first in all the peripheral uses, in which it can be easily eliminated. Only those that still remain would then be explicated through the idea of "acting from an identification." The analysis we have so far developed is, in other words, advanced with the claim that it clarifies the meaning of freedom which resists other, easier circumscriptions. One could also say that freedom in many cases is but a euphemism for something different, or less—as for the fact that a certain punishment will not be meted out—but that there are also occasions on which it is seriously and fully meant, and that it is only these which our earlier theory hopes to explain.

This sharpened re-understanding clarifies not only the direction of our over-all advance, but also our more immediate concern with choice, for exactly the same lines of thought which we just traced in relation to Free Speech can be developed in regard to the freedom of a choice. Just as we must utter every sentence in a context of risks and consequences but nonetheless refer to speech as "free" when in actual fact only some special risks have been removed, so also we make every choice, strictly speaking, in the face of obstacles and dangers, but nonetheless call some choices "free" when all we really mean is that some special pressures are not present.

One additional clarifying axiom we therefore can lay down is as follows: No choice is ever "free" precisely in the common, ordinary meaning of that word (as opposed to our "unusual" definition), for regardless of the question of determinism, there is no doubt that all choices are made in the presence of some pressures and some risks— that none are decided in a vacuum.

Yet the parallels run further: for just as the word "free" in Free Speech is (strictly speaking) an unnecessary and misleading euphemism, so with free choice. In both cases the actual situation can be described much more accurately if one turns one's back on the slippery idea of freedom and speaks instead of obstacles and risks that have either risen or grown smaller.

We choose our second instance from the opposite extreme of the spectrum, for if social institutions on the one side grant much less than we sometimes imagine, then they are on the other side similarly limited in what they can take away from us. Our customary language exaggerates both: the benefits we reap as well as the harm we suffer. Just as Freedom of Speech really does not set us "free," so we are not really "coerced" by much to which we ascribe the power of coercion: in one case the boon consists only in the lowering of certain painful consequences that we might incur, and the threat, in the other case, is merely that these painful consequences might be increased.

The stock, classroom example illustrating coercion is that of the man who aims a gun in my direction. The point is that in this situation I would "have no choice," that I would be helplessly in the hands of the other's will, and would have no alternative but to obey what he said. I wonder what Grade B Westerns the philosophers who use this example have been watching. For only in the least imaginatively written script do these things happen in quite such a simple dead-pan fashion. If the film-maker is the least bit ambitious, these moments become precisely the occasions on which his hero displays the full acrobatics of his cunning. He thinks fast, perceives undreamt-of possibilities out of the corner of his eye, and chooses between them in a flash. The barrel of the gun certainly does not transform him into a limply hanging marionette. So the overtones of the word "coercion" are really too crass even for these caricatured situations. And the threats that we normally face in our actual lives are not encountered so directly, nor are the stakes involved anything like as high. We say "publish or perish," but perishing often means only teaching at a less prestigious college.

I do not mean to make light of the instruments of force that governments and societies have at their disposal. Who, today, would still be fool enough for that? What I am trying to address lies on the other side, and has to do with facile, hand-me-down abdications. No matter how dangerous or difficult a situation may become, there always are, if we only look closely enough, an inexhaustible diversity of paths to take. Even a gesture can be infinitely modified, and a single sentence can be shaded in countless tones. And nothing at all that those who try to "coerce" us have in their arsenal, nothing in their array of instruments, from the deprecating puzzled look to prison and the threat of torture, can ever constitute itself as a final barrier, as a wall of sheer impossibility. To a realistic perception these things are never more than added consequences which in spite of their sometimes stupendous weight, can be assessed and accepted as costs that may be worth incurring. And in that sense even the cruelest government is subject to a kind of limitation: just as, strictly speaking, it cannot set us "free," so it cannot literally subject us to "coercion." The language of freedom magnifies the shadows on the wall. The simpler language involving the context in which an action takes place turns us back to the realities which cast these projections.

This now makes a somewhat subtler feature visible: when we are subjected to "coercion," the force to which we are exposed usually identifies itself. Normally, at any rate, we do possess the benefit of knowledge, of something that is like an advance notice. To that extent the qualities that we associate with human dignity are precisely not abrogated in these situations. The annulment of that dimension is more complete when we are "manipulated" without force and in the spirit of sweet consideration. So one could argue that the associations which these words have should be reversed: manipulation is not milder, but can be more "de-humanizing" than coercion.

In our first chapter we said that modern totalitarianism represents not just the collapse of freedom. The distinctive characteristic of the regimes of a Mussolini, a Hitler, or a Stalin—their murderous lawlessness, their jingoism, and their cult of a leader and of brutal might—remain uncomprehended if one's analysis operates in the polarity between the unfree and the free.

But not only does this conceptualization fall short in that it fails to consider other features besides the absence of freedom, it can be challenged even within its own limited circumference. One objection follows directly from the line of reasoning we have pursued: if the conditions under a totalitarian regime are characterized as the absence of freedom, then the people living under such regimes are reduced to helpless victims, and then the excuse that "one had no choice," that there was nothing to be done, that one was impotent and irresponsible, is granted in advance. And it is just this that I am concerned to reject.

If for a moment I may draw once more on my own experience: I lived my childhood and early adolescence under the Nazis. My mother was Jewish yet we remained in Germany throughout that period. I can only say that life was not bereft of choices. There always were conversations, on trains and in buses, to which one could either listen in silence, or in which one could ask a variety of risky questions. Even in the notorious salute, one could either lift one's hand as if one was very tired, or raise one's arm so that it snapped up like a triggered wooden board. The constant hum of choices never stopped, and they were anything but insignificant. To quickly throw a fruit to a prisoner, when his guard looked away, was a splendid moment; to laugh out loud during the showing of a newsreel was to perform an act that easily could have momentous consequences.

The more elaborate, theoretical positions developed by many writers (by Hannah Arendt, for example) which picture Fascism as a system of absolute control, and make of it an all-comprehending, inescapable and, in that sense, "total" order, from which no individual could possibly escape, have at their core a quite erroneous conception of this basic everyday experience, which the grandiose categories of their intellectual machinery then enlarge and cloak. This turns Fascism into a metaphysical melodrama, a philosophic version of the sorcerer's apprentice story, in which the initially benevolent demon of order goes berserk and swamps the world.

The opening strokes of a truer portrait would have to mark out precisely the disintegration of any sort of "order." The image of complete control is the wishful fantasy of those in power, and the notion with which they hope to put resistance into a deep sleep. But in reality the dissolution of the norms of legality naturally spreads, so that more and more of society is implicated in a warfare among thugs. This in-fighting corrodes the internal social structure, till the whole of society becomes the stage on which gangsters fight out their cabals.

A conception of Fascism along these lines would not hand out the excuses which defining it as the obliteration or even the diminishment of freedom would provide. Action is not rendered less possible, even by such conditions. No mystic transformation has occurred. The penalties one risks if one makes certain choices will be very high, yet that does not mean that the choices are not made.

It follows from this that governments cannot give or take away the dignity of man, any more than they can do this with his freedom. Even in slavery men can preserve a quality that some imagine to be the prerogative of kings; and a rule of inequality certainly does not possess the power to extinguish the dignity of all those against whom it discriminates. The quality in man that inspires humility and awe is not so fragile. Nor does it need the garden soil of particular social arrangements. It does not grow only in places that are protected or privileged. It can sustain itself even in the absence of democracy, and it was not invented in 1776. To suppose otherwise exaggerates once more the magnitude of the political.

The attitude which lends this quality to men has deeper and more wide-spread roots. It draws from a broader and more general soil, and is at the same time subtler, more intimate and more mysterious. To say this does not mean that these denials and infractions are less serious than we might have thought. It is the other way around: they should not be belittled, but that which gives man his dignity should be restored to its proper size.

One standard philosophical formulation says that a choice is free if I possessed all the relevant information, and was not subjected to (irrational) methods of persuasion and was not under duress. We could summarize much of what we have been saying in the form of a reply and a rejection of this definition. First, we never do possess all the relevant information, and we are never only influenced by rational arguments (even the most rational argument is advanced by a person, and not even his tone of voice can be completely separated from the "rational" weight of his reasons) and we are above all never free from all duress. Every choice has its consequences, and we always make a choice under certain kinds of pressure. To call choices that meet these (and perhaps other) conditions "free," and others not, is therefore fundamentally misleading. For, though we do speak of degrees of freedom, the word "free" all the same suggests a division, which in these terms cannot be drawn. If we continue to think along these lines, then in spite of all manner of precautions and the best of intentions we will continue to suggest that some choices are somehow not made under pressure, and that in some the subject was not influenced. And this is patently never the case.

Secondly, we could say that the difference between a choice made when someone points a gun at me, and any other choice (or, the contrast between my being brow-beaten or harangued or kept in some specific ignorance, and situations in which this is not the case) is distorted and obscured when I regard myself as "unfree" in the former and "free" in the rest. We can be more specific and precise, and nothing is gained by the pretense that our language has shrunk to two categories, or two words, and that these situations must be fitted into one or the other of these two. A threat does not render me "unfree." A threat simply raises the cost of some action I might take.

Yet another different question now presents itself. If prerogatives like Freedom of the Press or Speech give assurance only that some special risks or penalties or consequences will not be among the many which will unavoidably remain, if they do not literally guarantee a freedom, so that we cannot invoke that name—does this mean that we are less entitled to the protections they provide, that our claim to them has lost its force? It does not. On the contrary, these claims rest now on firmer ground and can now be advanced with greater strength.

If, in an actual political situation, your right to hand out a certain pamphlet is questioned and curtailed, then to protest against this in the name of freedom—to proclaim that man's glory now is imperiled—may be for the moment effectual or not, but the thought will have no real strength. Your case will have much greater force if it is understood that what you are demanding is precisely not something great and lofty—that you are not asking for the moon of freedom, which can be denied with a condescending smile—but that you are asking for something very small, for no more than a bone from the table, which it would be an outrage to deny. And that is closer to the facts: for no government can protect you against the loss of friends, the enmity of neighbors, and the myriad other burdens that you assume if you take one side in a genuine controversy. In truth, all you are demanding is that there not be still one more institutionalized addition to their weight; and that at least this paltry and perhaps ineffectual act not be made still harder by this one degree.

Even when larger actions are at stake, the switch from the

framework of freedom to that of an act with consequences clarifies the case and gives it greater power. One could say that to think in terms of a "freedom of choice" is twice confusing. Once, because of the word "freedom," but a second time because in actual situations what is at stake is not really the right to "choose," but the right to perform a certain action. In cases where the act is more material, where it consists not only in the expression of a view, or of the distribution of a leaflet, but where it becomes a matter of my right to attend one school rather than another, or of my right to live on a certain street, or of my right to engage in this or that sexual behavior, or of my right to refuse military service, what I ask and may receive is greater. The government may not just refrain from the imposition of a sanction, but may actively protect me from some dangers, or it may forego the imposition of a penalty even when I refuse my support to one of its major enterprises. Still, this does not change the general structure of our thought: the stronger reasons for "giving somebody a choice" do not flow from the high value of an abstract freedom. They grow upward from the ground of individual acts. They do not come with a pedigree that traces their line back to a first philosophical commitment. Rather they talk the harsh language of give and take.

Behind the detailed reasons which cry out against a specific burden stand more dispassionate and general concerns, yet even these are more of the earth than airy incantations of freedom in the abstract would suggest. That, for example, tolerance in general is good rests on the plainest grounds: harsh measures always make it difficult for people to bring their lives into some conformity with what they want. It is arduous to make one's way down from the surface till one's real needs and desires can even just be seen, and it is still harder to shape one's life into some accord with that perception, yet failing in this is so ruinous that there is no excuse for obstacles that could be lowered.

Most basically we have just performed a separation: we made the decision to distinguish the issue of having to face risks or obstacles from the idea of freedom, and to make this division permanent and sharp. Our motives for this were very plain: behind the writing of this essay stands more than anything the conviction that the idea of freedom is a shimmering lure, that it tricks and traps, and that to think in terms of it is always to skate on thin ice. That makes it only sensible to drain the murkiness of that idea out of areas where this can be done, to reclaim drier and less treacherous ground, and to confine that word to places where it cannot be avoided. But aside from this pragmatic fact it is also a matter of calling things by their right names; and obstacles are obstacles, risks risks, and difficulties difficulties. If we allow ourselves to imagine that obstacles or risks make us "unfree" we will conjure up the notion that they make it impossible for us "to act otherwise," that they can box us in until there is no, or only one, way out. Or conversely: as long as these ideas are linked, we will be mesmerized into the illusion that because one obstacle has been removed we now have several options when this was not the case before. And for the moment the point at stake is just to fix very firmly that this is not the case. We have seen in the examples of the Grade-B Western and of what life was like under the Nazis that if one looks only closely enough, there is always still, even when obstacles are terrifying, a mass of possible alternatives. Therefore we are merely undoing an exaggeration. Risks, difficulties and the rest do not ever reduce us to helpless victims, and the point of our disconnecting them from the idea of freedom is on one level just to etch this into our minds. On the same grounds we deny the reduction of freedom to the elimination of obstacles; we refuse to grant that this gives us, or even that it increases, our "freedom" because that again would do that favor too much honor; it would again insinuate that some lock which had us immobilized had now been sprung. In essence we are saying that the raising and the lowering of obstacles are not worth the name of freedom, that thinking this amounts to an inflation which is corrected when we insist that obstacles only make actions either easier or harder and have done with it. And there is no reason to switch horses when the difficulties rise very steeply or fall very low. That simply makes an action either very hard or very easy, and that is enough.

We trust no one suspects we overlooked the patent fact that this raising and reducing of obstacles is precisely what people very often do mean by freedom. On the contrary, we would insist that this is true of both the traditional "negative" and "positive" concepts of freedom. "Negative" freedom has always been associated with the absence of restraints, but "positive" freedom shares this preoccupation and is really just the other side of the same coin, since it measures the freedom of an individual in terms of his power to break through restraints. Our point is precisely that this is *all* that is at stake on one as well as on the other side of this distinction. We would go still further and affirm that this applies equally to much of our talk about "objective" or "real" freedom as opposed to the mere experience, the "feeling" of freedom. To speak of someone as "objectively" or "really" free means often only that some obstacles were lowered, and to identify just this with "real" freedom seems to us, for all the reasons we have given, thoroughly misleading.

We insist that this spade be called a spade. The veil of the word "freedom" needs to be lifted, and substituting the ping of the word "obstacle" for the boom of the word "freedom" does just that. It puts some of the cards of this game on the table, so we can see at once what a society has granted to us when it institutes, e.g., Freedom of the Press. It draws a far clearer line around what we may owe in return for this, but also around the indignity of having even this denied. For we are not using smaller and more sharp-edged words to minimize these things. Far from it. More basically, we are trying to cut away the pulp so we can hold on more firmly to the kernel that really counts.

That our thoughts aim in the general direction of a more disenchanted view of choice is by now probably quite plain. We have moved a considerable distance from the rhetoric of "I did not have a choice and therefore was unfree" and from its opposite, "You did have a choice and that means you were free"—but the single sum of our separate considerations should now be brought into relief.

Below the easily reached surface on which most philosophic debates deploy their chess-game strategies, one often finds mental pictures that are primordial in their simplicity, but also in the spell which they cast over our minds. The metaphor that dominates most of our thinking about freedom conjures up a tight and narrow corridor in which we are enclosed. We imagine ourselves walking down this straight, dark passageway, with no room to sway or curve or to turn back, with no other possibility but to go forward step by step. Only at great intervals—the nightmare makes it seem as if it could be miles—do we envision coming to a forking point, where at last two corridors go off in different directions, and where we then "have a choice" and decide between one or the other of these two. In that picture the occurrence of a decision or of a choice is fearfully rare, and because of that, extremely precious. Freedom thus becomes identified with the moments in which this prison hallway gives us at least this much room, and the entire issue converges on the question of whether moments like this do indeed exist at all. When it appears as if they do (or, when a social system makes provisions to guarantee that they will at least sometimes happen), then the general feeling is that all that could be hoped for has been granted, and that what freedom means has now been achieved.

We want to set against this a radically different metaphor. In this other picture there are no walls. Everything is open and what moves forward is almost like a cloud or a field of forces. Particles fly in all directions, come together, collide and shoot apart in no set pattern. As this inchoate whirl progresses, other forces or particles impinge on it, engage it, perhaps trail after it and then fall behind. This image makes vivid the one most crucial feature of our re-interpretation of what choices mean: most fundamentally, a choice is not something rare that offers itself to us only after a long wait. It happens constantly, at every second. Every step and every move we make we could have chosen to be otherwise. It is as if all of our life were carried forward to the constant and monotonous accompaniment of choice—choice drones on and on, like a buzz that will not stop. And it does not sway before only two alternatives, there is never just a simple fork, a mere either/or, but at every step one could move in countless possible directions. There is no corridor, but a whole sphere of not yet realized possibilities surrounds us, and every second we select one from this swarm and make it real.

This is so no matter what the circumstances of our life may be. It is true even for the slave, for even he chooses out of a thousand possibilities the one word he decides to speak—and the choice may be momentous—and shapes in the same way, as the seconds tick, the shade of meaning conveyed by every gesture. We always will be awash in the midst of uncountable alternatives. No one can ever take this from us, or grant it to us. It is simply a given, a brute fact.

The opportunity of doing otherwise, the sense of openness, of space, of not being "locked in" therefore does not at all signify the attainment of a goal, or of a privileged high status. On the contrary, it more nearly marks a level below which we cannot fall, a kind of lowest stratum that cannot be transgressed.

In a sense it therefore would be comic to think of the existence of alternatives as a necessary prerequisite for freedom—necessary, though not quite sufficient. Of course, this is true, but the idea that the existence of alternatives takes us three-quarters of the way and that some addition provides merely the remainder is quite wrong. The existence of alternatives, the possibility of doing something else is much more nearly always there. It is a constant, and not the more than half completed work.

Our main conclusions concerning choice are therefore:
1. That everyone always "has a choice"—that choices are as plentiful and ordinary as sand is on a beach.
2. That the "having of a choice" therefore does not make one free, since everyone would be always free if that constituted freedom.
3. That no choice is "free" precisely in the usual sense of freedom. "Free choices" (if this means choices made in the absence of duress) do not exist.
4. That everyone inevitably is always surrounded by obstacles and by constraints. If freedom is the absence of all constraints, then it is a kind of death.
5. Obstacles and risks do not make an act unfree—they only make it harder.

By now it should be clear that our definition is much stronger than one might have thought at first, for we have now rejected the three most powerful competing definitions: Freedom is not absolute independence, it is not the having of a choice, and it is not the absence of constraints.

The phenomenon of choice, moreover, fits our definition. It can be subsumed under it and requires no qualifications. Freedom is a function of identification, not of choice: an act can be free even if I did not "choose" it (if it expresses what I really am), and an act can be *un*free even if I did "choose" it (if I do not identify with the thought that moves me towards one of the alternatives).

5

Freedom and the Self

OUR RELATIONSHIP TO THE IDEA that we possess a permanent "real" self is strange in its extreme ambivalence. When we discuss childhood development, we find it natural and easy to imagine a consciousness which does not yet possess a self. That the self is not a given, but has to be achieved, that it is not fixed, but fluid and precarious, seems then a quite innocuous thought. But beyond that, if we are asked to identify and to locate the "real" inner self, or to describe it we quickly come to the confession that we imagined a complete but disembodied duplicate of ourselves, a ghost-dwarf that observes our minds from the inside— and then we laugh at our childishness, for surely that homunculus comes from a fairy tale.

Yet nonetheless the idea persists.

To "refute" this notion seems ineffectual. Arguments only prune the stem, but leave the root intact. Our strategy is therefore different. We developed from the very start an alternative interpretation, that was designed radically to undercut and literally to replace this image of an inner core, of the old Substance-Subject. We meant to substitute for this Gestalt the concept and the picture of identification, the pattern of a shifting, moving weight. In this view the "real" self is only a grouping into this or that configuration. The underlying thought has been that the inherited metaphor has to be supplanted, that we cannot expect our thinking to abandon its old home, until another place has been prepared.

Yet we have also been pursuing a second and more pointed tactic. Our whole investigation of the experience that we associated with the Undergroundman was an attempt to bring the idea of the Substance-Subject down from its abstractness and to make it concrete. The claim tacitly embedded in that analysis can now be openly advanced: our description of the completely disassociated self, of the identification with a mere point behind all actual experience represents an embodiment, an actualization of the Subject-self propounded by philosophers. The Undergroundman as we presented him is the psychological equivalent of that metaphysical conceptualization.

Our intention was to demystify the Subject, partly by substituting the vocabulary of identifications, but also through an explanation of the origins of the idea of the Subject, for we see in this notion the extreme extension of the phenomenon of identification. The idea of the Subject has its origin in the capacity for disassociation—it is the natural and unavoidable result when that capacity breaks all restraints.

We thus no longer view the Subject either as a core, or any other kind of entity. We see in it instead the empty other side of a wholesale negation: at once a logically prepared-for possibility (that of non-identification), but nonetheless a vacuous, mere postulate. It therefore is only a theoretical construction, without claim to actual existence— and thus precisely not the "real" or genuine self.

The greatest power of this effort to disarm lies in its direct confrontation: concretization allows us to see the ghost which haunted us during the night of a too abstract thinking. Our examination of the psychology of the Undergroundman had this as its main purpose: the self of the Undergroundman, that point without dimensions to which he escapes, is the philosopher's unchanging Subject seen by day.

These two extended strategies should leave no doubt that the imagined inner essence, the only actual seat of Subjectivity, is not what we mean by the self.

But how can we then conceive and understand the self?

Logic points onward from the contrast that has now emerged. We must no longer suppose that the self is something that we ever simply find. We have to free ourselves not just from the idea that it is a peculiarly baffling core-entity, which is always still one step beyond our grasp, but we must also abandon the notion that it is any special entity at all—and saying this is easy, but really thinking it is hard.

It means that the fantasy of our searching through a great many masks where we look and examine and then discover that this is sham or spurious, while that is genuine and authentic, does not apply. Nothing corresponds to it. There are no characteristics which we have to detect, as when we have in front of us ten paintings and know that nine are fake while one is an actual Monet. The real self from which we have to act in order to be free is basically not something endowed with certain qualities which make it "real." And even our metaphors of "further back" and "deeper down" are misleading, for they substitute a location, or an order of discovery for the possession of inherent properties. To deny all this and to emphasize in contrast that the self does not pre-exist, but is brought into being only through an act is part of the import of the idea of identification, and making this explicit should begin to clarify its meaning.

To go further: the stress is not on the aspect that we ourselves perform this act since this might generate the confusion of some self already being there to undertake this act which brings the real self into being. Nor are we in the main concerned to bring out that this is an active rather than a passive process or that some "decision" is involved, that "we choose to be what we are." These are all *under*statements that fall short of our target.

An analogy might bring us closer to it: numerous writers have remarked that in the case of the emotions a peculiar *intimacy*, a special connectedness exists between our investigating judgment on the one side, and the object of this judgment (that which it purports to describe) on the other. We think that we are in love, or angry, but our opinion is not a detachable and separate fact. That thought or conviction is itself a part of the event. Our believing that we are in love is itself a proof of the actuality of our love, just as a doubt also does not remain apart, but itself can be an indication that our feeling has begun to cool. This inclusion of the observer in the phenomenon observed has led some to say that in the realm of the emotions reality cannot be separated from appearance, that in this special case our "thinking so" indeed does "make it so," that our perception and the fact perceived merge into one.

One can obviously raise objections to this view. (What I believe may be part of the emotion, but it is not the whole, and therefore my perception can be mistaken: I may believe that I am in love, but still be wrong.) Yet for our purposes this is irrelevant; the remaining element of truth will still serve us as an illustration and at the moment this is all we want.

What is useful is the general conception of "self-constitutiveness"— which is proposed. How widely it applies, whether only to some minor portions of the emotions, or more likely, to many different aspects of the mind is not the issue. We are interested only in the principle involved, namely, that a mental phenomenon may be so constituted that it and our perception of it are not two separate components, but coincide, so that the phenomenon comes into being through our apprehension of it and has no existence apart from it. This exemplifies in general terms the more particular characteristic of the self which we are trying to explain.

The point of our insisting that we must set aside the image of an inspection through which the authentic or the sham reveals itself should now make itself felt: there is nothing there to be discovered. If we observed the river of experience and waited for something bearing a special mark to come floating past, we would be disappointed. Our identity, or our self, is not a collection of such premarked bits. The qualities in virtue of which something becomes part of the real self are not there beforehand, but are only brought into existence when the self is formed.

Yet it would be a disastrous misunderstanding to suppose that a mere opinion, or a judgment, or a thought were enough to "create" the self. It would be laughable to imagine that a child did not have a self or a sense of identity until it at some point thinks: "Ah, this must be me!" and that then, touched by the wand of this reflection, a self suddenly materializes. And it would be equally absurd to allege that every momentary judgment, or passing doubt, radically changes the identity of an adult. That would make the self too fickle and would rob it of all permanence.

No, the picture we are trying to create is best seen in two halves: on the one hand there is "self-constitutiveness"—to that extent the analogy to what we said about the emotions holds—but on the other hand it is not just a "thinking" that constitutes the self: it is the act that we from the outset called identification. It is crucial to understand that the self is literally "constituted" through this act of identification. There is no self apart from this or prior to it. The self—if we may put it so—has its being only in the fact that something is given that significance.

To render this thought more concrete one could envision a flow of elements that are initially "neutral." Then, gradually, some of these undergo a process of "attachment" and are invested with a special status; they receive an added significance. In a fashion analogous to this, the self is by degrees eventually constructed.

That the self is "built up" in this manner, and that this is its status should now throw some light on a terminological concern: we have been speaking of "the self" and of "the real self," but also of "the sense of self," and again of "identity" and "the sense of identity" as if they meant nearly the same. This was not unintentional, but was one expression of the contention we have just advanced. Despite all the finer-grained distinctions which can be drawn, we wanted to underscore that all of these are far more intimately related than one normally assumes.

This interpretation of the status of the self runs in many ways parallel to important psychological discussions, most prominently perhaps to those of Erickson and of Piaget, and this, too, is not accidental. It has been one of our aims to draft a philosophical perspective that would be more in harmony with the psychology of our own century than with that of three hundred years ago. But there are of course close kinships also to contemporary philosophic writings.

Sartre, both in the *Transcendence of the Ego* and in *Being and Nothingnesss*, elaborated a similar view of the self in incomparably greater detail. His notion of "pre-personal" experience is especially close to some thoughts we have just put forth, yet there are nonetheless major divergencies. For one, Sartre believed that the self is generated by "reflection," i.e., by the act of becoming aware of our consciousness, and we would disagree with this; but Sartre also, and importantly, places an "emptiness at the heart of Being" and often identifies consciousness with this "lack," this "nothingness." For us this represents essentially a remnant, an element which Sartre inherited from earlier philosophical positions which he transformed when he should have abandoned it completely. An accurate (let alone a "presuppositionless") phenomenological description does not discover any "emptiness" from which experience is perceived. This "hole in the core of Being" is either the hollow shell of the Subject otherwise repudiated by Sartre, or it is the postulated refuge to which the wholly alienated (disassociated) self withdraws. Far from being a part of the structure of "consciousness as such," it is merely a feature of the one extraordinary organization of consciousness which we named after the man from underground. Experience, therefore, does not enclose a vacuum into which it threatens to collapse, but is more like a compact, evenly supporting ground. From the essential sameness of this plain some things are gradually "raised" to become the self.

The actual process of this "personalization" of consciousness could be compared to an aspect of our relationship to language. Especially in traditional, still unspoiled settings, in mountain villages or among farmers, one frequently encounters an intriguing contrast: in their own speech, when they tell jokes or stories, these people often express themselves with marvelous vitality and color. But it is quite different when they turn to writing. Suddenly their tongues are tied, and only strangely stilted, bureaucratic phrases reach the page.

There is an analogy in this to how all of us experience language: at first it confronts us as a finished building made by others. The sentences we form, the words we overhear ourselves speak seem awkward and inflexible. We are like a farmer writing. Our medium of thought is still impersonal and copied. Then starts the arduous and never quite successful process of moving this crust back. One opens cracks, experiments and rearranges and gradually bits take on a character that is more private, until through continuous alterations we slowly make what we are saying more nearly our own. Some great writers persist in this effort till even a single sentence out of context is recognizable as Kafka or as Brecht.

Our experience is similarly impersonal at first. We do not progress outward from the private but grow in the reverse direction: away from a neutral, anonymous and glaringly public world that is not yet experienced from a point of view and is not yet divided into a self and its opposite.

The absence of any inherent self and the fact that it arises only when that significance is attached to some parts of an otherwise neutral experience lead us to speak of its "self-constitutiveness," but this does not mean that the self (or an identification) exists only in the thoughts we have about it, that it comes into being only through reflection, or that it is as we think or imagine it to be. The genesis of the self involves a rearranging of experience, and that reorganization exists and is real whether we are aware of it or not. In other words, the self is genuinely mental, it exists only in our minds and not apart from it, but it would simply be a blunder to confuse this with "the next level higher up," and to imagine that this reorganization has its being only in what we think about our minds—in the consciousness we have of our minds. Our identification does not appear in the instant in which we recognize it, and it does not vanish when we close our eyes.

From this it follows immediately that we can be mistaken about our own identifications. Not only that; in actual fact we never have a secure and settled sense of what our identity or our real self is. It remains elusive and unstable, and is always seen as through a veil. We guess at it, suspect an error, and grope in a new place.

This is of course not in conflict with our earlier contention that there is no self which could be discovered or detected. To put the difference concisely: we then said that there is no inherent "self-characteristic"—like a color, or a flashing red light—and that it would be folly to look for one. All we are now saying is that once this significance has been given to a content, or that reorganization of it has indeed occurred, then that different fact can be either missed or grasped. The process involved, however, is once again not an "inspection." We cannot discover who we are by something analogous to a mere "look," but only through certain kinds of actions.

The self crystallizes behind our back. Meanings attach themselves, experience is organized into new structures, and no announcements of the progress are made to us. It happens unobtrusively and in the background. To determine what we feel or want or hope or think is often hard enough, but these are ropes compared to cobwebs when the questions are: Is this feeling truly my own, or is it copied, borrowed from a book, invented or only a wish? Is this what I want, or is it a Pavlovian response, a knee-jerk of the brain? So the lines are blurred and seem to shift, and only fragments come into view and then disappear.

The actual "shape" of our identity is therefore more like the inkblots of a Rorschach test than the neat circles in our opening diagrams. The exact geometry of these drawings made the important logical relationships explicit, but in real life we do not actually identify with all of our reason and with nothing else, nor with the whole person, nor with none of the parts of our person, but more nearly with irregularly broken pieces of some or all of these. We also do not identify either totally or not at all. It is rather a matter of increasing and diminishing degrees, and even these are anything but permanent. At most the fluctuating patterns develop in a gradually stabilizing way.

Still, we should not suppose that we are trying to lay hold of nebulous and mocking wisps. On the contrary, the self, from one perspective, is for us in the end a simple and quite ordinary concept precisely because we think of it merely in terms of a set of identifications.

What we mean by the distinction between an element with which we identify and one from which we disassociate—and only this inclusion or exclusion has a direct relationship to freedom—has been exemplified already in our examination of the Undergroundman. But there we mainly described situations in which we disassociate from our thoughts. A different, very ordinary example in which the same division plays a role, though it is now drawn in quite another place, would be the case of an adolescent whose upbringing may have been extraordinarily puritanical and strict. Under such a tutelage an identification with one's sexual impulses would very likely not occur. During the onset of puberty the insurgence of these desires would then be experienced as an invasion by external forces, and the resulting actions would concomitantly signify the suffering of defeats and of compulsions.

The familiarity of what we mean by identifications can be brought home still more if we consider the manner in which they most commonly are changed by us. That, too, is at least in certain contexts a quite straightforward undertaking which, under different names, we all have performed many times. We know the steps and the extended strategies and procedures which someone might adopt so as to "accept" his sexuality more fully; they range from ordinary resolutions, to small deliberate changes in all sorts of patterns of behavior to various forms of therapy—and this would be the general picture of how many identifications can be altered.

The emphasis on the homespun, however, should also not be overdone. A very different illustration is needed to balance our picture. In his well-known "The Case of Ellen West," Ludwig Binswanger portrays a highly intelligent young woman. In her teens she was impatient with much of the dreariness of philistine everyday living, and was given to flights of romantic exuberance, but was otherwise "normal" enough. Yet around her twentieth year she developed with relative suddenness a most bizarre and wholly overpowering obsession for the eating of every kind of food. Her craving became so intense that after waking in the morning, she would wait for its arrival as a prisoner locked in a tin box might wait for the heat of the rising sun. But she attached at the same time a truly religious fervor to the thin and weightless and the fragile, and felt an intense loathing for anything suggesting the obese. Her struggle between these opposites took ever more desperate forms, and Binswanger's account traces the stages of her descent over several years, through extended periods of nearly total abstinence, close to starvation, interrupted by stretches in which she is wholly in the grip of her unnatural hunger, to her death at the age of 26.

We mention this case partly because the differentiation into self and non-self is in this instance so sharp and clear. In one sense Ellen West's original personality remains quite untransformed throughout her whole ordeal. She observes the subtlest changes in herself with astonishing lucidity, and reasons with acute intelligence about her situation. She is even quite aware of the macabre humor of her unusual affliction. Whatever advice is given to her she invariably has already considered. And this makes her utter helplessness more graphic. She is extremely conscious but is nonetheless moved by forces which she cannot control. And that is one aspect most immediately at issue: that this division, this "organization of experience" can be so powerful—that the phenomenon of identification can be so real.

But it is also true that nothing in this poignant story can be easily explained. We certainly do not imagine that the entire syndrome was caused by a particular identification, or that some change in it, perhaps the "acceptance" of her inhuman appetite, would have produced a cure. It is precisely the mysteriousness, the fact that we often do not understand how such splits are engendered, and that their shape can be so baffling which we mean to stress. So from a different perspective the phenomenon of identification is dark and obscure. Nothing in regard to it is "simple" except for the bare division drawn by it, but this is the only part of it that is to our purpose.

Our conception, though, would still be too one-sided unless we recognized that this example represents one extreme on an extended spectrum. The dividing line between that with which we identify and that from which we disassociate can be as overpowering and fixed as in the case of Ellen West, but the phenomenon itself reaches through subtly graduated steps to another pole, where it can be quite fluid and mobile, and where the area of identification or the locus of the self can be displaced with ease, through a sheer effort of our will. That end of this continuum is of special interest to our concern with freedom and we shall therefore illustrate it rather fully.

We can think of a relationship, perhaps a marriage, which one of the partners resisted from the start. Conceivably something established itself in the man's mind in the original encounter: this woman was not a "serious possibility" for him—why is quite unimportant; doors were shut, that is all. Every growth of the relationship was from then on for him an incursion, every demand an imposition, the whole a steadily increasing servitude. That might have been the situation up to the point at which the man experienced a kind of conversion. Having taken stock of his life, he realizes the absurdity of his reluctance, assesses his marriage and decides that it is good, and thus commits himself to it and identifies with it. Such a turn is within our power, and it can reverse the position of the self so abruptly that one has an acute experience as of a weight that suddenly is being lifted. It is as if one were now running downhill and no longer climbing upwards through the snow.

In a smaller form I have sometimes witnessed similarily immediate redirections in some of my students. To some, all facets of university life occasionally seem uniformly bleak; they feel that kindergarten was the beginning of a conveyor belt on which their parents laid them at the age of five and that so far they have been only holding still, while the hands they passed performed their operations. They themselves remained asleep, feeling dimly but one thing: that what was being done to them was ghastly. They are apt to say: "Everything I do is always accompanied by a monotonous, dull sound that keeps repeating: 'All of it should be different, none of this has any connection to what I really want.'"

The alternative thus is blank, a sheer negation. And just this sometimes opens the door, for an abrupt change can be effected by simply filling in the other options. As soon as the fantasies of a completely different life are spelled out, their seductiveness starts to pale— combing beaches in Hawaii becomes less attractive once the sand is real enough to get into one's food. With this the realization dawns that one's present life, as it is now, corresponds much more closely to what one oneself wants than one had supposed. And this can be decisive. For this, too, produces sometimes a reversal. One says: "Yes, this is part of me. What I am doing is not just due to outside pressures. It is something that I want and I am doing." And this can make the same startling difference as in the marriage we described.

This brings us back to the episode from my own life to which I referred in the last chapter. During the first few years in my profession I surrendered my time and energy to the demands of teaching philosophy with a sense of deprivation. I experienced it as a concession. The space I gave to it curtailed what I had meant to do. But then I gradually had to acknowledge that I never felt as alive as when I was discussing a question in philosophy. It seemed a grotesque admission: real aliveness was found not in love, not with nature, but in this—in the rearranging of abstractions. For a time I still resisted, and the more territory I gave over to philosophy the more barricaded in and corralled I felt. Eventually it came to a kind of crisis, for the disproportion had grown too absurd: the things I really wanted to do had shrunk to the point that everything else, which comprised nearly my whole life, was suspended, was placed between brackets, and rendered negative by a mere prefix. The change happened quickly. In one sense it was like leaping into the air and making in the fall of severed limbs a whole new body, but in another sense it was like simply putting one's pen from the left hand into the right one. I went on as before. Only the prefix was different—and yet nothing was the same.

This should not be misconstrued. There was no "real" self in the cellar. The idea is not that under false surface layers a more genuine self had all the time been hidden, one "destined" to teach philosophy from the very start, and that I came to terms with this inner essence. It was not as if some impulses were more "real" than others. One might better think in almost quantitative terms. It was just that my mind when left alone found itself spinning philosophic webs more and more of the time, and that these thickened and usurped increasingly more space until the significance attached to them had become a paradox which was resolved when their meaning was converted, and I said: "They and not the rest represent myself."

Inherent in these relatively sudden adoptions of a new identity is also the possibility of a cynical abuse. For if the locus of the self can be so wilfully displaced, if it can sometimes be shifted almost by command, then this creates the option of executing these dispositions calculatingly, like maneuvers in a war game. If in certain situations the opposing forces happen to be very strong then the conflict can be pre-empted and reversed through a crude sleight-of-hand. I simply join the stronger side, or even better, I pronounce it to be me (a mode of conquest that leaves even generals behind) and I now dismiss the former identity without so much as a skirmish.

These relatively rare instances in which the sense of what I really am can be maneuvered by my will, in which I can, so to speak, slip my identity under what I have been doing all along and can thereby reinforce and free in one fell swoop a region so far resisted and held down, capture once more the thrust of our whole discussion of the self and guide it further. For the general perspective in which the self is not originally given, where it comes into being only through the organization of experience, can be seen in a still different light. It is an irritation, a tongue stuck out at our intellects. It is somewhat humiliating to admit that there should be any such dichotomy between what we accept and what we reject about ourselves when both are, of course, part of the whole and when both sides obviously are entangled in much more complex relationships. That we in so many situations want, on top of that, to cleave along such school-boyish straight lines—as when we set reason on one side and the emotions on the other—makes it still worse. Yet, the real wound to our narcissicism is the realization that it is our self that is involved. We are deprived even of a place to rest, and only the shifting sands of a problematical "significance" remain.

The "radical reversals" in the marriage, student and philosophy teaching examples thus have a disturbing implication. How much weight can we attach to an identity that is so readily manipulated? What if no more than a phantom had been rearranged? Yet this, too, is only one face of a coin: for without the organization supplied by the self our experience would remain an inchoate sprawling flood.

But the entirety of this discussion of the self and of identification was for us in a sense preliminary. It should have clarified the base, or the source from which we must act in order to be free. Now we can develop the implications that this has for the idea of freedom. For to make it more palpable has all along been our main concern.

In the simplest terms we propose to think of a person as free to the extent to which his actions correspond to the identity, or to the self, which has all the various characteristics that we have been endeavoring to define. We have turned away from the envisioning of freedom as an absence, as the smoothing out of obstacles, as the removal of hindrances till the air becomes too thin to breathe, in favor of pursuing a very different goal: that of reaching, making contact with and even of submitting to the forces of the self, so that they may be expressed and released.

Everything that we have said about the self and about identification should now be applied, and should narrow down and clarify what is meant by these "inner forces" or this "nature" that must be expressed if we are to be free. Most obviously we do not accept the notion that man is endowed with an inner, let alone an eternal, essence, and we deny this even for the individual. When we speak of the "real self" we simply are not talking about an underlying, or hidden, or mysterious "inner nature"—either of man, or of the individual person—but only about the plain and, as it were, surface identifications. Freedom for us is the expression of what we are, of the qualities and characteristics we possess, but in an unpretentious sense: it is the expression of qualities with which we identify, and the totality of the section just concluded should have rendered sufficiently specific what this means.

This protects us at once against the situation in which someone else begins to dictate to us in the name of freedom; where we are told that our own experience of oppression is not to be trusted, that our mysterious real self is in fact extremely free, though some coercion of our lesser self unfortunately seemed required to force us into line with our truer nature. We are shielded against this kind of Newspeak by the categorical denial of any general, hidden human nature, which could be known or invoked by those who want to control us, while we ourselves are ignorant of it. (Even if there were a universal human nature, freedom according to our definition still would not be the expression of it, but would be action from our individual identification.) The fact that our identities are highly individuated thus puts a hurdle in the way of anyone who presumes to speak sweepingly for a great number. The fact is that it is extremely difficult for each of us to discover our areas of identification, and anyone else is at an incommensurately greater disadvantage.

But this also undergirds the critical dimension of our whole account of freedom, for a further implication is that freedom is now understood to be "no more" than the acting out of these diverse identities; and what we have said about their problematic status now affects—and was of course intended to affect—the status which freedom itself can claim.

But to sever the idea of freedom from any possible core-subject also places it on firmer ground, for it now can no longer fall together with that doubtful entity. Freedom for us, in other words, is viable and genuine—is not merely an illusion, but a reality to be reckoned with—even if the core-self with its traditional attributes cannot be defended. We have taken that millstone from freedom's neck. For us the phenomenon of identification is sufficient; if it is granted, then man can be free.

We have said that the simple idea of a correspondence should take the place of the customary associations of freedom with the absence of hindrances and that in their stead we now think fundamentally of a matching—our outward life has to match our identity or our self if we are to attain freedom. We have to achieve something like a geometrical congruence, a mutual fit, a kind of attunedness, like a harmony between two tones. There should therefore be a basic sense of ease, as when two gears spin without friction in a prearranged synchronization. The usual stress on the difficulty of freedom, on its weight-lifting muscularity and lonely heroism, should begin to have some slight ring of melodrama and of pathos, and just the reverse side should make itself felt: the absence of strain, the collapse of tension, the lightness of freedom, glorious as that of pure play. The now appropriate connections might be with the superb effortlessness of Bach's or Mozart's music, though the reverence and respectfulness can be dispensed with; one picture of the free person might be the figure of a baker, twirling soft disks of pizza-dough in a shop window, juggling elegantly to keep three of them simultaneously in the air.

Freedom should connote a natural flow, neither cramped nor forced, a shift away from the need to control, to compensate and to correct, and toward the exuberance of actions and words at last taking shape quite effortlessly, as if by themselves. This is, in the end, the most authentic prototype of the experience of freedom, and is at the same time the one most revealing tell-tale signal of where the boundaries of one's "real" self may lie. For nothing offers itself to the traveling glance of a mere introspection. No booms are lowered and no red flashing light says "self, self, self." We discover ourselves only indirectly, and often from the "feel" of certain actions. It is this increase in vitality and surefootedness, this undertaking of a shift that ends with the definite impression of one's now "having found one's stride," of one's now "functioning" that is by all accounts one of the surest indications that an accord with our nature has been found.

This in effect reverses the process of our self-discovery. We do not start from an unstably floating image of the self and then systematically close in on this elusive source. It is not as if the circle of the self were originally given, and some other circle, like in an experiment in perception, gradually had to be superimposed on the first. It is more the other way around: we first become aware of this experience of a "free flow," of a natural, heightened functioning and then work backwards from many observations of its appearance and its absence to the tentative formulation of what may be our self. This fact, that our identity, or our self, is largely discovered (and perhaps even comes into being) only through the process of an "acting out," that the possibility for expression is thus in a very stringent sense the necessary precondition for the very having of a self, is packed with social, political and also educational implications. But even now it should give us a new sense of how very intimately the self and freedom are related: the paradigmatic experience of freedom is not just a consequence, or a by-product of the expression of our nature; it is in fact the principal guide to the discovery of our identifications: we fashion our self from the mirror image of our freedom.

This close relationship between the self and freedom has of course everything to do with the extravagant valuation that is sometimes placed on freedom. The fact that the spontaneous flow of action is at once a signal of the self and our most immediate realization of freedom points toward some of the deeper reasons for the special relationship that artists and intellectuals have to freedom. Freedom often matters much more to them than to farmers and to workers, and the reason is not just that they are in many cases simply better off, let alone that they are more far-sighted or more idealistic. The kind of freedom which we have moved into the center of the stage is an indispensable necessity for their everyday work. For most serious writers, for example, it is an either/or over which they have not much control. Their writing either suits themselves, and is quite stringently a self-expression, which regardless of the arduous work it may require, nonetheless in some sense naturally flows from them, or it simply cannot be done at all. The degree to which this is not a matter of "principles" or of "integrity" is surprising. Quite often a writer may even want to write a casual potboiler, but it turns out to be impossible. He either writes in "his own style," or the individual sentences simply refuse to come. Thus artists and intellectuals in insisting on freedom defend more nearly the very thing that makes it possible for them to do their work, while the need of others to be attuned to the requirements of their nature is very much less, mainly because their work is of a fundamentally different kind, and can still be done even if the connection with the self has been disrupted. (I can build a table according to your specifications, and I can even write a doctoral dissertation in this way, but if I try this with a book for which I care, the conflict will become intolerable: either I stop altogether or I become a hack.)

The process through which an artist finds his own style or his own "voice" could thus be a symbol for much of what we have tried to say.

His experimenting and rejecting, the feeling-out of alternative modes of expression, and still more, of course, the eventual hours of "inspiration" where the otherwise foot-by-foot advance finally becomes a dance, a swift and flying rush, incarnates the concept we have tried to define.

If this is an embodiment of what freedom means, then it should be quite apparent that I can be in a situation in which I "have a choice," or in which I even can participate, by voice vote and quite directly, in the making of the rules that now govern me, where for all this I still do not experience anything like freedom, but may still be like an insect trapped in amber. The conditions which either make freedom possible or preclude it are therefore subtler and much more complex than the mere presence or absence of opportunities to choose or vote, and the notion that in arranging for these privileges one has done enough, that they are synonymous with freedom, cannot be defended.

Deeper than this still lies the general preconception that "order" or "community" somehow share a common quantity with freedom so that a measure of one of these must be taken away from the other, that they exist at their mutual expense; or again the similar presumption that an increase of freedom always risks the possibility of chaos and the disintegration of society into isolated atoms. Since this is one of the most facile justifications of those who rush at opportune occasions (often coinciding with moments at which their most material interests are at stake) to the defense of an abstract "order" it is important to say flatly that this opposition is in general terms entirely unreal. The analogies we have introduced make this palpably apparent: Why should an artist who has found his voice or style produce work which must be inimical in principle to "order"? Or why should the artist who comes closer to self-expression than his fellows be either more isolated, or with his actions put greater strain on the communal bonds? How easily one could argue just the reverse: namely, that the work of such an artist will be less erratic, and will be consonant with a "deep," "organic" order; or that his art, as it grows more authentic will at the same time speak more penetratingly to others, and will emanate from layers that are shared and common, if not "universal." And if for artists, then why not for ordinary mortals? The fact that my everyday actions accord with my own nature in no way suggests that they are in principle opposed either to order or to anything communal, but on the contrary holds out the promise of a harmony with others.

But of course there is an opposition, only it is specific and not general: a society naturally can mold a type and encourage in him a specific set of identifications which will, if acted out, produce perhaps not exactly chaos, but will at any rate oppose and undermine the social, and engender the hackneyed war of each against all others. But this does not inhere in freedom; it is a consequence of one peculiar identification—with those individual desires whose satisfaction perversely always spells another's loss. And this puts one aspect of our own society into the proper critical perspective: we have substituted "human nature" for an unfortunate type that the institutions of our culture foster; the calamity of this type comes to the surface in the paradox that he finds his freedom only in the anti-social. For him the exclusion indeed holds: he is so constituted that the communal always represents oppression, and his identity is expressed only in the advancement of his individual advantage. The opposition between freedom and community or order is thus not a general boundary of freedom, but is the symptom of a disease from which we suffer. Or it is an accusation: forces in our society have malformed us to the point where this is our freedom.

The same is true of the relationship between freedom and one's individual uniqueness: advocates of "autonomy" often sound as if all conformity is shameful, and as if sheer difference were already admirable. But even a crude common sense can see that this is comic: for in the name of independence from all others one ends up being guided by them. What others do is automatically precluded; the prevalent is ruled out, no matter how right or appropriate for oneself it actually might be, and one imagines oneself a gourmet while in fact feeding only on leftovers. But this is no requirement of freedom. If some accepted norms happen to accord with one's own nature, then their adoption does not diminish one's own freedom. If they really fit they may enhance one's self-expression and also make one more genuinely independent. The force of one's energies for resistance and rebellion can then concentrate on rules or customs which really do violence to one's nature—and there will be no dearth of those.

Part of the point of this "concretization" is to have done with empty praise of freedom. To throw around its shoulders a cloak of glittering superlatives is as fatuous as showering warm adjectives all over love, except that it is more of a travesty, since blind veneration begins to undo freedom, while love survives inanity.

A first step towards a genuine appraisal of freedom's actual value, relative to other goods, might be the realization that freedom is not just a matter of degree, that to think in terms of a continuum from less to more is to oversimplify. The facts approximate more closely the familiar bellshaped curve: a small proportion of our actions or of our lives approach the two extremes, and are genuinely one or the other, but the preponderant majority lie somewhere near the middle, neither coerced nor free but to roughly similar degrees both at once. In most everyday situations we would be hard put to deliver a clear verdict; and significantly not so much because the pros and cons balance each other out, but because the individual factors are themselves gray instead of black and white. This in a sense confirms what we earlier said about identifications, namely, that our identity is often vague, that only fragments crystallize and that the locus of the self is shifted as we hesitate and change. In modern culture this hedging of one's bets becomes in fact endemic so that even the occasional experience of real freedom or real oppression is bleached out. One no longer has a clearly defined identity, and therefore both enthusiasm and rejection are so toned down that one lives in a twilight world to which the categories of the free and the coerced hardly still apply.

But even aside from this vision of a grey apocalypse, people in their ordinary lives probably never felt particularly free. And this is important only because it stresses once more the contrast between rhetoric and truth: when we decide on a career or on a marriage the quantity of freedom we gain or lose is just one of many factors that can be easily outweighed. In these contexts we rather casually surrender some of our freedom in exchange for the greater fascination or the greater usefulness of a certain job, and we of course make such decisions in our personal relationships at every point. To recall these homey truths might be of some help when freedom-or-death oratory threatens to sweep us off our feet.

To gain a better notion of the relative worth of freedom we might give more body to its counterpart, and see whether we cannot render, concretely and briefly, the meaning of being unfree. Here, too, we reject the commonly accepted picture which raises hurdles, piles up obstacles and pressures, and sees the unfree man essentially as a man "boxed in." We have been suggesting that these words as they stand conceptualize much more adequately what they represent than any translation into degrees of diminished freedom would. But we also advanced the consideration that freedom should not be identified with the mere smoothing out of obstacles, since liberation then dissolves into mere ease. But if we are not to imagine the unfree man as fenced in then how shall we picture him?

We can outline him with an inversion: if freedom could be symbolized as a correspondence, as a harmony, and if the free man basically expresses what he really is, then unfreedom is a conflict, a dissonance. The outward life and conduct of the unfree man are unattuned and grate against his inner nature. If the free man has found the channels through which his forces can flow out, so that his gestures are animated with an energy that comes from within, then the vitality of the unfree man either lies unused and fallow, a pool of stagnant, brackish water, or it is bottled up and kept under pressure, while the outward conduct is disconnected from it, shaped by unassimilated, arbitrary and external strictures which render it mechanical and dessicated.

The analogy to Freud's concept of repression is here consciously intended, but a major difference should be observed at once. We have already indicated that the sense of self comes into existence only through its expression, that the sense of identity develops and becomes known to us only as it is acted out. The exact opposite is true of Freud's libidinal forces. The main burden of Freud's conception is that these forces have a permanent existence so that they will manifest themselves in the form of neurotic symptoms if other avenues are blocked. Our vision of the self is radically different. The self is extremely fragile; it can wither from sheer lack of use, a little dust can suffocate it. The problem of freedom is in large part the problem of how to keep the self alive, how to devise a mode of education and a society which do not extinguish it.

There can be no question of an absence of influence or pressures, and a free man in any case might encounter obstacles with exuberance or contempt. What renders a man unfree is therefore not constraints—these are inevitable—but the increasing distance from, and the eventual loss of a foundation in himself. The less motivated and organic, the more arbitrary the controlling forces are, the less relationship they have to anything within the self and the more freedom is crushed.

In proportional terms, freedom decreases as the dominion of the forces which I can integrate and accept is reduced and as the controlling forces become more alien and remote. If there is an absolute, a Black Mass of oppression, it would be the final betrayal of the self; the moment in which what is most loathed conquers the last defended sanctity: an act like the one in George Orwell's novel, when Winston screams that they should hold Julia's face into the cage with the rats.

One general understanding, that really should be obvious, nonetheless has to be made explicit at this point: what value I should place on freedom has to be at the very least a complex question that one flip of the oar cannot decide. Maybe every language needs some sound to signify the last resolution and the placid sea, but freedom in any case is not its name. So the where and when and what kind of freedom must be delicately calculated. And not just because "circumstances vary" but for deeper reasons that bear spelling out.

For one thing there is no "correct" identity—not even in the individual case. How could there be? It is not as if an original self lay there, waiting as a measure, so that my identification can approximate its contours till the two eventually coincide. My acts can fit my identification, but for my identity there is no model to be copied. The slowly forming pattern is therefore never simply right or wrong. I can never say: this is me, here I stand, I cannot help it, this I must express—it is instead a tenuous construction whose benefits and disadvantages call for elaborate evaluations. We traced earlier the outlines of this kind of weighing when we pursued the implications of the "Platonic" and of the "Aristotelian" and of the "Undergroundman's" identification. And in our own case we similarly have to ask: What will be the whole web of psychological and other consequences if I accept this or that as my self, and how will these compare to the freedom obtained by acting this self out?

This suspendedness, even of the very self, the fact that it is included in the calculation and in the flux that knows no ultimate firm ground, separates our framework most sharply from all forms of a wistful "return to nature." It precludes any abdication to a mysterious, primordial source whose outflow could be of overshadowing importance, and demands instead a restless care and circumspection that is aware of the duality we faced before: that the self whose release is freedom is both, a mere shadow, and nonetheless also the pulse of our life.

But any simple lifting of freedom unto a shield, or plunging forward with a cry of "Freedom at any price" is ruled out by a still more powerful consideration. To say it harshly, parts of my self or of my nature are bound to be unappealing or mean or retrograde or evil, and the chances are that I simply will not want to act these out. Expressing those would not just be a slight and easily outweighed advantage, but would be a straight detriment. It is the hindrance or the extirpation of these impulses that represents the immediate gain. So freedom needs to be limited not only for the sake of others. The requirement to curtail it originates in each of us alone and is determined by our own individual evaluation.

This does mean that we are a battleground. And it is downright curious that the idea of freedom responds with such obtuseness to this toddler's truth. For despite the habitual association of freedom with the upward rising and the transcendence of the self, these are precisely the aspirations with which freedom seems to reckon least. To give the reins to all my facets, alike to the attractive and to the repugnant, might maximize my freedom but it would also signify the end of any further growth. It is this and not just compromises with the social order or the rights of others that imposes limits on my freedom. The more basic question is: With what value is a particular identification, or more simply, a given impulse endowed? If it is generous or beneficial, then giving expression to it is (if I hold these values) good; but if it is mean or ugly or destructive, then providing for its unhindered expression is plainly bad.

The evaluation of the identification (or of my nature) by moral, human or whatever other standards is therefore always primary and dominant. And this means that freedom is anything but a categorical or unquestionable good. How great or small its value is depends decisively on the value of the force that is to be released.

This, it seems to me, is how each of us individually almost has to think, and we are also, in my judgment, entitled to apply this mode of adjudication when it comes to others. This implies (to give, for now, just one example) that the free pursuit of one's material gain deserves perhaps only a very lowly status. And with that one of the classical reasoning-tricks, astounding in its artlessness, should be exposed: the invocation of the general sanctity of freedom whenever property runs the danger of being in some way restricted. The whole gamut of restraints placed on "free" enterprise, from the basic right to ownership down to graduated income taxes, were all along protested from the high plank of freedom's inviolability. Could society in the abstract or particular citizens ever interfere with the full exercise of this impulse to acquire, and how could such intrusion possibly be justified? The tacit assumption behind this question is almost farcical, since there is not a single thought or wink of our eye that is not influenced and shaped by the environment in which we move. We are constantly "interfered with." So why not in regard to what we own—especially since large accumulations are wholly interwoven with complex social arrangements, and with the contributions made by others? To take advantage of every manner of interdependency while one acquires, but then to shout "freedom" at the sign of the first claim by others should by now provoke a laugh, or maybe anger—but not a philosophical debate.

But let us nonetheless point to another premise which lies behind these ratiocinations: it is the assumption that the very high significance of freedom applies with equal force to all parts of the self that want to be acted out. Would the trepidations when limits on property are to be "justified" have any motive if one did not believe that with the frustration of any impulse freedom is equally at stake? But we know from our own individual case that one or another part of us has to be checked at every moment, and, more decisively, we know that the exercise of some specific inclinations represents anything but an awesome value. On the contrary, they may be wretched to begin with so that it is their discouragement (and not their freedom) which represents a good. Why then can we not think more sanely about others—and about society? Every expression of the self is obviously not of equal value, and to limit some may be hardly ever, or even never, justified, but in the case of other impulses this may not be true. We might place small value on the desire for excessive property. Or we may decide that it is baleful in itself and that its exhibition is a lapse which we should combat in ourselves and help others to avoid.

In short: it is not true or legitimate to say simply, "The more freedom the better." I know that some parts of me are pretty vile and that expressing those will make me worse. And the same goes for others: they, too, have some foul qualities and it is natural that these should be restrained. A great deal more about how, and by whom, this would have to be decided needs to be said, but by now we at least should be prepared to resist those who use the idea of freedom as an instrument of intimidation. If some people can express their identifications only through the manipulation of great economic power, then we might point out to them that not every expression of the self is sacred. If the identifications of some happen to be such that the social discouragement of these impulses would cramp their self-expression, then the time may have come where they should cultivate a different self.

One can think of freedom as a luxury. None of the qualities it stands for—neither the consonance between my life and my nature or my identifications, nor the richer flow of energy released by this, nor any of the other signs it might bring in its train are brutal, bare necessities. In many cultures most have lived their lives in hostile circumstances, and were cramped and misshapen by their molds. To demand otherwise is in a sense presumptuous; to want more than others were content with rings of being spoiled. For most people the advantages of freedom do not come first, nor should they. Naturally this, too, can be frivolously misconstrued. But if survival itself is at stake, if the example is that of a man looking for food and shelter, then the expression of his individual nature, and the attunedness to his self can wait. Freedom becomes a consideration only after the few brute needs of life are met; it belongs to the plenitude of the "superfluous" that gives life splendor.

But I mean the word luxury to have also another and more ominous overtone. Think of two boys in a fairly serious fight, evenly matched. One of them knows that staying close to his own style might mean that he will lose, while forgetting this, and concentrating on what seems to work might give him the upper hand. We know that he will decide that this is not the time to experiment with self-expression, that he cannot afford this luxury just now. And this is the point: that freedom is a subtle and refined attunement, easily lost and speedily abandoned by most when things get raw. Very few are clearheaded and controlled enough to know what their nature is and to stay close to it, not only under strain, but even just in the confusion and the "too much" of modern culture. And this has serious implications. For if one is tired of calloused exhortations but actually wants ordinary people to possess some freedom, then the creation of a general setting which makes this possible will have to be among the first and main requirements. This would have to be like a benevolent, mild climate, with long and pleasant summers and winters not too harsh; the soil would have to be fertile and harvests easy. Only in a milieu corresponding to this image—with the necessities provided, and sustenance secured, with the calamities muted as far as can be—will most men find it possible to act more nearly in accord with what they really are. Certainly they will be forced away from this in the middle of a "struggle for survival." And this shows that the conception of freedom which our society adopted is on this score reversed: for we link the idea of freedom to the Darwinian jungle, and imagine that any moderation of it limits freedom, when it is just the other way around: freedom becomes possible only after the fight over the bare necessities has stopped.

Our version of freedom is in some ways less presuming than others. We do not see man as solitary, autonomous, or independent; he is for us inseparable from his culture. In other respects, however, our concept demands much more and places freedom higher; that his actions cannot be predicted, that he makes choices, that he is self-conscious, does not distinguish man and does not make him free. It is not obvious that every detail of how a plant will grow can be predicted either; even a dog chooses one food and refuses others, and that we alone are self-conscious is a curious claim: it is constantly repeated with bland self-certainty, and yet, if the capacity to be aware of one's experience is meant by this, then this too is patently not a prerogative of man. No cat and no mouse could survive a single hour if it did not experience its own pain. So these cannot be the unique attributes on which freedom rests. All of these fall short and lie on too low a level. What we have singled out is by comparison rarer, subtler and more mysterious: that man forms a self, that he creates an image of his own identity and acts this out—nothing less than this is the foundation of his freedom.

The idea of freedom does not ask us to pass beyond the limits, and to transcend the fixedness of the self. It represents a warning not to lose touch with our nature. As we move on from one embodiment to others, it writes on the wall the place from where we have come. That is its power, but also its worst failing. For the will to self-transformation, the hope to travel far into the distance must conflict with it. Freedom advocates the expression of what we already are. Since this includes the struggle among the parts which make us up, it does not enjoin the surrender to any one of these, or the pretense of a false consensus. Yet it also does not teach us to burn bridges, to leave whatever we are now behind, to become "arrows of longing for the other shore." In the face of such departures it warns of calamities. And the refusal to embark with us on these high journeys, the fact that it wants to stay at home, is probably its most disenchanting trait.

Still, freedom is nonetheless entitled to a superbly high rank among other values, and the full force of its great claim becomes most clearly felt when the absolute extinction, the total loss of freedom is conjured up, not as a hyperbolic phrase, but as a fact. Perhaps one can imagine it like an encirclement: despite one's mute or clamorous resistance one is quite gradually driven back. A force, in no way affected by us, deprives us slowly of more and still more ground. It moves like a wall of ice, takes from us this and then another area of our life, till nothing is any longer our own: till even the last refuge is surrendered and the ice has closed.

Freedom thus is, but it is also *not*, a "luxury." One place of self-expression can be exchanged for others rather lightly. In this it is similar to food: whether we eat bread or rice is of debatable importance, and to have both is finally to have more than we need. But we must eat; and in the same way we must have some self, and something that is our own, and some small area in which what we are can be expressed.

The extinction of freedom, when it is complete, thus spells much more than just the loss of the privilege to be different, or to be unique. Gone would be not merely the recognition of oneself as an individual or as a person. The deprivation would be more absolute. At stake is not only the ease with which the self can be singular, or the acknowledgment of its high status—at stake is its existence: if everything is taken from the self, nothing remains.

One image of a truly unfree person would be that of a human being who can no longer say: this is a bench that I have made, this is my feeling, this is a moment I have for myself. It would be someone who has nothing left after the sham and trash of life has been discarded.

6

Freedom and Education

SOME PARENTS WANT to break away from the stunting middle-class conventions by which they were raised, but they are at the same time serious and high-intentioned. At least in the sphere of their own family they want to act on something in which they believe. Not surprisingly, they find that freedom is the one value in which they still have some confidence and so they decide that they will give it to their children.

This high resolve easily leads to the unfolding of a pattern which we all know. For such parents the conflict with an impulse of their child, becomes the abridgment of an ethereal good, and they, therefore, make desperate efforts to move impediments out of the way, to avoid collisions and to give more room. Yet inescapably a cycle starts to form. As the parents pursue this policy of non-interference, and press themselves more and more against the wall, even the most minimal requirements of everyday living begin to collapse. There no longer can be scheduled common meals, and the housework stops having even intermittent breaks; toys and dropped clothes pile up in heaps, and plants and pictures bite the dust. Soon all attempts at serious conversations drown before they have been launched, and in the end all parts of the parents' lives not connected to their children either must eke out an escape, or bog down to a halt. Sooner or later, however, the merely human nature of the parents is bound to reassert itself. Waking to the realization that their own lives have been surrendered, they will strike back—and now go too far in their exasperation. Their sense of guilt then steers them back to their original course, only this time with a still more adamant determination: the ritual of their touch-me-not religion will be once more punctiliously performed, till the stretched string of someone's patience again snaps, and the wheel is given another, and more vicious, turn.

This would be bad enough. Yet the twist that really hurts lies not in the parents' failure to sustain their first direction, or in the price it exacts from them, but in the cross-purposedness of their first intent. If they follow it with bent devotion, they do no favor to the child, even in the periods in which they do abide by their resolve. Their attempt never to stop the child, to eliminate the causes of "repression," to avoid resistance, create for the child a spooky, ghostlike world, in which everything retreats as soon as it is touched. It is like a game of blindman's buff in which all others always stay out of one's reach, or like a corridor that does not echo even one's own shouts. It is the "empty space" to which the idea of freedom dominant in our culture leads if its prescription is for once consistently applied.

But one might go still further back, and look at the earliest infancy, at a newborn of only some few days. In his book *The Empty Fortress*, Bruno Bettelheim argues that the "perfect," wholly loving mother might do her baby almost as much harm as a preoccupied, harsh or indifferent parent. We need not go through the experimental data (drawn in large part from his treatment of autistic children) and the complex reasoning that leads Bettelheim to this conclusion. Only the central point matters for us: how is this harm done? What deprivation would a new-born, swaddled in complete love, still suffer? What is the "not enough" in Bettelheim's other title, *Love is Not Enough*?

The answer lies in the fact that this idealized mother anticipates the infant's every desire; that the wish is already sated before it has had the chance properly to take shape. Under the care of such a mother, the wish in effect collapses instantly into its satisfaction and this deprives the baby of the opportunity to become aware of its own impulse, and even more of the possibility to experience the interplay between itself and a separate, distinct person who responds to it. In the extreme case the baby's wish and the world it meets remain so blended and so intermingled that no demarcation, no self or sense of identity develops.

The situation Bettelheim envisions thus involves a too perfect "fit." Before the content in the infant has fully crystallized, the mother already replies to it in a fashion that produces a match so conclusive and so pat that the baby is cheated of the one event which Bettelheim regards as most vital: the experience of its own will achieving an effect, of seeing that it is capable of working a real alteration.

Bettelheim singles out the event of the baby's being nursed and makes of it a kind of paradigm. The *im*perfect mother, who does not conform to the ideal, and is not a "model mother," gives the breast a little clumsily to start with. The infant, therefore, is uncomfortable. Perhaps it cannot breathe as freely as it wants to. If this discomfort goes unperceived, or if the mother should ignore it, then that would be the worst of three alternatives. But if this slight displeasure of the baby becomes recognized and the mother makes adjustments to it by attempting one or a series of subtle small modifications, all of which follow the baby's lead—that would be the best situation. In terms of the experience of achieving an effect, this mother gives more to her child than does her apparently superior counterpart who performs with such astonishing éclat that every action of the baby is pre-empted and every instant where the infant can affect the world and experience itself as producing this result is invariably undercut.

The salient point is that the rank order is reversed: the supposedly ideal mother is in actuality a second best, and the somewhat (not, of course, grossly) less adept and less giving mother should hold the first place. As Bettelheim says: the image of our self takes shape only from the denials, from the refusals and resistances we meet—this birth, too, occurs in pain.

In the picture of these two ways of nursing, the radical opposition between the two ideas of freedom which has emerged as one of the main polarities of our thinking becomes still more definite and firm. In the one case, the concern closes in on the removal of all hindrances. The radical fulfillment of this idea can be consummated therefore only in a vacuum. The concept which we have set against this notion is condensed into an emblem in the less perfect mother's way of nursing. Here the encountering of opposition is not necessarily an evil. It is acknowledged that barriers and resistances cannot be avoided and also recognized that some are sometimes positively needed. An obstacle is not by definition the denial of a freedom, and freedom does not gain its meaning from the contradiction of its limitations. The core of its significance is distinct and separate from the concern with hurdles and frustrations. The good or ill they represent, whether they augment or diminish freedom, depends on something else. Neither are choices and the making of decisions constitutive of freedom. Whether they contribute or detract is a function of a separate magnitude. The center to which all of these are hinged is the fact of *my* acting, or *my* making a difference, of *my* having an effect. That the baby meets some resistance does not undo its freedom, but is, on the contrary, a condition and prerequisite for it. That it is given choices and makes decisions is similarly beside the point. To achieve the rudiments of freedom it must have that less adept, less "perfect" mother: when showing its discomfort brings about a slight shift in the mother's posture, then it has acted, and in that has tasted freedom.

In the narrow compass of this situation the two ideas confront each other and we find that carried to their limits they exclude each other; the absolute attainment of the commonsensical idea of freedom, which derives from the image of an "open space," destroys precisely the conditions needed for what we have argued to be genuine freedom.

This most elementary, almost laboratory-like context also brings to light an important corollary. In the "liberal" tradition it is an axiomatic postulate that the freedom of one person should be restricted only to protect others against possible infringements. This assumption sets the stage on which much of the later theorizing is played out, and shapes especially the psychology of most of the subsequent discussion. It portrays freedom as a good that cannot be exceeded—the more the individual has of it, the better it will be for him. Restraints are not imposed for his sake, but only for the sake of others. In fact the most immediate purpose of these restraints is again to protect the freedom of those others, to ensure that they, too, are surrounded by an "open space."

This, from the start, casts all other human beings into unappealing roles. The "Other" constitutes most fundamentally a limitation; his existence extracts from us a series of concessions. Society confronts us as a multiplicity of centers that insist on restraints which are organized into a web of encircling negativity.

Our contrast between two ways of nursing exposes the folly of this conceptualization. On the larger screen of the political with its higher level of abstraction, the error is no longer easily detected. This is one reason for our reversing the Platonic order, and proceeding from the inner self outward, to the social and to the "larger canvas" of the state. But in the concrete and immediate instance of the relationship between one infant and its mother, the mistake is immediately apparent: the impulse of the baby must meet with some "limitations," the gestures of its hands must encounter some "resistance," and this of course must happen for its own sake. If its "freedom"—precisely in the meaning of the liberal tradition—were not limited, it would not make contact with anything whatever, and that would not only hinder its development—it would quite literally die. So the grand and justly famous argument from the Master-Slave relationship of Hegel's *Phenomenology of the Spirit*, that one consciousness needs a second, other consciousness, to gain from it the recognition of its subjectivity in order to become a genuine Subject (an argument which Hegel almost certainly directed against the political philosophy of his predecessors), is actually still an enormous *under*statement. We need the Other not just for the achievement of reaching our own full subjectivity; we have need of him from the earliest beginnings and for the most rudimentary accomplishments.

The recognition of our acute and continuous need exactly *not* to have freedom in the inherited and long-habituated sense thus opens a perhaps grotesque perspective. For now an earlier consideration comes back to us with much greater force: in the chapter on "Freedom and Absolute Independence" we tried to make more vivid what complete and total freedom in this sense would actually mean and we concluded that it would be dreadful. But now we no longer have to travel to these theoretical extremes. Once the extent to which we need constant contact and response has been acknowledged, once we admit that we must have a never-ending interaction and steadily increased attunement— which Bettelheim calls "mutuality"—and that it is we and not the Other who benefit from this, the traditional idea of freedom shows a gargoyle's face. Now not only its complete fulfillment appears terrifying, but even its mundane day-to-day enactment, the ordinary pull it exercises, seems inverted and prone to guide us in the wrong direction. The pursuit of this miscomprehended value now suggests tales of steering by a compass that leads north when one wants to be heading south; of traveling with every step deeper into a frozen wasteland because the very instruments of guidance are perverted.

Just as the withdrawal of all obstacles would suffocate a baby, and would turn life for a three-year-old into sometimes tumbling, suspended in weightlessness, and then crashing in fury, so would this leveling of all obstacles make for abortive pre-schools. If, in the name of maximizing freedom, all interference on the teacher's part is simple-mindedly reduced, a void results. But now it does not remain hollow, as it might between one set of parents and their children. With more children in the situation, the vacuum inevitably will be filled. The first to rush in will naturally not be the more subtle and complex and frail, but the crude and strong, so that in such situations, a kind of *pax* of the most muscular is soon established. Some, nonetheless, manage to convince themselves that even this represents a kind of freedom. This feat of verbal magic turns abdication and even just mere sleepiness into the highest act a teacher can perform. Rest, on the teacher's part, becomes his supreme virtue. He now sits, undisturbed, for days in the same chair, while the five-year-olds around him battle in a jungle.

The children on whom this *laissez-faire* for bullies is unleashed have to encase themselves in cumbersome protective crusts. And this would be bad enough. But in our context it is just as serious that the kindergarten, or the day-care center, shaped by this philosophy—and they are full of missionaries who preach this emptiness to others—pours grist on the mills of those who want to elevate authority and harshness. Their instinct for dominance and for assertion jumps at the chance. "That's proof enough for me," one hears them saying, "better to have a school that's run like a tight ship." This is the real disaster; this misconstrual of what a free school ought to mean gives the idea of freedom a bad name; it makes it easier for those whose natural inclination is to impose governance and order to feel justified. They point to this kind of school and hold it up for general refutation.

That many form their general political positions from the model which they see in schools makes it doubly important to realize fully that this abdication of the teacher does not establish "too much," let alone "complete" freedom. Rather it simply gives way to the pecking order of the crudest. This is in no sense a high degree of freedom, but comes close to its general destruction. And this cuts both ways: it means that those who think that mere withdrawal creates freedom for the children in their care are simply wrong—this self-indulgent recipe produces nearly the opposite effect. But it also means that in this version the possibility of a genuine "free school" has not yet been tried, and that it, therefore, has not begun to be refuted.

We should remember that these judgments rest on the support of our general analysis. If the essence of freedom lies in a self that finds expression rather than in the eradication of all obstacles, then the misguidedness at stake is fundamental. The divergence is not just a matter of degree or of the niceties of this or that procedure. If the possibility of acting from a sense of self is freedom, then any version of the teacher who hides his head beneath his wings is in principle no longer a means to that end. Then a categorically different approach is called for.

The educators who confidently flaunt their "old-fashioned" views have mainly played an easy game. Blithely they imagine that the only real alternative to their own practice is the caricature of freedom we have just described and this supports the fantasy that they have won without a fight. But the real alternatives, which actually would embody freedom, have not yet been confronted. The schools which confused freedom with mere unhinderedness were clay-ducks for those who basically wanted barracks. Schools built on the firmer ground of a more thought-out idea of freedom would be a less easy target.

The same problem extends from kindergartens all the way to the universities: a large proportion of the changes instituted in recent years were guided by the same to my mind misconceived idea of freedom. This is true of many of the features of some open classrooms in the lower grades, and of a whole diversity of changes in high schools, ranging from having the students sit in circles instead of in straight rows to revamping their time-schedule into "modular arrangements." It applies as well to many colleges, which proliferated their programs to provide more choices, dropped requirements, and so on. Some of these changes certainly were steps forward, especially if one remembers the rigor mortis of what they replaced. But others were abortive and opened bigger holes on one side, while they closed a small crack on the other.

For instance, this idea of freedom clearly discriminated against teachers with ideas or powerful enthusiasms, and to an extent against all who seriously meant to teach. And this was inevitable as long as every form of influence was perceived as a curtailment. Conversely, it placed a premium on those who offered mainly long disclaimers. It hung a cape around the fact that they often simply did not have much to say. They could not be accused of imposing their own or anybody else's views on students, since they had nothing to inflict. Similarly, it lent color to the daydream that all discussions, no matter how insipid or stage-managed, are somehow less "authoritarian" than even the most haltingly presented lecture, and led to the institutional provision of countless "options" which actually gave the students very little from which to choose. In many situations, it helped along the step-by-step process in which the intellectual content of a set of courses was ruled out because it was regarded as too rigid and confining. The predictable result was that the students felt still more degraded, since now indeed the school did nothing more than condition them to live by time-schedules and to accept the patient and well-mannered habits that fit one nicely into the consumer apparatus. (And there was irony in this, for precisely those who rebelled most sharply against the previous intellectual dead weight, were also those who felt most keenly the humiliations of being treated to the remnant.)

The forced march back into the past, which we now witness, was almost predetermined by the logic built into this way of construing freedom. For the principal imperative which issues from it, by its very nature, cannot be satisfied. The attempt to fulfill it radically slips into the nightmare of its absolute denial. Small wonder that a pull in one direction, once it goes far enough, brings on a counterpull that drags the center back till the original impulse once more digs in its heels and starts a repetition of the process. The inner conflict of this notion thus makes for the futility, the teeter-tottering, the indecisive remaining in one place, the permanent loggerheadedness of the debate between the "traditional" and the "progressive" factions. It hardly could be otherwise, for if one's idea of freedom turns into counterfeit as soon as one has really staked oneself on it, then some such rope-pulling contest must result.

This general stagnation and cultural paralysis makes itself manifest in an accumulation of ordinary, everyday facts. From school to school one syndrome unfailingly recurs: from the most occasional encounter in the cafeteria, to the intermittent but interminable main conversation in the common teachers' room, to the full-dress battles between groups of incensed parents and school boards, and beyond that to the talk in the plenary sessions of the big conventions, and most obviously in the huge body of the current literature on education—in all of these different settings, the same arm-wrestling duel is fought out. The teachers in most schools wearily line up on the opposing sides, and carry this tug-of-war on during countless lunches, while spates of books exert their force to move this issue by a foot in this or that direction.

The most appalling aspect of this is the enormous waste of energy and time. Yet, as long as the issue is anything like: "Stand back!" "Do not interfere or influence!" "Let the kids do what they want!" on the one side, and "By God, I want to teach them something!" on the other, this deadcentered immobility can be the only outcome. And not because this is a head-on clash, but mainly because the wrong metaphors and concepts have split the minds on both sides of this fence. The "progressive" wing, of course, really does want to influence and teach, and has no intention of letting the kids do what they really want (which might be not to come to school at all), and the "traditionalists" are often more kind and more intelligent than they allow themselves to sound. But hooked on the wrong image, they circle around each other in one spot.

Some of my earlier examples might have left the impression that the difficulty lay merely in a going to extremes. One might have thought that the parents just went too far in giving space, that the perfect nursing mother was simply the rare case of an unlikely flawlessness, and that the kinds of pre-schools we described showed only that even the idea of freedom has to be taken with some salt. The cultural rope-pulling contest to which we have just pointed should begin to put this into a different light. For the deeper failing of this idea of freedom is precisely that it gives no real guidance, that one is forced to abandon it if one wants to stay sane. That this idea leaves one in the middle ground is therefore the more serious disease, and not the cure.

Moreover, the mere toning down, the universal give-and-take does not really help. Most parents, of course, realize what a disaster for their children full freedom (on the terms of this idea) would spell. They anticipate the paradoxes we have traced and naturally stop well short of them. But for the most part they do not attribute this to anything in the idea itself. Instead they make the excuses of practicality, of general human weakness, and of the exigencies of their own, not easy, lives. On Sundays they still look to this idea of freedom, and on weekdays they capitulate. Secretly they feel guilty and wish for a truer and more consistent way of bringing up their children. They do not turn roundly on the idea itself, but lay the blame instead upon themselves.

Yet this still falls short of the accusation which we mean to raise. Of course our fingers have been burnt enough, and our culture generally is so respectful of the pragmatic and the practical that old age came to it right after childhood; we know that one has to be cautious with ideas, that only a carefully balanced diet, a pinch of this and a teaspoon of the other is healthy for weak stomachs. And with most ideas this may be wise. Yet this is just the charge we want to bring: that this is not the case with this idea of freedom, that in its instance the celebrated compromise is no way out, that in its case the middle-road is even worse than some of the extremes, and that something, therefore, is amiss that no more drawing in of all the horns can fix.

Let me give two examples to illustrate this allegation.

One, perhaps most typical—half-and-half between authority and this kind of freedom—is the shift from clear-cut prohibitions, from letting the child's will plow headlong into a firm interdiction to the calm and sensible "discussion." One no longer says, "I will not stand for this," but has recourse to remonstrations. One "persuades" Tommy that all things considered, he really did not want to pound the nail into the cocktail table. This way of cushioning the impact, of guiding the child not with a stick but with a gentle hand, seems such a natural safe course between the extravagance of freedom, and the demented stunting of old-fashioned discipline that it becomes for many the obvious path of least resistance; so much so, that the thing looks settled, that the case seems closed.

To see how wide open it in fact still is one only has to hold the older, harsher stance against this mellowed counterpart. For even the authoritarian approach is on two counts superior to this smoothing of the waves—of course on the assumption that it may be strict but not sadistic. For one, it at least allows the impulse of the child to form. It gives time and room to it so it can crystallize. Whatever else the crasser blocking of the child may fail to do, at least the child gains clarity about the nature of its will. Usually only the action is prohibited or punished, and that gives a kind of sanctuary to the wish while it takes shape. The later clash might well assist this even further, for the negation reflects back and brings the contrast into sharper focus.

The seemingly more enlightened but in truth only gloved forebearance does just the reverse. Its milder, more insinuating interference intercepts the formation of the impulse. The adult's wish blends into the incipient urge, so that the two cannot be sorted out. The chance of any genuine self-discovery or sharply defined self-expression is thereby ruined from the start. The child's internal situation becomes murky. It no longer knows where the persuasion of the grown-up ends, and where its own will starts.

The other advantage of the unmodulated sharp reaction is that it secures the crucial gain of keeping the conflict in the light and clarity of the external world. The battle is not staged within the child, but takes place in the open space between it and the adult. This again helps to engrave the demarcating lines so that the emerging sense of self becomes solidified. The more soft-spoken rule, in contrast, lays the burden of the conflict much more on the child. At its worst, it splits one part of the young human being off and hires it into the service of the adult's demand. The task of turning the original impulse back is shifted from the external social world and is now assigned to that part of the youngster. This division is bound to have a weakening effect. The energies now work against each other and cancel out. (One could even wonder whether the internalization of these conflicts is not one version of Gregory Bateson's "double-bind," and whether there might not be a connection between the coming of this general dispensation and the increase of schizophrenia in the middle-class.) But consider a second and more complex example of a compromise with that idea of freedom.

Open classrooms, in actual practice, have been unboundedly diverse. Still, one general tendency stands out, and one could think of it in terms of a "selection." No open classroom, for obvious reasons, can depart in all respects from the methods, norms and habits of the surrounding community or school. Some selection is inevitable, and the first changes instituted are in nearly every case the obvious and familiar ones: the confinement of sitting in assigned chairs is abolished, the children are allowed to move about more freely in the room. In the perception of some, this more than any other single step marks the definition of an open class. Naturally, this goes hand-in-hand with taking the children off a uniform time-schedule, so that they can read or draw or do mathematics, not at one predetermined time, but more at their own discretion. In addition, one also includes activities that engage the affective talents—one sets up corners for "pretend" or "fantasy," equipped with puppets, costumes and the like, encourages the writing of poems, the performance of music and so forth. But importantly one also changes the whole general tone: one becomes more supportive, just plain friendlier, more humane.

So far the emphasis has not been on the core of the actual teaching, namely on how reading, writing or mathematics are presented. The physical mobility of the child, the time-framework, the emotional relationship between teacher and student, and the imaginative and affective capacities of the child seem to have been singled out. One is careful not to inhibit the impulse of the child when it wants to move, but is very much less concerned with what happens to his intellect, when the moment of instruction does take place. One is, for instance, quite unembarrassed by the use of the kind of "skill-books" now in vogue, and seems not to be aware of the contradiction between a general regard for freedom and these instruments which force the child's mind into a rigidly preprinted mode, and steer it like a wind-up toy to put an "X" into exactly this small box, or to draw a line between two things that start with the letter "c". Here the effort at individuation, the sensitivity to the distinctive character of each separate child seems suddenly to break down. Exactly the same set of exercises, in the same sequence, executed in the most deadening routine, seems to be good enough. The possibility that a first- or second-grader already has his own manner of structuring and of absorbing information, and that his categories and procedures might conflict so seriously with this choreography that they could be warped or destroyed by it, is not considered.

This imbalance has again a strong connection to the traditional idea of freedom, for in relation to the child's emotions the teacher can give freedom, and still retain a definite and concretely conceived role: he is not harsh, but gentle, he is not intimidating but makes an effort to draw the child out. But not so with the intellect. If the teacher does not want to inflict his knowledge, and the child turns a deaf ear, then in a sense the teacher can do nothing except wait. The giving of freedom in the intellectual sphere (on this idea of freedom) in other words runs the risk of plain not teaching, of getting paid though one is not working, of perpetuating ignorance; while the giving of kinesthetic freedom still leaves one a place. And that is one cause of the imbalance: one gives emotional freedom because that is not too compromising, but one continues to teach in rote ways, because the only alternative envisioned is not to teach and that would end the school.

Below the surface of this lies the fact that we still somehow imagine the mind to be a blank. We picture the teaching of knowledge as a filling in of empty spots. We have no analogous image in regard to the emotions where an organization of forces is acknowledged to be present before we come upon the scene. Everyone agrees that we at most shape and form the affective side and that we must reckon with an already given constitution, which we improve or botch. When dealing with the intellect, however, some regard this as less problematic, as if no consideration for the previously operating structure was needed, as if the definition of success were simply that this or that had now been taught. This underlying attitude contributes to the greater caution adopted vis-à-vis the affective parts, and the much more mechanical, rough-and-ready methods employed to impart "information."

Originally, the stress on action, in Dewey for example, was coupled to an equally emphatic critique of intellectual straitjackets. But, oddly, the tendency has been to tone down this aspect of his program, even when other portions were adopted. Yet, if anything, the order should have been reversed. The constraining mode of teaching that aims at getting the right answer from the students—that sets him pointless little tasks and rewards him with "correct" in one case, and with "wrong" in all the others—violates his liberty much more than does making him sit in one chair. So the most frequently practiced version of the open class moved where it might well have stayed in place, and left unchanged what it should have leveled to the ground.

Certainly, any opening up at all is preferable to the closing of all doors, but one could easily maintain that this general emotional blandness is at best ambiguous. Does this approach really help to bring individuality out into the open, or does it in fact hinder real individuality? Are the original concerns for interaction and community still served if authentic action, involving real risks and real errors, is discouraged, and mainly small and private impulses are actually accomodated? Might the effect not be the opposite from the one hoped for: namely, an isolating and introspective preoccupation with the self? In any case, as long as only relatively trivial inclinations can be acted out inside this setting would it not be better to hinder those? In fact a measure of control over these surface impulses is absolutely needed if countless things from genuine relationships with others to self-respect are to develop; and more basically, because no sane or at all satisfying life is possible without that.

The case for a radical reconstruction of the methods of intellectual instruction is, in sharp contrast to this, very strong. Every advance in our understanding of the cognitive powers of the mind raises the estimate of how complex and finely structured its modes of operation are. To force these processes into simplistic patterns must do more damage to them than we can adequately comprehend, though one could guess that it resembles the crippled feet of Chinese women. Moreover, this drilling of the mind does not produce clear benefits, at least none comparable to those gained through a minimal control over superficial inclinations. On the contrary, both real life and genuine academic excellence require a mobile, open and spontaneous mind, capacities of balance, of synthesis and of reorganization, which this training on isolated bits is likely to destroy.

The simple fact that nearly all children learn how to speak a language, while many bog down when it comes to reading brings this home. For the feat of acquiring a language, of grasping the rules and meanings to actually use a language in the world is vastly more impressive than the relatively simple step of merely correlating words to signs on paper. One could not master the earlier, more demanding task, unless a very high degree of intelligence were present. If some cannot manage the far easier subsequent transition, then this has very likely some connection to the very different manner in which it is taught. A two- or three-year-old does not learn how to speak at special times or in a special place; and he does not first memorize the "alphabet" of possible component sounds, nor does he group words into those that start with "p", or perform exercises that fill in "missing links." He learns his language as the need arises and through natural use. But the key difference may well be that the operation of his intelligence is not controlled; that it is left alone, and has the chance to structure this material and these tasks in accord with its own rules, in line with principles that either inhere in it or were organically evolved. If an intelligence capable of learning language has difficulty with the step to reading, then this may be because the imposed organization frustrates and cramps the assimilative procedures of the mind to such a point that they no longer function.

Intellectual hoop-jumping thus cannot be defended with the argument that ignorance will be the lot of those who have not been put through it. An intelligence able to acquire language in the first place could make the substance of our public school curricula its own in other and much less debilitating ways. Those who are most prepared to lay down the specific "goals" which every student should be required to attain belie their professed concern for "competence" through the crude, manhandling methods which they advocate. The disciplinarian mode of instruction should be opposed precisely on the ground which it preposterously claims to monopolize. The link that ties the authoritarian to knowledge exists only in propagandistic rhetoric. These methods do not teach enough; that is the heart of what is wrong with them. What fraction of the subject matter "covered" in this fashion does anybody still remember five years later? And what effects on the intellectual powers does their application really have? That question becomes haunting if one has ever been awed by the sheer brightness and rapidity of four-year-olds and has made the comparison to graduate students.

To what conclusions do these considerations point? There are mainly two: the first is that any attempt at the complete enactment of the idea of freedom which identifies the lowering of hindrances as the principal goal to its realization and which therefore tends toward the establishment of an "open space" is bound to bring on grotesque deformations, and further, that this is in itself a cause of much wasted motion. The second is the realization that even compromises with this idea do not work. We saw that they infect with guilt and seduce into resignation and that the injunctions of that conception lead often to an inverted practice: one will yield just where this will do damage, and one will remain immobile where changes would have been most urgent.

Our earlier, theoretical criticisms of the traditional concept of freedom have now been applied. If these are some of the traps, impasses and blind alleys into which it leads, then its hold over us should be resisted. Since its high prestige still exercises controlling power in the political domain, one has to go back to the ground of the very simple situation between one parent and one child to see sharply the flaws of its illogic. One purpose of the foregoing lies therefore in the further observation of the contrast between two opposed ideas of freedom: as the weakness of one becomes more evident, the strength of the other makes itself more felt.

But at stake is not just that concept. Our more immediate concern is with the day-to-day conduct of education, and there most particularly with the fact that it receives no definite direction from that notion. And this represents a waste of the idea of freedom. It is invoked much, but to no effect; its potential force is left unstrung. The advances made so far have been confused and the likelihood increases that they may again be lost.

Can this be remedied? Is the interpretation of freedom which we have evolved more capable of guiding education? Are its directives less confounding, and could they be implemented? Is that concept a foundation on which a stronger and more definite demand could rest? In any case, what are its implications? How would one educate a child in freedom on the terms of our notion? What would one have to do to make it free?

One way of thinking about teaching would go like this: imagine an accomplished juggler. He had talent to begin with, but through practice he has now reached a point where he is able to keep six dinner plates up in the air. With his face strained in concentration, his quickly moving hands toss up disk after disk as they descend. Someone else stands next to him with still more plates, ready to hand him the seventh, and after that perhaps the eighth. If it is done at the wrong moment, either before the juggler's skill is far enough advanced, or clumsily, off by a split second, the result will be that with a crash all of the plates fall to the ground. The new plate has to be offered at exactly the right time and in precisely the right manner for it to be included and to stay aloft together with the others.

It is good to think of the student not as idle or passive, but to imagine that his mind is as skilled and as engaged with its own problems as is that juggler's. To thrust a new piece of knowledge on him is not obviously an improvement, is not guaranteed to make him better. In fact, the wrong addition will bring everything that he could so far do to a collapse. Early on in teaching, one must come to the recognition that only some very few out of the ideas one has to offer will be of real use to the student, that the most important and most demanding part of teaching concerns this process of assimilation, the creation of the unlikely circumstance which allows a student to incorporate one more idea into his own thinking.

There is a second, similar analogy: perhaps the most crucial difference in teaching is not adequately captured by the opposition between the "authoritarian" and the "permissive." Perhaps it would be better to think in terms of a comparison between two ways of gardening. One could be called the "Prussian" method of growing something. It first flattens the terrain with a bulldozer. Nothing is left standing, the ground is leveled and laid out in geometric squares.

Then one sprays the earth with various weed-killers to make sure that nothing unexpected sprouts, and only after that does one cut straight furrows, neat like rows of chairs, in which one then plants turnips.

The other way of gardening has been perfected by the Japanese. Typically, they start from the trees and shrubs and stones that are already there, and in a very delicate and careful process prune and trim and rearrange till the surprising beauty of an ordinary moss, or of a root curling through it, has been clarified. Of course, new plants and rocks are added, but the whole evolves with a great care for the previous arrangement.

That difference, applied to education, shows in sharper outlines where the real oppositions lie. The main objection to what is usually labeled the "authoritarian" may be its eradication of the natural pre-dispositions of the mind, or of the whole person—the pretense that the mind is a *tabula rasa*, or worse, the making sure that it becomes one. And so, too, for the advocates of freedom. The talk about not interfering and not exercising influence (not "molding" students) conveys the absurdity of a mere abstention and misrepresents what they really mean, which is expressed far better by the image of that other way of gardening, which sees itself as a ministration, as an enhancement, of that which is already there.

Given this, one might think of the basic educational situation along the following lines: one fundamental premise should be the idea that the child (and, perhaps, the person in general) is if anything too exposed to influences from the outside world. The problem is not the gathering of forces great enough to still have an effect, but the other way around: the danger is that they will be too strong. Man's powerful neurological endowment gives him a much greater sensitivity; he is more receptive, more exposed, more vulnerable than the rest of nature. One could compare him to a skier who has to shield himself against the excess of light in order not to become snow-blind.

The second correlative premise should be that the child hears his own voice only in a "whisper." The sights and sounds from the outside world are intense and vivid and strike it with a great force. They nearly drown out the perceptions of the child's own feelings and desires. Here, too, the traditional picture has to be reversed: we do not, as a great many philosophers maintain, see our own minds, our inner subjective impressions, with assurance. On the contrary it is the physical, the public and objective that presents itself to us with great clarity.

Our internal sense is by comparison extremely faint and frail, and the danger is that this "connection to the center" will be cut altogether, that our subjectivity will be overpowered, so that only the outward shell of objectivity is left.

Nothing is more misplaced, on this general orientation, than the often encountered fear of the child. One has not been handed a rapacious tiger cub that now by hook or crook has to be "socialized." The forces on the side of culture and the grownup are so much stronger than those of the isolated, individual child's that the encouragement to "crack down on him" is almost comic.

Not just that: the more general perspective which thinks of man as "egoistic," and as naturally satisfying his own instinctual appetites, and which looks to education (and particularly to morality) primarily for the taming of this selfishness, should be confronted with a wholly opposite perception. A truer starting-point might be the observation that all too many at some midpoint in their lives feel that they have not once done anything they really wanted: that in everything so far they have been led by expectations and considerations of and for others, so that they now at last want to do one thing for themselves—a decision frequently expressed in therapeutic contexts. The threat lies in an excess of taming; it takes very little to sever a human being from his own inclinations, or beliefs, or feelings, and the fear of not being able to "control" the child becomes in that light downright silly. One, if not the principal enterprise of education becomes, therefore, not the diversion of the promptings of the self into more social channels, but on the contrary their enhancement and protection. If our own self is more obscure for us than the external world in the sense that what we want, or feel, or have a talent for is not presented to us in evident and easily read signs but always so that we must guess at it—then much has to be done to overcome this. Ways must be found to amplify the fainter signals; some may need help to penetrate through to awareness; others that have been overlaid need perhaps to be restored; outside interference might have to be warded off. More generally, the arduous task of building an interpretation, of assigning meanings, and of structuring from them a larger pattern needs to be assisted.

In practice this means that the student must be enabled to make all manner of discoveries. But these cannot be achieved unless he has sufficient room to act, for neither talents nor emotions nor even appetites can be assessed and given precise definition till we possess the clarifying information that only their expression furnishes. Mere intro-spection drifts into fantasy and wish-fulfillment. There is no way of knowing our talents apart from actual undertakings that put them to the test. Emotions, too, show their true nature only when they are released; held back, they turn into mythic monsters. The simplest appetite is only a blind urge till it is acted out, and the surprise of satisfaction or of disappointment tells us that what we wanted was indeed an apple and not soup.

In this need for experience lie the much stronger reasons for creating schools in which the child can move. For at stake is more than just the unblocking of an impulse that should not be stopped. It is not as if some inward crystal were already fully formed and only had to see the light of day. The inside is only soft dark mud until the process of exposure gives it contour and shape. Providing the chance to engage in action, to put the imprint of one's own desire on the external world and to observe that interaction, is therefore not a matter of indulgently allowing whims to pass. At issue is literally the coming into existence of the child's individuality and self. For the process of that formation advances inward from an outer crust. At first no more than the surface is structured and articulated, and inch by inch the protoplasmic inward-lying mass has to be sculpted.

In the first instance, this raises the requirements by several notches. To lift the constraints of a uniform time schedule, and to allow mobility from one chair to the next is obviously not enough. At the very least the student must be provided with the wherewithal to pursue the greatest possible variety of "projects." And these should be not pre-tailored, but be open to the most unexpected explorations, and they should give sufficient room for the eventuality of genuine reac-tions, for the astonishment of seeing the material assert its own inher-ent limitations. The child must have the opportunity to carry on an enterprise through several stages until an insight, perhaps quite inac-cessible to all bystanders, finally congeals—though the child of course must also have the privilege to drop at once a game with which it has grown bored.

But a second reason complements this first. The child must not sit—a convenient vessel holding still while the teacher pours—just on its own account, but as much for the benefit of the instructor. For how can the teacher know the substance on which he practices his art, if the child like all the others only looks up to him with placid eyes? There must be a constant rise and fall of enterprises started and abandoned if his own ignorance is to be cured. Only from their activity can he surmise the attributes his children might possess. So he had better grant them the prerequisites for their display, and for the most empirical of reasons: it would be utterly "unscientific" to operate on material which one has not understood.

This clarifies one fundamental difference between the mode of teaching based on the traditional idea of freedom as against one premised on the comprehension we have reached. The former notion thinks of every resistance as curtailing freedom and, therefore, leads to a general reduction of all obstacles and places the student into an insipid foam-rubber world. For us a blanket leniency is not a superior achievement. We do not measure the approach to freedom by this standard. Sometimes vigor and robustness—which naturally must never become cruel—are plainly called for, while in other situations an averaged-out mildness is far too paltry and a great deal more has to be given. Thus our concept does not enjoin one common compromised denominator. On the contrary, it supports sharply drawn discriminations and thereby leaves the student in a world that has character and weight. If a flat refusal strengthens the child's sense of self, then it might well contribute to its freedom, and if mere forbearance still smothers and absorbs, then only more extravagant support will suffice.

But the contrast runs still deeper. We apply not only a different calibration when severity is measured; our previous analysis exposes the preoccupation with that issue as itself an error. The determination of just how mild or harsh one ought to be, should not be *the* question in which philosophy of education exhausts itself. That nothing general can be said on this score should have been transparent all along. Life and the difficulties one meets in education would have to be simple and uniform indeed to justify the mere instruction that one's tune should always be played mutedly. So we prescribe not just diversity and contrasts where the other concept monotonously prefers the bland; we demote the quarrel over the degree of soft- or hardness to the subordinate position it deserves.

To rear a child is first of all to live with it, and living with it is no different from doing that with any other human being. There cannot be a safe railing to be followed hand over hand. No "manual" with clear diagrams can possibly be written. All attempts at this are foolishness because they are specific where this should not be done. And the case in point, which offers just one "How to . . ." rule and in addition recommends no more than an abstention, merely drives this thought to its absurd extreme.

Within the framework we have developed, the opposition between the gentle and the crass is only one among an indefinite many, and where on this polarity one should place oneself, where one should "draw the line," can be answered only with: that depends. More than that, the genuine anguish over how one should really raise a child has for us no such easy resolution. Whatever can be said must be expressed so that it allows for the particularity of this one teacher or parent and this one child, and for the uniqueness of this one situation. This gives notice that being a good parent or teacher requires a rare talent. If freedom were just a matter of not being in the way, then anyone could give it: nimbleness would be the only precondition. But if a self capable of expression is to develop then the teacher and parent will need, among many other things, an alert intuitive (not scholarly) intelligence. One will have to understand the child; one will have to gauge what some gesture or expression means, and often that is only possible if one's imagination can still leap. Rarer yet is the talent of knowing how to react, for that means to invent and execute an action on the spot.

The one man who more than any other seems to hold out an answer to the question of what we should actually do is A. S. Neill, the founder of Summerhill. His books have received wide attention and much applause. Yet Neill himself admits that he is quite often categorically misunderstood. Why should this be, given his extraordinary literary talents?

Some have suggested that it happens simply because he is a marvelous practitioner, a grand and glorious man, who knows what to do but who unfortunately is not a properly trained theoretician, and who therefore bungles as soon as principles and abstractions come on the scene. I must confess that there seems to me to be a deeper and a good deal more intriguing reason. Obviously it stands not alone, but it may have much to do with the idea of freedom. Neill, of course, uses the word on almost every page, and my suggestion is basically that he means one thing, while his readers expect and substitute another. His audience, not surprisingly, comes to him with the traditional associations: no hindrances and no resistance, no obstacles if it can be helped. But this is miles from what is on Neill's mind, and the indications of this crop up so constantly that one can pick and choose among the evidence.

One example is the anecdote about some visitors who were shocked and disappointed to discover that even Neill will not allow his children to climb up on roofs, and that poisonous medicines are locked away in cabinets even at Summerhill. In their eyes this meant that Neill lived by less than he preached. He in turn writes that they were "damn fools."

Another is the incident in which Neill went to the Covent Garden Theater together with a friend. Apparently a child, one or two rows in front of them, talked in a loud voice throughout the first ballet. During the intermission Neill and his friend looked for a pair of different seats, and as they settled into them the friend asked what he would do if one of his kids behaved like that? To which Neill's answer was: "I'd tell him to shut up!"

Or again, there is the passage in which Neill discusses the harm that lying parents do to children, and in which he writes: "Instead of saying, 'Mommy has a headache, be quiet,' it is much better and more honest to *shout* 'Stop that damned row!'" (italics added.)

One visitor reacts with surprise when Neill raises his voice sternly at a boy because he kicked a cat. In still a different place he refers to the fuss that he (Neill) made when a child upset his potato patch, or when his chisels, saws or planes were damaged. In all of these and a hundred other situations, Neill flies in the face of just what giving freedom is supposed to mean. Far from practicing abstinence or hanging like a punching bag, he can be drastic without violating what he means by freedom.

That there has been this general misapprehension is a genuine calamity. There is no way of counting the day-care centers and small communal, high-intentioned schools that invoke him as their patron saint, and that in his name have cooked a sugary sauce which would have made him sick. If Neill had not been transformed into a sweet phantom, some might not have led a march of children down a fly-paper-covered road. And, therefore, it must be said sharply that this is not his advocacy, that this is neither what he preached nor practiced and that it is not what Summerhill stands for.

The personal character of Neill alone—all broad straight lines—should have ruined that watery interpretation. (Recall the incident where a father, a member of the higher English aristocracy, decides that he just might unbend enough to give his son a try at Summerhill, though he still needs reassurance on one reservation, namely, that his son will be protected against the vice of masturbation. To which Neill replied: "But why should he, since apparently it did no harm to you or me.")

But Neill in any case combatted this version of his thinking as directly as he could. He devoted a whole separate section in his most famous book to the "Spoiled Child" and writes: "A child should not be given everything he asks for. Generally speaking, children today get far too much, so much that they cease having appreciation for a gift." Or just before that: "The spoiled child is a nuisance to himself and to society. You see him in trains scrambling over passengers' feet, yelling in corridors, never paying attention to his harassed parents' request for quiet." And in still stronger terms: "Later in life, as the spoiled brat grows older, he has even a worse time of it than one subjected to too much discipline." In yet another context, in which Neill deals with the harm done by "bossing" children, he reiterates this in terms reminiscent of a point we made before: "This applies even more to the benevolent boss than to the disciplinarian. The child of spirit can rebel against the hard boss, but the soft boss merely makes the child impotently soft and unsure of his real feelings." Or once again in clear-cut and general terms: "To have a community of mixed ages and for everyone to sacrifice all to the young children would be to completely spoil these children."

So far this drives forward only the thought that freedom is for Neill not at all the same as the mere giving of endless rope. I stress this because the worst practice calling down his blessing is in actuality indistinguishable from neglect. Young parents who themselves were spoiled read Neill, substitute their own ideas for what he means by freedom, and simply do not seem to notice the countless passages of which I just gave a small sample. In the upshot Summerhill becomes the scripture that sanctifies their lethargy: their child is in effect abandoned, but with self-righteousness.

On a more theoretic level Neill tries to correct the dogged misunderstandings through the distinction between freedom and license. And here he does show himself to be technically inept, for that division, as he draws it, leaves what he actually means in bad confusion. He draws the line in the time-honored fashion: freedom is doing what you please inside the circle that surrounds you; it becomes license when that circle is transgressed, and your actions have adverse effects on others. Since Neill adopts this differentiation straight from philosophic classics (it occurs almost verbatim in J. S. Mill), a closer look at what is wrong with that demarcation may be worthwhile.

First, it seems to promise more than it in fact delivers. To say that you will not be interfered with as long as your doings will not inflict harm on others sounds only generous till one asks the question: just what specific actions does this make immune? Does not anything at all that I can do, or even think, have effects on others, and are not some of these bound to be "harmful?" Does not even my most private nightmare dampen the mood of others across the breakfast table? So the privileged sanctuary I am being granted shrinks till nothing is included in it. By this criterion no act whatever is firmly exempted or protected. Anything at all can be legitimately interfered with.

But it may be even more important to realize that the idea of "interference" can of course be flexed from prison penalties down to remonstrations and consternated looks. The proclamation that one will not be influenced in the sphere of freedom is therefore doubly overblown, for even if there were actions that had no effects on others, it would still not be possible to shield these acts against every form of interference. We have already mentioned this consideration in the context of politics. But clarity, or rather, honesty, on this point may be still more crucial in the domain of education since the arsenal of hidden, subtle penalties at the disposal of parents is quite bottomless, and since the image of immunity in this more intimate and private setting is, therefore, even more deceptive.

A second objection would question this criterion on straightforward moral grounds. We have already clashed with the notion that interference can be justified only when it occurs on behalf of the Other, and proposed that, on the contrary, the subject himself constantly needs influence and contact for his own sake and even his survival. But here again, one is free as long as one does not impinge on Others, but becomes guilty of "license" when this is the case. Odd as this may at first sound, I would argue that it should be more the other way around. What a cynical principle of education it is to say in effect: "We shall

stand by and watch, as long as all the harm you do is done to yourself."
(In other words, about you we really do not care.) "But when you
touch another, then watch out! We will intercede though the damage
for the Other might be rather minor, but we will abstain even if the
harm to yourself is beyond repair." Is this not a formulation of the
maxim that on the political and social level turns a culture into a
butcher's shop? And should not, in the context of education—and not
as a high standard, but rather as a minimum—the focus be first and
foremost on the individual child so that when and how influence is to
be exerted is assessed first in terms of the child's own requirements, and
only after that, and often as a last resort, in terms of the protection
Others may require.

A third charge against Neill's use of that distinction is that it does not
begin to fit or clarify his practice. You do not have prohibitions against
climbing on roofs, or swimming in the absence of a lifeguard for the
sake of Others, and it is primarily for the individual's own sake that you
do not want to spoil a child. Neill does not for a moment follow the
general rule that his children are left utterly unhindered in their own
regard, nor does he intercede only to protect them from each other.

In short, the distinction between freedom and license which Neill
himself advances in order to block the misunderstanding that "everything is permitted" in Summerhill is no help at all. But then what does
he mean by freedom, which is so different from the customary expectations, and by what guidance is he led?

There is one particular example that, more than any other, leads to
the right answer: this is the wonderful little story in which Neill paints
a door. He writes that if Robert came along and started to sling mud at
his fresh paint then he would "swear at him heartily." But then Neill
envisions a slightly different situation. What if Robert were not the boy
he has known for years, but were new to Summerhill and had in the
past been smothered by the weight of stern authority, and Neill detected that this flinging of some mud was his first act of rebellion and
was of vast significance to him, because for the first time in that
moment he threw off his yoke and stood up? What would Neill do in
that case? Neill answers that he would drop his brush and join him,
that he too would reach down for wet earth and throw it at the paint,
since the boy's "salvation is more important than the door."

It could not be clearer that the decisive consideration here is not the protection of the Other, but that everything hinges on what the self of that one boy requires; and it is also evident that a fatuous and tepid, nicely averaged "permissiveness" is not what Summerhill represents. In one case Neill would "swear heartily," and in the other, patient indulgence is not nearly good enough! The calibration of the proper degree of discipline, of where to "draw the line" is obviously not the issue. Neill would not measure out his swearing cautiously in the first instance. It is unproblematic, does not violate the youngster's freedom, is simply part of the wear and tear of normal life together. The distinctive element that singles Neill out from the general run of educators is that in the other case he is not simply indulgent, but he actually would join the boy in throwing mud at the door he had just been painting because he sees in this the boy's "salvation."

From this beginning we can look at the kind of authority which Neill rejects. He is not against authority in every form, but attaches to it his own special meaning, just as he does to freedom. Apropos of the ruined potato patch he writes that an authoritarian would have "dragged in the question of morality," but that he did not say that it was wrong to steal his spuds; he refused to make it a matter of good and evil, but kept it entirely a question of his spuds; they were his spuds and should be left alone. This distinction touches a theme that runs through the entire book. If one seriously wants to understand Neill's thinking, one has to grasp that his assaults on the "authoritarian," far from endorsing a general capitulation, are meant to draw a very different line: the point is that the confrontation must be personal, that the adult who stops a child should do it in the name of his own person. Neill has no objection as long as one self clashes with another self. He directs his sarcasm and anger against the adult who drapes around his individual desire the cloak of a seemingly impersonal world order, who puts the child on one side and himself, in alliance with a universal rightness, on the other. It is only this exclusion of the child, and this grotesquely imbalanced duel, that he castigates. And we already know the underlying reasons: the danger in education is that the external, shaping forces will be too great, and in this alignment they surely would be crushing.

These also are the reasons for the radical equality which is so marked in Summerhill. And I am not referring to the formal equality embodied in the democratic institutions of the school. That seems pedestrian and ordinary. Some almost casual demonstrations of it show much more vividly what is involved. Twice incidents are mentioned in which a child asks Neill to "leave the room." Once a five-year-old says that he does not want him at his birthday party, and in another instance Neill explains that he would only ask his daughter Zoe "not to bring that mud and water into our parlor" because if she told him to get out of her room, he would "of course obey her wish without a word." The "mutuality" is here of great significance: Neill feels that he can insist on his own space, and that he can do this firmly, but only in an equitable trade—so the privilege of sometimes wielding discipline comes at a price. That ties a thread back to Bettelheim: the obedience shown to its own desire gives the child the crucial experience of having a real effect upon the world, and at the same time it confirms the child's knowledge of what the specific nature of its own desire is. The respect shown to its own internal world and the direct force with which it meets the Other assist powerfully in the crystallization of the child's sense of self.

In the same unselfconscious way Neill also writes: "I have never demanded good manners nor polite language. I never ask if faces have been washed. In short, I treat children with the dignity that adults expect to be treated with." Or, "We adults do not demand that Uncle Bill must clear his plate when he dislikes carrots, or that father must wash his hands before he sits down to a meal. By continuously correcting children, we make them feel inferior. We injure their natural dignity. It is all a question of relative values. In heaven's name, what does it really matter if Tommy sits down to a meal with unwashed hands?"

If the idea of freedom for Neill does not rule out a certain harshness, there is still something which it does preclude: namely humiliation. For "dignity" is here obviously the key word, and the connection to the forming of an identity is again impossible to miss.

And the same could be said about Neill's continuous reprobation of the use of fear. His reiteration of all the harmful consequences which frightening a child is bound to have, and his enumeration of the ways in which adults, often unwittingly, inspire terror, together with the long line of particular recommendations of how the instilling of fear is to be avoided, becomes almost wearisome. But if one asks why this concern is so pivotal to Neill's thinking, then the answer is again quite patent. Obviously not every frightful experience is to be eliminated. The child should not be coddled in an unrealistic cotton-candy world.

What has to be avoided is a permanent, deep-seated fearfulness which is very easily created. Neill's description of the positive counterpart to the timid child bears this out and one can see why much of the hope he has for Summerhill turns on this opposition. He says that one must always be "on the child's side," and when he gives his own assessment of what is best about the children reared in Summerhill he ranks most highly that they have "complete self-confidence," that they are "not afraid to be themselves," that they are "natural," "spontaneous" and, above all, "sincere." I think this shows that Neill opposes the kind of fear that—in our language—produces a "displacement" or a "disassociation" from the self, and that when he speaks of being "natural" and "spontaneous" and "sincere" he comes very close to what we mean by "having an identity or self, and acting from it."

Neill's book has been so frequently misunderstood because the meaning freedom has for him is not the traditional one that centers most on the reduction of all obstacles. And his thinking cannot be clarified by simply cutting off some piece of that idea and relegating that to "license." The difference goes much deeper, for what he actually intends is much closer to the idea of freedom which we have evolved. I am not claiming that Neill thought his way through the whole underbrush we have tried to clear but that there is in large terms a surprisingly close correspondence; that one could imagine his and our work as two independently elaborated parts—one philosophical, the other practical and oriented towards education—two components, which now can be linked up.

This is tantamount to the assertion of a symmetrical relationship: *Summerhill* becomes a much less paradoxical and much less misleading book; the disparate pieces of it "fall into place" as soon as our general analysis of freedom is offered to it as its understructure. Perhaps one could even say that without all the previous clarification of how obstacles and choices relate to freedom, and all the rest, Neill's book cannot be fully understood, but that once this is done it makes very natural and easy sense.

Yet large parts of the practice envisioned and performed by Neill represent, as well, an enumeration of the implications for education of our abstract idea of freedom. If one does not pervert Summerhill into a merely "permissive" school, and if one also ceases to imagine that this is its basic message, though it "does not go to extremes"—if one can shake oneself loose from that interpretation and from that defense of it—and one instead perceives it on the base which we have laid, then one will come closer to grasping what Neill had in mind, and also to knowing what it would be to rear a child in freedom, in our sense of free.

Passage after passage shows how closely Neill's idea of freedom approximates our own. He asks, for example, "How much of our education is real doing, real self-expression?" (where the phrase "real doing" seems to underscore the most central point of our discussion of "identification"—that it must be "I" who acts). Or, he writes: "Winifred found herself by being allowed to be herself"; or again: "At Summerhill it is love that cures, it is approval, and the freedom to be true to oneself." This carries over even into his concern with the phenomenon of self-rejection, which for us was typified by the Undergroundman. At one point he puts down the reflection: "I find that my chief job is to sit still and approve of all the things that a child disapproves of in himself—that is, I try to break down the child's superimposed conscience, his self-hatred." So that he, too, makes the same connection between the act of self-acceptance and the attainment of freedom. This he stresses not just once but again in these terms: "When a mother teaches a child to be good, she suppresses the child's natural instincts. She is saying to the child, 'What you want to do is wrong.' This is equivalent to teaching the child to hate himself. To love others while hating yourself is impossible. We can only love others if we love ourselves."

How far he is from preaching mere non-resistance and indulgence is still further indicated by paragraphs like these: "In almost every home, there is always at least one ungrownup grownup who rushes to show Tommy how his engine works. There is always someone to lift the baby up on a chair when the baby wants to examine something on the wall. Every time we show Tommy how his engine works we are stealing from that child the joy of life—the joy of discovery—the joy of overcoming an obstacle. Worse! We make that child come to believe that he is inferior and must depend on help." Here "obstacles" quite in line with our own discussion do not diminish freedom, but, on the contrary, are at times its precondition, for their conquest provides the occasion for the "discovery" of the self.

What Neill means by freedom does not resemble therefore any mere unhinderedness. His vision of it finds expression when he writes: "This business of being sincere in life and to life is a vital one. It is really the most vital one in the world. If you have sincerity, all things will be added to you." This is the attribute which finally counts for more than all else; this "absolute sincerity" is the goal; and sincerity is here only another name for the capacity to be oneself.

It might seem as if this chapter should now be concluded. But actually we still have to negotiate a very major turn, for temporarily the entire critical burden of our previous work has been left behind. Neill is obviously an evangelist for freedom. He preaches it without qualifications and sets it as the force of life in opposition to the armies of the night. So there is after all a deep disagreement between Neill and us.

Specifically, *Summerhill* is full of affirmations of the purity of children. If they are sometimes mean or cruel, then this is always due to harmful outside influences, and most commonly of course to "repression." Their basic nature is altogether good. Prior to their "conditioning" they were sweet Rousseauean savages in swaddling clothes. This stands in flat contradiction to everything we said about the self. We emphasized that the self (and even the "true" self) is a questionable mixture, that identifications can be gruesome as easily as they can turn out admirably, that their value is an open question, which can be answered only through an assessment of the individual case. (All we would say concerning "human nature" is that it is obviously neither so depraved that an auspicious culture cannot occasionally produce fine results, nor so splendid that the wrong circumstances cannot turn most men into monsters.)

This implies two logical connections: Neill needs his faith in the immaculate, pristine human nature to justify the absolute value he ascribes to freedom, while we, conversely, proposed to weigh the pros and cons of freedom's value, and in exchange for this obtained the advantage of being able to dispense with that precarious premise. Concomitantly we can lay aside the insupportable distinction between the "conditioned" and some exempt territory. And this is important, for Neill fogs the entire landscape when he consistently speaks of "conditioned children," and sets these into contrast with those reared in Summerhill, implying that Summerhill, and especially he himself despite the great robustness of his character, had no effect on children.

This contrast is pervasive and is constantly invoked by others; and it produces at once a mystification, or a cynicism, which chloroforms all thinking. From our point of view this is quite unnecessary. Of course, there is no sanctuary immune from influence. And naturally the formation of the self is just as "influenced" as is the rest. The only questions are what relationship that "self-image" has to one's actual empirical characteristics, and most crucially, to what extent this inner self is outwardly expressed. The children in Summerhill naturally are "conditioned," too, but the crux of the difference lies in the fact that they are influenced to shape their self-conception after the attributes or potentialities which they in fact possess; and that they are given help to bring their lives into an accord with their now-forming selves.

Just as we discard the whitewashed image of the angelic, "unconditioned" child, so we can also drop the crutches that Neill rents from Freud. (By, incidentally, *mis*reading Freud!) We refuse to turn "repression" into the sin against the holy spirit of mankind, and we can do without the magical prescription that the emotionally crippled can almost all be cured through "abreaction." For us, the possibility of acting the self out does not spell "salvation," but we continue to insist that it has neither more nor less than the earlier, empirically assessed value. Nor do we surrender now any other parts of what we previously established: our position is still that the self develops out of congealing identifications, whose merit is inevitably relative, whose demarcation we can only guess at from faint indications, and whose expression is therefore always problematic. In short, we still hold to the stand that freedom is no mere illusion, yet that it all the same is a most elusive and sometimes treacherous notion.

The disagreement with Neill is therefore not just over the value of freedom, while we concur on its meaning. At stake is something much more fundamental, namely the general status of that idea.

This difference needs to be explained: Certainly we have proposed an interpretation of freedom and have attempted to clarify its meaning. But, when all is said and done, this is the smaller and less ambitious portion of the task we chose. Deeper than this goes our effort to challenge and to weaken and perhaps to subdue one modality of thought, and to strengthen and possibly make way for another. For Neill, freedom is a categorical and final answer, and thus Summerhill is for him, at least in part, a utopian school. Our principal assertion is not merely that it is something less, but rather that freedom is no measure, that its base in the shifting self is so fluid that no firm judgment, and no determination of a definite direction can be based on it.

We have carried this theme forward from its first statement in the parable of the village whose inhabitants were deafened by the sound of a gargantuan brass gong; we pursued it when we separated obstacles from the idea of freedom; we pressed this same thought further through our long discussion of the self, and of the concept of identification. The whole of this extended exploration was meant to set off islands of clarity from the sea of confusion. But there was a second, underlying purpose that should now be rendered more explicit. Think of it as a kind of twofold motion: one part was this elimination of the peripheral and surface obfuscations, this removal of the outer shells, but the other part was to expose—precisely through this stripping away of the outer layers—that even the inner core was dubious and soft. This is not to say that the idea of freedom is only a conundrum, or that a few cuts by a philosophic surgeon will show it to be an empty hoax. What lies at the center is quite real and precious, but it is evanescent and fabulously difficult to know (not one whit easier than it is to know who we "really" are, and whether we do now "express" it) and therefore next to impossible to reach or fix or to provide. To use just the idea of freedom, therefore, for practical assessments, for overall appraisals, either of a culture or a country, or indeed (and that is the present point) in the evaluation of a school, and most of all to try to wield this notion when brute decisions are to be made, is a calamitous mistake. A violin has its uses, but it is not a baseball bat.

This is what I have in mind when I speak of the "status of the concept" and say that our more ambitious goal is the achievement of a "different modality of thought." A great deal more will be said about this, but let me for the moment give one first illustration.

One instance of the posture we are trying to attain might take the following form: when someone in an otherwise high-powered intellectual context blandly says that something or other makes a nation or children "free," then there should be by now a kind of shock reaction. One should feel that the conversation has just gone into a spinning fall, and that instantly measures have to be taken if disaster is to be averted. The first and most obvious of these might be an attempt to switch to other, sturdier categories, though this will naturally depend on the context.

In practical terms, this comes to saying that the gross and basic questions in the case of a government might be questions like: Who in this society is murdered, either tacitly, so that he dies from hunger or avoidable disease, or overtly and through explicit action, so that he dies in a camp or by a firing squad? Who and how many eat, and who goes hungry? Who must go without the barest sustenance while others raise heaps of waste? Who works and at what sorts of tasks, and who is idle? What punishments are there and for what transgressions? Are the laws administered fairly, or is there bottomless corruption? And even, what purposes and goals does this society as a whole pursue?

I am suggesting that all of these are relatively answerable questions, that we lay hold of definite characteristics in posing them, and that these are the questions we must ask if we want a first rough estimate. Of course some of these more specific questions are often subsumed under the idea of a "free society"—this is part of the point. One should realize that using the word "freedom" to assess these matters leads one out on the thinnest ice; that one is now most apt to fall again into any of the errors that we earlier uncovered—from imagining that one is "free" because one had a choice, to thinking that some part of oneself has not been influenced, to the fantasy that totalitarian governments turn their subjects into helpless robots, to indefinitely many more.

The general tendency of our total project is therefore not the philosophically customary one: we are not searching for a tidy definition so that one can then go ahead and talk with greater confidence. It is more the reverse. We are performing this examination to increase our scepticism, to *dis*courage the reliance on the concept of freedom; in a sense to wean us from it.

How this applies to education should be evident: it means that many of the concrete and immediate issues about education should not be discussed in terms of freedom. We argued earlier that the preoccupying debate, between the "disciplinarian" and the "permissive," was bequeathed to us by the traditional idea of freedom and that it was bound to remain a stalemated Indian-wrestling bout. We can now follow through on this and add that if the issue is the prevention of cruelty to the children, then we should not mince our words but put the matter in these words, as the humane opposed to the sadistic. To allow this conflict to usurp all our thinking about education, and to turn it into an interminable "philosophic" problem by casting it into the more "polite" language of freedom versus authority, protracts a social and an intellectual disease.

From at least one perspective this should be seen as a reversal: for precisely the one polarity under which all other questions in the debate about schools have often been subsumed has just been set aside. But two misunderstandings have to be forestalled. First, I am not merely giving the platitudinous advice that it is better to be concrete and specific rather than abstract and vague, and that it is therefore more strategic in front of conservative and upset parents to speak of "individuated" or "humane" teaching than of giving "freedom to the kids." There are far more serious reasons for abstaining from the idea of freedom than just that it is "vague." These other reasons will still emerge, and their eventual consideration will be the crux of this book.

Secondly, and more pertinent to our next few steps, it is not a matter of simply translating from the general to the more specific. In fact a major feature of the situation, as we see it, is that some of the worst flaws of our educational system and some of the grossest errors committed by both parents and teachers stay hidden as long as we pull towards greater or less freedom. One reason for our wanting to shift away from this polarity is that the most patent wrongs do not lie on its line. Several of these seem to us at once so obvious and so crucial that we shall take the time to develop at least one extended illustration.

One of the most glaring faults that is rarely raised in the countless conversations on the topic of "What is wrong with our schools" is the simple fact that teachers in high schools are normally expected to teach six or seven hours every day.

To place this into some perspective one should recall that we have a penchant to speak as if the worst outcome of a class would be that nothing was learned in it; that it was a "waste of time." But this is much too optimistic. The bottom level is not a situation of no change, for the student can be weakened and debilitated and made less intelligent: a teacher may not only fail to teach but may do serious damage.

The prevailing time-arrangement is enough to make the infliction of real harm inevitable. No one could possibly be interesting for six whole hours day after day. No one, no matter how well read or how intelligent, can be genuinely stimulating and exercise the students' minds with new information or new ideas at this relentless pace. To hold someone's attention, especially if that person is disinclined or tired or a little restless, makes extraordinary demands on one's energy. To do it at all one has to function at a peak of one's capacity, with nearly total concentration, and give of oneself with both hands. Who can do this on a 9 to 3 o'clock basis? College professors in the main are only expected to hold between four and six lectures in a whole week, and even then the students do not always sit on the edges of their seats.

Part of the peculiarity of this situation lies in its relationship to some strange general assumptions about the nature of intellectual work. No one in our culture would dream of measuring a stand-up comic, or a jazz musician, against a forty-hour week. It is quite understood that playing a few sets might leave a man exhausted, and no one would suggest that anyone working such short hours does not earn his keep. Has anyone proposed that the exertions of a football or a baseball player should be assessed in terms of time? Imagine someone saying of a soccer goalie that making those breathtaking "saves" was, after all, only six minutes of work!

But when it comes to teachers an altogether different framework is applied. School boards and parents ring the alarm when "contact hours" are to be reduced. The presumption is that teachers get their pay so that they will teach, and if one cannot check on their busy hands, one at least wants to make sure that their mouths keep moving. The expectation is "a full day's work." This is the thinking that was developed for assembly lines.

Apart from the niceties—such as that teachers often double as athletic coaches or bus-drivers—teachers in most schools do not have a quiet corner of their own, not to speak of a separate office. They only have the continuously noisy teachers' lounge, which means that there is no place for a few minutes to regain one's concentration or even just to read. And that cuts deep. Take a little survey and find out what and how much the average high school teacher reads! But when should they do it? After they have done their seven classes and have maybe coached and—if they are women—have cooked for and fed their families and graded papers and done their "lesson plans"? Yet, they are not teaching six-year-olds; their students have been in school for twelve whole years. What is the supposition? That they remember enough from fifteen years ago, when they were in college? But even then most of their courses were not in the discipline they teach, but in "secondary education."

Under this regime there is no hope whatever of maintaining an even tolerable level, and the teachers themselves cannot help but know this. In any case, even if they had illusions, these would be quickly cured by one look at the dazed faces of their brighter students. These circumstances virtually force a teacher to lose his self-respect.

The students in turn cannot esteem their teachers for the performance of their essential function, and therefore they see them as shams, who look taller only because they sit on institutional pillows. Yet the discouragement of countless students represents the most serious damage. They lounge month after month in a bemused and weary patience, watching the hours, while they sip the proffered sugar water, and gradually a heavy crust of hopelessness, a firm conviction that nothing good could ever happen in a school, is built up. It seems as if a never-ending snow were falling till little caps of white grow even on the student's eyelids. This frozen cover is the greatest obstacle when they finally do have a chance encounter with a genuine thought. To thaw through this thick layer and get to the point where the student is at least awake becomes the task of the occasional exceptional teacher, and may require the better part of a semester. As if recovering from a long illness, the student does not trust his legs. He is feeble from his long confinement, and cannot believe that a school is not a hospital, in which one simply waits till one is at the end discharged.

This, far more than any other factor, is the major cause inside the schools for the battery of much-enumerated wrongs; from the proverbial "apathy" down to the fact that some schools are places of quite literal, and mortal, warfare. But how could it be otherwise? Fifteen- to eighteen-year-olds, with energy enough to break down walls, are given just enough to keep them "occupied," enough to prevent their turning fully towards something else, but not sufficient to take a real bite. How often students say that they hate school most of all because it steals their time! Those from poor families mean bluntly that it takes time away from their jobs and that they need the money; and the remainder feel that the insipid fare strings them along, that they are being teased. Emphatically, this is in no way the individual teacher's fault. On the contrary, under the present dispensation the teachers are condemned in advance.

Note the key assumption: Must an adolescent be taught for seven hours every day? Even if we grant for the moment that they have to be kept in school (to stay off the streets and the labor market), is it necessary that there be that many classes, and that each is a lecture plus discussion with thirty students and one teacher? That monotony inevitably makes the gruel very thin. But a lecture could be a festive and wonderful occasion, like a concert. To witness something shining and coherent after the dross and drabness of much talk could revive one's courage. For that to occur, however, there should be no more than three or four lectures in a week. They would require preparation, and one would also need time to digest them. Still, would not this exchange of quality for mindless quantity be extremely beneficial? Surely the most crucial thing is not to kill off the curiosity of students who possess some, and to awaken it in those who don't. But how can the slow trickle of inanities be anything but a Chinese water torture? The trouble with the schools we have is not that they are either too permissive or too authoritarian but that they are too boring.

But to speak in the present tense of schools in which children will be raised in freedom is also a cultural presumption. True, our meaning of freedom is considerably more down-to-earth than ideas of autonomy or of self-determination, yet even a regard for self-expression stands sky-high above our present level. The danger is that we suppose ourselves to be far advanced, and engaged in reaching for a prize that other cultures could not grasp. But that ignores the radical novelty of our problems and the fact that we have so far not begun to deal with them. A first step towards realism would be the acknowledgment that enormous alterations are required—not to attain some lofty value, but just to bring us two steps closer to a sane situation. We need some idea of what schools would have to be like to respond at all to the demands now made upon them.

Ivan Illich argues that schools should be abolished, and spending a single day in an average school should be enough to make one see his point. Nonetheless, my disagreement is that this seems too great a capitulation. The social order which we have evolved imposes on us a multiplicity of deprivations. One of the few compensations it could offer is the possibility of spending the first twenty years of our lives on our own development. To surrender this because we lack the wit to devise a set of decent schools seems an incredible failure of imagination—

we simply cannot be that inept and stupid. But the rearrangement will have to be fundamental if there is any thought of bringing the institution of schools up to date.

To gain some historical perspective one might recall that the kind of school which we in essence still accept, arose originally in the Middle Ages, and was designed for a small clerical elite who were taught by monks. In "primitive" cultures all knowledge was almost entirely communicated through parents and elders, and most teaching still occurred inside the family setting as recently as about 200 years ago (the "tutors" in aristocratic houses). So, in outline, we took an immensely specialized and idiosyncratic institution and stretched it to encompass everybody. Ever greater numbers of increasingly diverse children, whose goals in life were ever more removed from those this kind of school originally served, were processed through it, while at the same time spates of new disciplines and different kinds of knowledge were reduced to one and the same model of transmission. Walking through endless corridors in high schools, one sees through the windows in the classroom doors exactly the same scene in every room: one teacher talking to approximately the same size group of students. Is there any real excuse for this depressing uniformity? If one starts from the immense diversity of what these students will eventually do and from the fact that this is how they spend the biggest part of their first eighteen years, the monotony of the format seems grotesque.

When the one-sidedness of schools which cater to the aptitudes and backgrounds of an already absurdly privileged small faction is assailed or lamented, the customary remedy is always the introduction of yet another set of courses. If enacted, the result is one more teacher with a group of thirty students going through fifteen weeks of lecture and discussion. But this is a trap. There is no correlation between the importance of a subject, or the intensity of one's concern, and the amount of intellectual interest that can possibly be said about it. There is no ground for the presumption that everything can be chopped into the bits that will be grist for this quite special mill. This may be the one instance where McLuhan is right: that medium powerfully modifies the message. It is superbly suited for some few tasks, but that great strength puts the ill-adapted at an equally large disadvantage. The attempt to rebel against academic narrowness by forcing the essentially non-scholastic into that very mode, therefore, leads it into a contest which it is foredoomed to lose, and subjects it still more to just the constraints one means to break. This grinding up of everything into a pulp to fill one kind of skin and the concomitant reduction of a human being to a monotonous single-wave reception apparatus is also the one calamity that Illich most deplores. And if the only possible advance were towards a still more expanded "schooling" in this sense—if one could only annex still further territories to the fifteen-week discussion-group empire—then I would agree: then even the abolition of schools would be preferable to their continuing expansion.

The alternative does just the reverse. It would confine that method to much less space than it now holds—two or three lectures in a week, but those as good as first-rate concerts, and not by every teacher but only by those who have a gift for it, and not on any subject but only in the few that call for it. And it would insist on the greatest possible diversity in the modes of training. It would not press still more into a quasi-academic format, but would develop other equally legitimate formats. It would explicitly acknowledge that we have reached a point where close to a third of everybody's life can be, but also must be, spent outside the mainstream of the culture. Given this, there is of course no reason why everybody should spend all or most of this long time in mainly one activity and setting.

From this perspective all justification for placing this whole period entirely into childhood and adolescence, and especially for arranging it into one uninterrupted sequence, disappears. Under the present form of schooling a majority spends the first twelve of their more energetic years primarily with books and then avoids them after that. Dropping out of school is treated like an epidemic, when it would be far more important to make arrangements so one can again "drop in." But education could be a constantly available alternative to the ordinary social order. It would be natural to leave one's usual life at any given point, and for whatever reasons—whether to overcome some particular deficiency or simply for a period of internal reconstruction—and to find the means to fit one's purpose. This might be anything from just an empty room in which one could find silence, to someone who in one half-hour could give advice so that in six weeks one could learn by oneself what one is now *not* taught in as many months, to an individual craftsman with whom one could apprentice, to participating for a time in every kind of manual work about which one is curious.

To return once more to Neill: the one feature of his school that branded it as just "permissive" more than any other is probably the fact that his children are not required to attend classes. They take lessons when they choose to, and some few students go without them for as long as several years. Many find this shocking. To those one could point out that Neill's book is full of examples of youngsters who eventually catch up and far surpass the level they would have reached in other schools, which bears out that knowledge can be assimilated with astonishing rapidity when the child is awake and not somnambulant from rote drudgery. But then an often wistful comparison to the rigorous European high schools is brought into the discussion with the suggestion that a solid grounding in foreign languages and "general education" must be acquired in one's teens and that this requires pressure. It could be replied that those who benefitted from these schools represent survivors; that there is no way of measuring the talents destroyed in, for instance, German and Austrian Gymnasia, since the failures remain invisible, and only the successes later on in life "make their mark." But it could also be argued that these schools had disastrous social consequences; they produced an unrealistic and often warped elite, quite out of touch with any of the practical requirements of life, and a separate mass of essentially uneducated people who were "eliminated" by this system with the result that both of these groups were vulnerable to Fascism. Recall how many intellectuals, especially lawyers, doctors, ministers and teachers were Nazis. Moreover, Neill's adage might be invoked that it is better "to be a good bricklayer than to be a neurotic scholar"; and this gains poignancy if one is not blind to the insecurity and lack of self-respect suffered by those who end up in professions which make demands beyond their intellectual means, or if one has an eye for the damage done by muddleheaded lawyers, incompetent physicians, bored teachers and dull academicians.

But we are actually far from agreeing with Neill on this matter. Our objection, however, comes from the other side. For the impression given is deceptive. Nearly all students in fact stay away from classes for at most a period of three months. Coming largely from disciplinarian institutions, the external constraints suddenly are lifted, and for a stretch of time they bolt, but soon enough nearly all return "voluntarily" to the fold. In fact, there is an interesting small provision: once a child does decide to take a class, he or she is expected to attend regularly, and this is primarily enforced by the other children, who presumably would be held back by someone who had missed the intervening work.

From one point of view this seems splendidly reasonable and even economic: in exchange for three months of vacation, one gets children who no longer need to be regimented, but who have come to see their lessons as preferable to the other available alternatives; who therefore come now with much more cheerfulness and no doubt learn faster, while they in addition develop also much more wholesomely in other ways. Something important can be learned from this.

Still, from another perspective it is much more problematic. Why are so many of the children so quickly reduced to docility? Largely because they are caught in an Either/Or dilemma. No genuine alternatives to the taking of lessons are provided. They are left on their own, to do as they wish. They are given the run of the fields and essentially must forage for themselves. Since nearly all the others already have made their adjustment, they are quite isolated and under social pressure. So it really is small wonder that they are soon bored and willingly enroll.

To allow children not to attend lessons is therefore not "too permissive" or "too radical." Our response would be quite different: for one thing, a more reasonable system (and that is all we are discussing, not an ideal) would be far more seriously and evenly diverse than Summerhill. To offer children a choice between the moss-covered format of the ordinary class and a solitary search for their entertainment may be fathoms above the current practice, but it is still fearfully imbalanced. One modality of learning and development receives full official sanction and requires an elaborate apparatus which engages, obviously, most of the energies of the entire personnel. All other forms are more or less abandoned. In these everything is left to the improvisation of the student and this demands so much that he soon opts for the corral. To make it at all fair, an approximately equal effort would have to be devoted to other modes or formats of learning and instruction. This applies at least as much to intellectual as to other topics. It is absurd to imagine that reading or writing or a foreign language or history must be learned from a single teacher who regularly meets with thirty students. A majority might profit far more from very brief irregularly spaced encounters. Conceivably these might be even rather far apart, for their intensity and individual attunement would more than compensate for what is saved in "contact hours." In the periods in between the child would, of course, not be completely without "supervision," but would be in a setting that would allow him to work on his own, but with help when he needs help.

If even just this minimum were consistently enacted, the whole general "feel" and aspect of a school would change. Instead of the corridor-long flights of drowsy classes, one might have individual teachers talking to one student at a time, and a few larger areas in which individual students pursue their own tasks. The objection to Neill is, therefore, that he still puts far too much stock in classes, that instead of giving full room and attention to alternative formats of teaching, he advances only to the point where the children have a choice between "lessons" on the one side and something close to nothing on the other.

From here it becomes apparent that still another side, which also strikes many as "too radical," is actually anything but that. Throughout his book, Neill breaks a whole sheath of lances against the all-importance of sheer learning, particularly when it comes from books, and sets into opposition to this the high value of pure play. To fume against this "anti-intellectualism" misses the main point, for historically, against the background of the English "public schools," much of this was desperately needed and was a courageously advanced, fully justified corrective. Neill might have recognized much better than his missionaries that the situation in America, with its long-standing disparagement of learning, needs to be tilted in the opposite direction. But the kernel of the difficulty is again that Neill is actually too conventional. He has to poke fun at those who take lessons and books and teaching all too seriously, because the kind of teaching done at Summerhill is by his own admission not very different from that of any other school. Not even the most elementary constraints, which we discussed before as far from sufficient—the physical mobility of children and their not having to be synchronized to one metronomic pace—are questioned and ruled out. This makes the fact that their own peers will enforce regular attendance so revealing! In sum, behind that iconoclasm stands, in truth, a faith in the archaic mode of classroom teaching.

A more nearly sensible arrangement would have to develop in essentially the opposite direction from the one in which we have so far moved: not towards the ever more complete assimilation to and encompassment into classroom schooling, but away from it. If it were firmly and clearly understood that every member of the society, regardless of parental income, was constrained as part of his "compulsory" education to spend about fifteen years, not inside the usual productive process, but in an educational cultural alternative—if the magnitude of what we are already doing were in short accepted—then the simple, functional necessity of this diversity would, I think, be obvious. It would not have to base itself on high aspirations to equality, but would be no more than an implication brought on by one's starting premise.

At the moment much of what is done from the day-care center and the kindergarten through grade and high schools is principally a training for further education, i.e., a preparation for more classroom learning. We instill the habits and develop the capacities that make the student ready for what at most should be one means and which even at that is highly overrated. If we took the small step to seeing this instrument for what it is, kindergarten would no longer have to be mainly a preparation for first grade, and grade school for high school, and high school for college (and then what?), but all this time could be spent straightforwardly on the development of whatever talents or capacities this or that person has.

The last few pages show by example that the problem of our educational institutions can be discussed much more incisively when it is not done in terms of freedom. They add still another post to the fence we are erecting against the idea of freedom. More specifically, they follow through on our earlier claim that the battle between more authority and more freedom hides very basic problems from our view and that these problems can be attacked with much greater force if they are severed from the entanglements of that rope-pulling contest. In the wings stands, of course, the implication that this is also true of other matters. Still, where does this leave us?

What if someone asked us bluntly: do you want an education and schools that promote freedom or do you not? What would be our answer?

Certainly it would not be simple. So let us go through it step by step.

As a first step, we can say quite definitely that if freedom were still associated mainly with the reduction of hindrances, or the creation of more space, we would not advocate it as a goal. That, on the one hand, is not what we mean by freedom, but it is also, and quite apart from that, a disastrous program. By focusing on the example of a newborn infant, we saw the actual results of the rigorous adherence to this path. The examination of that small-scaled instance dispelled for us the enchanting mist that enveloped this ideal. We now know that, consistently pursued, it leads to an emptiness in which one cannot breathe. That in itself places this value, and this meaning of freedom, into an even darker shadow than our previous objections. But we added still further criticisms: we brought forward that it lies in the very nature of this aim that the imperatives which issue from it cannot possibly be satisfied; we indicated that parents who model themselves after it are drawn into a vicious cycle of surrender and then harsh reassertion; we argued that schools guided by this principle are likely to descend from intelligent and subtle modes of exercising influence to crude and deceptive modes. We submitted beyond that, that even toned-down versions of this policy have negative effects; that they relocate conflicts in the child which are better confronted openly; that they warp desires before they have a chance to form; that they thwart the possibility of gaining accurate self-knowledge.

The sum total of these considerations has a cumulative effect. We are no closer to making our peace with cruelty disguised as "discipline," or with destructiveness performed in the name of a "tradition" or of "excellence"; but as a general platform or a programmatic vision this idea of freedom will no longer serve. More than that: we have now reached the point where we must acknowledge that the premises of this ideal deny the elementary need for contact, for response, and for all "mutuality." They make an idol of sheer distance; they conceptualize the other principally as a limitation and at the same time postulate a ruinous image of the self—armored in self-sufficiency it stands complete, prior to society and separate from it. These premises, moreover, bracket the whole human world behind one endlessly debunking prefix: that everything is an obstacle. In exchange for this they offer an advantage that cannot be grasped even in thought. Seeing this leads us not just to reject this idea as a credo: in this version of freedom we now perceive a genuine calamity, a blind obsession whose spell we hope to break.

If this much can be set aside, then what of the idea of freedom which we have developed? For us neither hindrances nor empty space is any longer the main metaphor. If any image has come to the fore, it is the picture of working from the periphery towards a center: that there must be a self and that this self has to be "expressed" are for us the principal requirements of freedom. Are we prepared to make of this idea a program for education or for the schools?

We cannot begin to answer to this question till the implications of this idea have been condensed and brought into relief. We said that the parent or the teacher should view the child or student as a juggler who already performs with great skill. In our story the "new plate" had to be added at exactly the right moment and in exactly the right way. We also made a comparison to two ways of gardening, one where everything was first bulldozed to the ground, while the other cautiously enhanced the growth that was already there. From these two analogies we proceeded into a description of the basic, postulated orientation that our concept would enjoin. The most central thought in this setting of the stage was a reversal of perspectives: we emphasized that the child's own perception of its feelings and desires and even more of what corresponds to its own "nature" is extraordinarily difficult and weak, and that the danger therefore is not that the child will stay a savage but, on the contrary, that the whisper of its subjectivity will be drowned out.

The strongest common denominator running through these elements is a high respect for whatever is already "there" before any deliberate teaching or educating would begin and, concomitantly with that, a greater seriousness about the actual incorporation of what is newly offered and its integration into the previously existing and functioning personality or intelligence.

A single illustration will sharpen the point that is at stake. Take the example of teaching how to read. One particularly fascinating phenomenon in this domain is the fact that children often perform a quite specific variation that one could call a "half-reading." They will sit with a book and move their finger from one word to the next, but the words which they pronounce seem to have no relationship to any that are printed on the page. From listening to them one could get the impression that they are only babbling, that they merely mimic a pose which they have much observed. What makes this an intriguing instance is that this is not the case. In situations in which someone actually compiled an exact record of the words these children speak, a subtle and hidden correlation between the printed and the spoken words was eventually discovered. This is never a matter of a direct one-to-one correspondence, where one and the same "wrong" word is always said in place of the "correct" one, but the child nonetheless substitutes a new set of words for those printed on the page. The reports say that astoundingly more rapid teaching can take place once these "rules of substitutions" have been understood. The teacher no longer needs to correct mechanically every individual mistake, but is now in a position to suggest the modification of a general principle, or rule, which then allows the child to make a leap to full-fledged reading.

Such "rules of substitution" would be illustrations of the general type on which we have to focus. When we speak of a respect for the pre-existing and of an incorporation of the new into the old, then what we have in mind are features of this type. This is quite different from what phrases like "teaching must be adapted to the individual student" usually convey. The capacities which the child already exercises—the plates already in the air—are in our view not comparable to appetites that mere benevolence will satisfy. They should be imagined in analogy to these "rules of substitution," and one measure of the deference appropriate to them would be the difficulty they present to our understanding. That even our greatest efforts give us barely an inkling of how the child's intelligence and psyche actually works puts the caution and the patience that needs to be exercised on a more stringent level. Similarly with the "whisper" of subjectivity that is easily drowned out: this simile is not intended to enjoin constant approval and the building of "self-confidence." The individuality that we mean to protect is again more adequately represented by the example of these hidden principles, and if one wanted to ensure the possibility of their "natural" development, then the requirements obviously would be high.

If the performance in which the child or student is engaged prior to all teaching is comparable to his use of such rules, then it is extremely difficult to meet the standards which our idea of a free education sets. If we include in our notion of the "nature" of the individual child characteristics of this complexity, and if these are not to be destroyed but enhanced, so that the child eventually will be able to identify with them and to express them, then what needs to be done is very hard.

The general structure of the activity of teaching, accordingly, would have to be quite different from the now customary one. The first and very major stage would be a study on the teacher's part; namely, his study of the student. Far from insisting on his syllabus or his curriculum, the teacher would, to begin with, spend much time on the most careful observation of the child. Before he "intervenes" he would first have to know what the youngster in front of him is doing, how the child's mind operates. (One might have supposed that this would be a minimal requirement.)

On the basis of this understanding the teacher would then have to find the one next step or idea which could be fitted into the already operating psyche or intelligence; and he would then have to assist with the assimilation or the integration of this new element so that the previous performance is not handicapped and the connection with the "center" of the child is not weakened or downright cut.

This is equally removed from both of the practices now in vogue. It neither abandons the child to its own devices while the teacher in effect does nothing nor does it foist new principles or materials on the student which only bring the "plates" he already juggles down with a crash.

In terms of the example of teaching a child how to read, our general view is on the one side utterly opposed to the model of the teacher who mindlessly "corrects" the child whenever he speaks a word that is not on the page. That method operates from ignorance and uses degradingly simplistic methods which may be excusable when teaching rats (though one could probably proceed with more sophistication even then). Furthermore, it is extremely slow. But the crux of our opposition is that it dismantles the tools which the child employed before. From a cognitive perspective it is therefore apt to leave the child in a helpless and literally "stupified" condition—blind, like a Kantian mind without its categories. And from the point of view of freedom it violates the single most essential condition laid down by our concept: it does not foster the identification of a child with its own nature, but instead destroys a part of it.

But we would be equally critical of anything approximating a mere waiting on the teacher's part while the whole burden falls upon the child. From our perspective this represents a fundamental misunderstanding of what freedom means, and also a general capitulation. Teaching as a whole would do better to model itself after the example in which one first makes a study of the principles the child employs, and then assists the child, on the basis of this understanding, to take the leap to genuine reading.

We have already said that this poses immense difficulties for the teacher. How could one ever reach an adequate interpretation of the performance in which the child's mind is engaged? How could one come to an assessment of what is "natural" for it, and how will one invent the "intervention" that might help the child to hear this "whisper," to amplify it and to transform it, and eventually to come closer to adhering to it till the child might acknowledge it to be his own? Yet, it is vital that what needs doing, nonetheless, can be defined as one specific project, different from those pursued by other forms of education. For example, it would not be at all the same as an attempt to realize to some maximum a given person's "total potentialities." That kind of full development would have quite different aims and would not result in the greatest possible degree of freedom. "Self-realization" in this sense postulates a very nebulous and almost unimaginable goal—what would it mean to use even just the full capacities of one's brain, if there is any truth to the often heard conjecture that we normally employ only a tiny fraction of our potential intelligence? Our concept would not lead in this direction any more than it would strive for the well-rounded person in the more colloquial sense. If what we have come to mean by freedom were taken quite at its word, then potentialities and aptitudes would no longer be enhanced for their own sake. There would only be one purpose to their development and that would be the elaboration of a "center" which the individual can accept and from which he can act. The criteria to be used would thus be very definite: the question would no longer be, what in this person is most valuable (by either moral or some other standards), but what will lead to the strongest possible identification—what, for instance, is the person most ready to accept—and what could be most completely and most naturally or even most easily "expressed"? To put it still more strongly: the only issue would be whether a person is "himself"; all else would be of subordinate importance.

This synopsis of some of the main implications which our conception of freedom would have for education is still very general and too abstract. But that is the reason for the long and close look we took at *Summerhill*. Our reinterpretation of it complements this geometric outline with a more lifelike account of the actual practice that would be involved—only, however, if the usual "permissive" picture of Neill's school really is crossed out. But even then one large qualification opens a wide gap: the intellectual training given in that school falls very short of the standard set by our concept. Paradoxically or not, it is the non-intellectual aspects—the emotional climate, the extracurricular everyday life, and most of all Neill himself (and especially Neill in his rôle as "therapist") that meet the requirements of fostering freedom in our sense. It is these other sides that give us a detailed picture of this form of education. Still, most of the stories which the book relates— from the anecdote in which Neill paints a door and in which he himself joins the flinging of the mud, through incidents like those in which Neill steals something together with one of his boys, or where he has the courage to tell another one to go ahead and jump from some high place, because the dignity of that boy is at that moment more important than a sprained ankle, and a hundred other wonderful examples—show through the actuality of living characters, and not only through dry precepts, how a firm sense of self is formed, and how the possibility of its expression could be fostered.

The general principle which has to be followed to educate a child towards freedom in our sense can be formulated in almost banal terms: on one level we all know when children are "acting" and when they are "themselves"—and one way of putting what needs to be done is therefore simple: to encourage them in the one and to discourage the other. The most mindless way of living up to this instruction would be to say to a child: "Now you are faking, and I wish you would not do that; I like you much better when you are yourself." What makes Neill impressive and his book instructive is that he not only goes far beyond this in his actions but that he has also thought his way through to the not so obvious extensions implied by it.

One example of this is Neill's insistence that conflicts need to be kept immediate and personal, that the adult should not set an abstract moral order against the child, but should confront him with his own emotions and desires, not camouflaged, but in the flesh. (Not: "This is wrong," but "I will not stand for this.") On this perception, morality becomes a refuge in an impersonal, object world which bestows upon those who escape into it an unfair power. This in turn obliterates the "Subjectivity" of those against whom this strategy is employed. Thus the usual view of morality is inverted: it is no longer the encomium of man's distinguished status, but is its abrogation. We have here an instance of Neill's "thinking through" which at the same time is part of the answer to the question of how an education towards development of a "self" would have to proceed.

So is the sharp line which Neill draws against the use of fear, which is not a protection against all dangers but which depends again on a very precise comprehension of the particular individual involved. What Neill rules out is only the specific use of fear that would displace a child from its own "center," that might cow the child into adopting a permanent disguise. The avoidance of this kind of fear is one of the steps that an education aiming at self-expression would have to take.

This applies as well to the meaning of equality to which Neill adheres. The fact that children have a vote, that the school is democratically governed, barely touches the intended measure. The form of equality required is illustrated by the examples in which the child's wish (to be left alone) has no less weight than those of an adult (so that Neill leaves the room).

Again there are the anecdotes in which the damage done by humiliation is marked out, the situations in which most of us would not notice that the child's dignity had been affronted, but where this nonetheless is done. There are stories that define when an extreme honesty is mandatory and still other instances in which the importance of letting a child "go to extremes," of not interrupting its explorations before the crucial self-discovery happens, is brought into relief.

This list gives us, I hope, a more definite idea of how an education for freedom, on our understanding of the word, would have to proceed. We have now translated some of the abstractions into practice and could rather easily fill in the rest. This lays the base for the logically next question: if this understanding circumscribes the meaning of education for freedom, then to what extent are we prepared to advocate it? How close or how distant are we from the point where we could say: "This must be done!" "This is the credo to be followed!"

Let us bring together some of our major reservations, and measure the length that separates us from an unqualified endorsement.

We certainly would not favor the emulation of Neill's Summerhill. There are, in summary, three reasons for this. The first is that the entire aspect of Summerhill which has to do with teaching and instruction, the side of it that is a school, does not live up to what we mean by freedom; in the end the intellectual training given is surprisingly traditional. Our second main objection is that Summerhill patterns itself too much into a single Either/Or, with the additional problem that each of the two alternatives is seriously defective. On one side it offers the possibility of coming to terms with only conventional classes, and on the other it gives mainly lots of rope.

But the third point is the most important: Whether and to what extent education should aim at freedom is for us a genuine and problematic question. This is the deepest difference between Neill and us: for him that value is categorical and final, while it is not for us.

But what then are the factors that for us circumscribe and narrow the claim of that value? Why can we not, like Neill, raise it up as the summation of what is needed for "salvation"?

The list is long.

For one, there is a "tactical" consideration. We saw that the idea of freedom constantly produces a stultifying and discouraging cross-purposedness and that this notion, even after much clarification, is still, like Gulliver, tied to the ground with apprehensions. This makes a real difference if the advocacy of reforms and programs is at issue. It means that resting one's case for any actual measure on that ground places it on the proverbial sand. To advance, in the context of our present culture, some particular proposal—such as the elimination or restriction of the uniform format of classes—in the name of greater freedom, simply does not cut much ice. Typically, many in the audience are apt to feel that "the kids already have too much of that," and this reason will therefore not affect the unconverted. (It is a great mistake for philosophers to imagine that the not-to-be persuaded have wax in their moral ears. This kind of condescension has shut the door to the internal complexities of the idea of freedom and has reduced philosophy to a shuffling of blank cards.) When we discussed our examples of particular proposals, the greater force of a whole range of reasons became evident. Hoisting up that concept, and marshalling the changes that one wants to make in one single line that leads up to its promise is, in the context of education, at least a forensic error. On that territory only lame and stumbling arguments can be arrayed. One will have given weak support when much stronger buttresses were close at hand.

But this practical difficulty is only the superficial symptom of deeper and authentically philosophical perplexities. The most blatant of these is the fact that the self is for us not the innocent and noble savage which remains if one strips off the corrupting crust of culture. Such attempts to whitewash human nature are aimed at preserving the dogmatic sanctity of the idea of freedom. A mystified conception of the self is needed to suppress the real questions freedom raises. This path we have deliberately blocked. For us the self is on one level an ambiguous and questionable mixture of both good and evil, and on another level an elusive "significance" established through our identification. To bring about the "expression" of this self is therefore for us obviously not the highest goal of education; when this should be done and where and to what degree, is still, as we have said before, subject to the court of other—moral or pragmatic—standards.

This should clarify one extended strategy that we have pursued throughout this book. Some might have felt that our idea of identification did not put freedom on a "solid" enough base, and to their minds this may have been a criticism. But that thoroughly misconstrues our actual intent. We had recourse to this conceptualization because it illuminates the element of what is real and gives plausibility to the idea of freedom (and it is not an illusion, it does have meaning), but at the same time we wanted to prepare for just this "turning of the table," for the moment where we would no longer be on trial before it but where we would judge and assess this idea. We wanted to stress the contrast between a stable and autonomous conception of the self, which we regard as antiquated, and an alternative, that is more up-to-date and can still be defended. And our endeavor was precisely to bring out into the open that the more "solid" base indeed has disintegrated. In short, the absence of a firmer foundation is not a flaw in our proposed interpretation. On the contrary, that the idea of freedom needs a foundation which has become so problematic—a kind of noble substance self—constitutes an objection to which it is vulnerable, and our account was consciously designed to lay this bare.

Next, there is the epistemic quandary. What our "nature" is—from the determination of a plain desire to the discovery of one's "true" self—is hazardous to guess; and whether and when we do "act from it" is also barely within the reach of our knowledge. To make of this a guide for the difficult decisions that attend education gives to a one-eyed man an almost totally blind dog. That measure is so difficult to read, the indications so oracular and dark, that it offers us no clear advice.

Further, there is the question of just in what sense action from a self is to be "maximized"—and if the devising of a program is at stake, then everything depends on that. Should we aim at the most sharply defined, most clearly visible and most intense "identification"? Is it preferable to have sometimes an *un*ambiguous and heightened sense of freedom—to really know that now, for once, one really is oneself, and that one does do what one wants—or should one opt for something more diffuse and flexible? If the former, are not the disadvantages of such a localized, and perhaps fanatically held identity only too obvious? Should one, alternatively, integrate the greatest possible diversity of facets into a single whole, and strive literally for the "largest" and most encompassing image of the self? Would that furnish "greater" freedom? But how could that be established, and what if the result were too bland? Or again, should one direct the effort with one eye on the social context and the other on a given individual, and try for some more complicated, calculated balance, which incorporates what one individual person can accept with what he can express most easily in his own context? But would this maximum—even if we could achieve it—not have the appearance of a shabby piece of social engineering, or of a cheap opportunistic trick that only needs a good nose for the path of least resistance? And does the spelling out of these alternatives not raise up the comic underside of these pretended quasi-mathematical deliberations? Is this measuring not reminiscent of the man who lost a penny in the dark, but searched for it two blocks away under the next light? Yet with all this admitted, how can we possibly still say that we are for "more freedom" if even the word "more" twists and turns in our hands?

Under these formal difficulties stand still other, more material doubts. If one could come close to "living from one's own center," would a great sincerity and naturalness (as Neill supposes) be the only consequences, or would there not also be quite different results? Would it not mean that even the most trivial actions now embodied and contained the self, and that therefore every smallest gesture was invested with an excess of weight? Perhaps one would be released from the sense that one's outward behavior inescapably turns into a pretense, that it is always only a distended and therefore "nauseating" sham; maybe it would finally have that compactness and that density which Sartre associates with the "opaqueness" of sheer Being, and which others see as that quality, found in nature, of harmony with itself, in contrast to man's restlessness. But would not the other side of this stillness be that at every point your total force comes into play: that you, in being yourself so completely, turn every request into an ultimatum? For if in every conflict your "true" and central self is all at stake, then all room for any negotiation is eliminated. There would be nothing that you could shrug off as inessential. You could never say that something only touches an outward room in which you occasionally like to play but does not affect you where you really live. There no longer would be any structure of protective shells that gives you and the other the middle ground on which the two of you can meet, and with this gone, only total coalescence or absolute negation still remain; the possibility of "relationships" has been excluded. Is not the other side of this "sincerity" that "I cannot help it, this is me" becomes a constant cry of "sanctuary!"

And this is only some few steps away from the critique of the idolatry of self-expression that Hegel sketched in the "Animal Kingdom" chapter of his *Phenomenology*. He argued there that if this attitude is carried through to its extreme, it of necessity collapses from an internal contradiction. What he had in mind is simply that the requirement of self-expression, if it is really driven to its limit and made absolute, becomes tautological and empty; that it no longer is a "standard" but turns into a truth by definition. The example of anyone who writes poetry merely to express himself illustrates this nicely, for no matter how wretchedly he writes, that goal, taken literally, has still been satisfied. Even in the face of the worst drivel, he can still say: "This is me," and be content. In the further development of this "dialectical inversion" Hegel then suggests that self-expression consistently pursued leads in the sphere of action to the same impasse that in the epistemological domain amounts to solipsism. All public and external categories that make genuine action possible in the first place fall to the ground, in a fashion that is analogous to the breakdown of all of the criteria on which the claim to genuine knowledge has to rest.

Next to these reservations that concern the actual content or the substance of this ideal, we find still other scruples, namely, those that address the feasibility of its translation into institutions. If an excess of acting from the self would be disastrous, if too much freedom, even in our sense would be ruinous, and not just for others but for the agent, then how can we establish in general terms how much of it would be desirable? But if not, then how are we to design the blueprints by which we could begin to build?

Each of the separate thoughts we have listed compounds the force of this question. If we explicitly recognize that the child's self is not pure and undefiled even in its first beginning, and that we must, in the light of other complex standards, decide which parts should be enhanced and which reformulated, then how can these be reduced to a compendium of simple rules? How could one specify the criteria by which the contest between the various and quite different senses in which "more" freedom can be realized is to be adjudicated? And if there is a genuine epistemic difficulty, even under the most favorable circumstances, how could these be overcome in the painting by numbers that is our social engineering and our politics?

More specifically: we said that the achievement of a certain self-acceptance would be a primary prerequisite, and we said that nothing was further from the proper method for attaining this than indiscriminate "indulgence"; that on the contrary, a going to extremes, which can be harsh in the right moment, but which also has to go much further than mere tolerance, again in the right moment, is indispensable. But how can this be formulated for cafeteria-style consumption? How could one give directions through which these very special moments would be indicated? And, further, how would one measure how far in these two opposite directions one should go? Yet even such a calibration would be of no use, for everything still hinges on the invention of the actual concrete act—on Neill's having the imagination to join in the flinging of the mud.

Similarly, we proposed that some specific forms of intimidation and humiliation do great damage. Yet, the translation of this injunction into the obtuse material of social arrangements again presents great difficulties. Recall the plays of Ibsen or of Strindberg, in which the meanings of subservience and domination in their genteel, domestic and sexual guises are explored. If one remembers how very fine the gloves worn by those who strangle others sometimes can be, then it become clear that no safe recipe can be set down even for an individual case, and therefore even less one by which whole factories could cook.

One could think of a poet as someone who has the gift to express some small portion of himself in words. In one narrow section, he has through practiced skills reached the point where in one medium a congruence between the self and its embodiment can be obtained. To cast what a poet does into these terms puts the ambition that has been before us into a different light, for it amounts to the presumption that one can achieve this expression for the whole of a human being, and not in mere words, but in his actions and his life. Obviously this cannot be done in any wholesale fashion, and surely not on an assembly line. Yet, in different words, this points to the same impasse,

namely, that the steps to this end would have to be extremely individuated. They would have to be taken with such sensitivity and sharp
perception that no rules will be of much help, and no general institutional arrangement could hope to offer guarantees.

This is not just one further reason why "more freedom" cannot be
the basis of a program in the sphere of education. It has larger implications concerning our culture and our politics. For one, this difficulty
has a converse side: if no ham-fisted rules can tell us how freedom is to
be achieved, if whatever is needed is so subtle and so finely tuned that
it slips through the meshes of these nets, then we can understand the
seeming paradox that some cultures, which we consider "primitive"
and in which no rules and no institutions consciously foster
freedom—cultures in which that concept simply is not known—
nonetheless realize in their members more actual freedom than do
other cultures where this is the intent. This is one of the main theses of
Dorothy Lee's fascinating book, *Freedom and Culture*, in which she
gives a spate of different examples. (Incidentally, she often stresses that
the prerogative to initiate action is carefully protected in certain cultures, especially in regard to children—among the Zuni Indians or the
Eskimos a parent does not "explain" how a toy works to a child—
which indicates that her idea of freedom is akin to ours.) The more
overt and formal structures of a culture may not just be insufficient and
in need of other supplements such as correspond to the sensitivity or
the individual judgment or the required tact, or the inventive imagination referred to in our previous paragraphs, but the more delicately
spun, informal and non-institutional "understandings"—something
for which we use the vague idea of the "ethos" of a culture—are
sometimes so potent, that they reach further, even by themselves, than
our intentionally designed apparatus.

Yet this importance of elusive cultural "attitudes"—the kind of thing
that makes a Zuni mother say of her two-year-old: "He talks already,
but I don't understand him yet"—the fact that something so mysterious
in its origins and so difficult to inculcate is central for the development
of a free person brings to light one crucible in which the West is
caught. The oft-repeated diagnoses which start from the "loss of community" may miss the far more stringent paradox that the West, which
is pre-eminently an intentional culture—it represents in essence the

first attempt consciously to design a culture—nonetheless chose, for its most highly situated value, an aim that cannot be realized by intention, a goal to which no clear-cut and rational rules will lead, which cannot be secured through the construction of institutional arrangements! The medium of operation that gives the West its definition thus proves ineffectual precisely at the most decisive moment.

This throws a great deal into a new perspective. Much of what we explicitly separated off from the core of the idea of freedom, and also much that we criticized as falling short of freedom must now be viewed more sympathetically. The provision of open alternatives and of situations in which one has a choice, the general strategy of reducing obstacles, and also more particular arrangements, like those involved in the protection of free speech, and even the clumsy efforts at creating a warmer climate in the open classroom are still inadequate. But we can now recognize that their failure is inevitable, that no institutionalized rule-of-thumb can reach the goal at which we aim. And if there is an inherent contradiction between the achievement of real freedom and any intentionally designed general social arrangement—if every generalized policy is bound to be too heavy-handed—then these may be the tortured and yet admirable efforts at an approximation. They may be attempts at mixing the fire of the idea of freedom with the water of artificially created institutions; and they may be undertaken in a situation in which no alternative to them exists; for in the absence of an "ethos" one can only either make intentional proposals or fold one's hands and pray.

In the same way it casts new light on the long line that stretches from "the tree of liberty, that ever anew must be watered with the blood of tyrants" down to the idea of a "permanent revolution." If every fixed social form is predestined to be an inadequate vessel, then only an explicit recognition of their impermanence can capture that transcendence. The need, however, is not just for the preservation and the maintenance of liberty. The picture of the constant danger of its loss is much too optimistic. More truly it calls for a permanent surmounting of all frozen institutions: none of them represents more than a makeshift pontoon bridge to another shore.

The same thought also evokes a much less ravishing perception. The West could be seen as well as the culture that made extravagantly precious sacrifices to capture the one goal of individual liberty. The extent of these burdens can perhaps be most quickly summarized through the acknowledgment that every feature which fascinates us in the study of a "primitive" culture stands in opposition to this freedom: the one characteristic of rituals on which most anthropologists agree is that they have to be performed exactly; the rules of kinship are, one and all, a set of constraints; social roles are fixed; etiquette inhibits; myth disintegrates under the impact of intellectual alternatives; the stability and coherence of a culture exists only as long as the interpretations which define it are not changed. Now, part of this is from our point of view a calamitous misunderstanding. On our view of freedom, but only on it, the formal structures as well as the "tacit understandings" of the Pygmy or the Maring culture do make positive contributions to the forming of an identity, and to the possibility of its expression. But this has of course not been the governing idea of freedom in the last three hundred years of Western history, and on the more customary meaning, all these features have been considered as curtailing freedom. So, on the one side, much was razed to the ground in the name of what to us is by now a misbegotten idol. But there is still the other side: the price has been paid, but where is the reward? If freedom is self-expression and not a life in which one does not meet much resistance, then one reason why the reward has eluded us must be this misperception. Yet we must go even further: for we have come to face the fact that all general or social tools are in principle insufficient for this task, which means that the instruments the West chose above all others simply cannot secure for it what it most wants.

This leaves us with the picture that the West, on the one hand, has denied itself more than was actually required. One could say it misunderstood the idea of freedom, and on that account practiced an excessive cultural asceticism. In Kafka's image, it pounded the whole landscape into dust; but much of what gave it shape obstructed only a chimera, and in fact would have been needed for freedom properly understood. On the other hand, it did not obtain the reward for which it bartered, and it failed in this for two separate reasons: in the first place because it misconstrued the nature of freedom, and further because the institutions designed to furnish freedom cannot do so.

This imbalance puts the demand for freedom on a different base. To ask for it in the name of "progress," to see it as the fulfillment of an aspiration, elevates the claim to it into rosy clouds, and muffles the tone in which one should insist. The situation may be more one of at last gaining compensation for losses long incurred. We live with the deprivations, but the return has been withheld. The mutilations of living in a modern culture we have to accept. If the one boon in the name of which they were inflicted is not handed over, then the time to seize it may have come.

Thus one major factor in the list of those that prevent us from making the demand for "more freedom" our platform in the sphere of education is the difficulty of translating freedom into intentionally devised, general institutions. Yet we could still add another set of strictures. Earlier we did make the advantages of freedom as empirical and as concrete as we could—recall the increased vitality, and the spontaneous flow of actions—but part of the point of this enumeration was of course to give them a specific weight, and to show that they had limits. This is now relevant, for it means that in the formulation of a program these advantages would have to be weighed against others. How, for example, should one balance the firm composure, the reserve and self-restraint and the control over the passions, to which classical Chinese education was dedicated, against the benefits of self-expression? That sort of quick cross-cultural comparison tones down our brashness, when it comes to our own society. At a greater distance we can see more clearly that the issue is not simple, that there are both pros and cons, and that whether a turn in the direction of more self-expression is the next best step from every present situation, regardless of all characteristics of an existing culture, is patently an open question. The dogmatic advocacy of "more freedom" thus comes close to lacking seriousness. In the context of education, at any rate, it is not much more than a narcissistic posture that puts those who hold it into a shining light; in its abstractness it is almost empty and is soon dropped when one begins to think in earnest about any concrete or specific situation.

We could go yet further, and look into the fine-spun and troubling paradoxes of the self. That for long spans of time these exercised primarily literature and religious thought and only rarely the social sciences, is a misleading measure of their force. The experiences from which they arise are not ethereal but are as earthy as burlap. The most ordinary of these paradoxes simply inverts our philistine expectations. The self, so it suggests, cannot be crystallized through an immersion in it. The attempt to tunnel downwards, like a miner, buries and dissolves the ore. It stunts the incipient formation, and leaves a grey and shape-less mass. The sculpting of the self needs indirection. Only in the flight from the self can it be captured; only in the surrender of the self to the work of building the external world does it gain form.

No end of great fugues have been written on this theme. One cultural corollary runs towards the apparent contradiction that the more elaborate and embellished the cultural categorization which could be expected to give contour and definition to the self, the more firmly drawn the lines of rank and caste and ritual prerogative and of taboo, the less developed is, surprisingly, the division that separates the outside world from the world of individual, emotional perception. Oddly, it seems that a very rich system of social positioning precludes the emergence of the more basic articulation between the "I" and the world. The word "I" is, for example, only very rarely used in tra-ditional Balinese culture. The lack of sharpness in this separation, the blending and fluidity across it, which is a kind of absence of the much-deplored Subject/Object distinction and which has obvious im-plications for the possibility of a genuine community, shows itself, on the one hand, in a very much less pronounced sense of agency (not "I did"—but "It happened") and, on the other hand, in the presence of a "subjective foreground" that runs across experience. This is strikingly illustrated by Ghandi's autobiography, in which his own life is narrated almost entirely in terms of small anxieties, and in which descriptions of other people or even of landscapes, barely occur. But we associate the variations on this theme more closely with lyrical and introspective literature. The paradoxes of sincerity, of masks becoming the faces which they hide—that world in which mirrors reflect mirror images of other mirrors—form the privileged sanctuary of a whole gallery of modern writers.

More flagrant yet, from our present point of view, is the explicit and direct negation of the self: the deliberate attempt not to fulfill or realize it, but with cultivated and sustained endeavor, to drain and empty and dismantle it in the hope that the curse of consciousness might be undone, that the individuation of the self could be dissolved, and that submersion in a larger and more quiet flow might be achieved.

Each of these forces on us a sudden reversal of perspectives. Their common element is that the climb upward takes on the aspect of a possible descent. Each, therefore, opens holes where we expected solid ground, and each in a different way makes the call for self-expression still more problematic.

Now, at last, we may be ready for a further step, for which, in a sense, the whole length of this book has been one extended preparation. To see the idea of freedom shaken, to recognize that its foundations might not carry, was in the past a cause for panic. It threatened a calamity. But this is no longer true for us at this turn in our thinking. We can go through the register of doubts and reservations we have just compiled and look it in the face. It is not even an embarrassment that we must hide.

Why is this?

Let me first try to say it in a metaphor: one could liken the idea of freedom to a vortex. A great deal that was really separate and independent and viable in its own right was drawn into the spinning circle of its spell and was then pulled under. Or, in a different picture: there was a soft and marshy center that steadily seeped further out, till the buildings on its edge collapsed; so one erected structures at a greater distance but since the morass spread, these, too, crumbled. Now, if one saw the idea of freedom at all in this way, then to have it restricted and contained and to have limits placed around it would of course not cause one to "panic." On the contrary, one would be reassured. And this is the perspective in which we view the "strictures" and the "reservations" that we listed. Most important is for us the fact that what we have separated off from freedom is now more secure and stands on firmer ground.

That it has been the entire strategy of this whole book on the one side, to almost literally "fill in" the idea of freedom (as one would a swamp), to give it harder and more concrete content while at the same time, along the entire length of our path, we have piece by piece separated territories off from it—that, I trust, has been impossible to miss. But the deeper intent of this design can be fully apprehended only now, in retrospect.

It has been a large part of our purpose to reclaim those structures or values or concerns, that have melted into the idea of freedom. In the process it had to be narrowed down. But this was done so as to strengthen the concept of freedom, not to make it weaker, and so as to place the remainder, to which it could not give firm support, also on a more secure foundation.

We wanted to find a way out of the fog, in which both the defenders and the detractors of freedom walk in circles, till the "brass gong, big as a pond," from our earlier story about the ancient village is struck and deafens them, and they fall to the ground. And we could not see any method for doing this, except that of going as far as possible inside the idea of freedom, and at the same time circumscribing it and building walls of separation between it and that which lies outside it. To stop the vortex, freedom had to be understood. The doubts and strictures that we have rehearsed no longer frighten us, because we now know what it is.

It is possible that previously there have been other similar spinning vortex notions, and that the small hands of rationality slowly built containing walls around them, but that we have so far failed to calm this last idea. If so, the breaking of the spell of this idea (which is not its destruction but its inclusion into the sphere of rationality) has become mandatory.

But this necessity can also be perceived in a less optimistic and less eighteenth-century fashion. Whether it was altogether wise to entrust ourselves to the guide of reason may be a very open question. But even if this is admitted, one thing cannot be denied: that it is dangerously foolish to follow reason and yet to tie a cloth around its eyes just when the climbing becomes hard. Our dilemma is that all other forms of knowledge—from those accumulated through tradition to those that we once possessed through "intuition"—have been so mutilated that they no longer serve us well. Yet nothing is quite as myopic and ignorant as a curtailed and limited and partial reason. In this way reason is exacting. If it can lead at all, it can do so only if it is unhindered and not interfered with. As in Kafka's story of the Hunger Artist who says that the only cure for the affliction of his art is still more art, so reason can only heal itself through still more reason, through a larger and more sensitive and more daring rationality. And therefore there can be no mystery in its own center. If there is a paradox of freedom, then it may be that freedom was the herald of rationality and yet became a darkness in which reason lost its way. That paradox had to be dispelled, for reason will be the noose from which we hang unless we can reach up and climb that rope.

To make this now more concrete:

The first and most obvious example which illustrates this general design is our extended consideration of the relationship of "obstacles" and "hindrances" to freedom (in Chapter 4). We ended this discussion on the idea that we would make a sharp and permanent separation between the two. We decided that the situation of facing a difficulty or a risk could be much better understood if we thought of it in its own terms, and not by means of the confounding and difficult idea of freedom. There may have been an uneasy reservation that splitting the idea of obstacles off from the idea of freedom in effect slighted their seriousness. The impression might have been that this classification reduced them to mere obstacles, and that the severance from freedom (with its imposing association) meant they were now adrift and would be swept under the carpet. One might have felt that we were coming dangerously close to saying that putting obstacles into people's way did not count for much, since it did not make them unfree. And this is not completely wrong. Part of the point was to underscore that obstacles do not transform us into helpless victims. But the retrospective re-understanding of the whole climb we undertook should now show that precisely the opposite was the far more important underlying aim. We, so to speak, knew in advance that the idea of freedom even on our interpretation of it would turn out to be as problematic as the just-assembled list of "strictures" and of "reservations" has now shown. And the intent was, therefore, to rescue that more incisive mode of thought. The ties had to be cut so as to salvage it, just because obstacles do matter, and because the less slippery conceptual instrument of their own language, namely, that of "hindrances" and "risks," gives us a much firmer grip on them than does the terminology of freedom.

This puts that concern, which had been part of the idea of freedom, on much firmer ground. And what we mean by this, in still more detail, should be very plain. We said, throughout, that it was terribly misleading to offer the reduction of obstacles "in the name" of freedom, since this was bound to raise false hopes and to disappoint expectations; that it unavoidably seemed to promise more than could eventually be delivered. Now, however, the time has come to face the other side of this same coin, which is simply that not to speak of them in terms of freedom, but to call them obstacles and hindrances and risks, does tell us what we have a right to ask and what we should not accept with resignation and how we must act.

In the context of raising children, this is to say that it is a mistake to try to find one's way through the maze of questions which ask: "When should I yield, and when should I be harsh?" by the light of the idea of freedom. It is a mistake to settle these decisions by this standard or even by the hope of its attainment, or to justify what one is doing by reference to it; that leads into all the perplexities our list of reservations summarized. But this error can be easily avoided by staying with the plainer words we have and by making our judgments and taking our actions and justifying them in these, their own names. So when it comes to obstacles, those that discourage and reduce the spirit and destroy should be levelled to the ground; those that stupefy and make less sensitive and do crush and diminish should be done away with. But those that are intriguing, that make contact possible, that may be fun to overcome—those that strengthen and enhance should be left alone. Even these terms will of course not always lead us comfortably by the hand, but at least we will have a chance, for in these terms we can think. This, and not "more freedom," would, therefore, be a part of our "program."

A second instance, that again makes our larger picture more specific, is our re-interpretation of how choice relates to freedom. Here, too, we performed a kind of severance, and the first impression might have been that this disjunction placed the importance of "giving people choices" into jeopardy. And we said, just as we did with obstacles, that to offer choices "in the name" of freedom was confusing and even treacherous, for that, too, seemed to hold out more than would be given. But now, in retrospect, one should see that here, too, this diminishment of the significance of choice was only the first step towards a badly needed clarity and that the second step, again, was meant to place it on a firmer ground.

Choices, as we said before, are as plentiful as sand is on the beach. We choose at every moment. The "narrow hallway" in which we cannot move a single step to the left or right, but only forwards, is only an image from a philosophic nightmare. The fact that we constantly confront alternatives and choose is so rudimentary and basic that nothing can possibly deprive us of it. It is so permanently "given" that it is much less than freedom, but it is also so secure that the idea of freedom is not needed to shore it up. We can look calmly at all the difficulties that remain even in our version of the idea of freedom, for choice remains untouched by them. It rests easily and safely on a much deeper-lying rock.

And for the bringing up of children the implications are once more analogous. To let them choose between two flavors of ice cream with the pretense that this gives them freedom is more than a ludicrous overvaluation. Now that we fully realize how elusive and resistant to predictions freedom actually is, we can turn this coin, too, on its other side. To hinge the offering of choices to the cloudy goal of freedom and to justify the right to them in terms of that chance-ridden expectation hangs them indeed from a most vaporous ceiling. The more forceful reasons are here, too, a great deal plainer. To give a child (and the same applies of course to grownups) an opportunity to choose simply increases the likelihood that it will be doing what it wants. That correspondence between action and desire puts the reasons for letting someone choose on a solid, earthy floor. Choice gives some increment of power, and some power is one prerequisite of self-respect. That, and others like it, are the stronger girders on which the demand for choices can now take its stand.

Once these are the name in which choices are presented, instead of in the name of freedom, we will find our way through the decisions in this sphere as well. It will still be hard enough but at least we will have honest and sharp tools.

Similarly, we can examine in this new light the notion that freedom requires absolute and total independence (in Chapter 3), that to be "really" free requires an autonomous, sacrosant and separate ego, which from some point "above" surveys the flow of events and, seeing alternatives, intervenes to steer them down one path rather than the other. In that regard we pointed out that this Ego is of course a figment but one that may be nearly ineradicable, since it has its roots in the Subject/Predicate structure of our language and in the capacity of our consciousness to "step back" from every object, till nothing but a point, i.e., a point of view, remains. But we placed more weight on an array of other thoughts. Two of these can now be rapidly condensed.

For one, we insisted that this degree of independence was actually not a prerequisite for freedom. Instead, it represented the demand of one bizarre identification. Only if this "limiting case" among all possible identities is adopted, does one need this total independence to be free. With any of the other (and more sensible) identities, freedom requires harmony with (and not independence from) that which one accepts as one's own self.

And secondly, we maintained that the enactment of this self, and of this independence, would be a terrible affliction. It would entail an unheard-of metaphysical isolation. Even on its own terms it would experience every contact as subjugation and only the madness of a Caligula as "free."

This case, like the other two, exemplifies our description of freedom as a vortex, but we have not put this idea (unlike the other two) on firmer ground; we have merely built a wall around it. The fantasy of such a total independence and of an Ego that possesses it is for many the very paradigm of freedom. But essentially we drew a line and severed it from anything that freedom should legitimately mean. We did not want to "salvage" or to "rescue" it, but on the contrary both that idea of independence and that conception of the self seemed to us liabilities and burdens which had to be dispelled. Our design in this instance thus did not have two sides, and there is consequently no need of a retrospective re-understanding. We marked off obstacles and choices from freedom so as to put them on a more solid base. But the idea of total independence we have allowed to sink.

The strengthening that we were trying to perform in this regard aimed in the opposite direction. The notions of obstacles and choices are in the end less elusive and more definite than that of freedom, and therefore they gained greater force by being amputated from it. Here the situation is the other way around: fragile and problematic as the idea of freedom may well be, the ideas of this independence and of this "point"-self are still more dubious and murky. Their severance, therefore, relieved the idea of freedom of a dead weight and strengthened it.

This, too, contributes to our equanimity in the face of our doubts concerning freedom. Others might feel that the long line of open and moot questions which we asked threatens their belief in the "absolute autonomy of man." But we do not perceive this as a "danger." The belief in this total and isolating independence has nothing to do with man's ability to make choices or to surmount obstacles or to resist influences or to think critically or to swim against the stream. On the contrary, it stakes man's dignity on a dream that will not support it. The peril lies precisely in having man stand on this bubble of blown glass when the earth would carry him much better.

We could pursue this retrospect over our previous chapters further, and could add many more examples. Our discussion of being influenced or "conditioned," for instance, could be re-interpreted analogously. Here, too, we argued that the expectation of not being influenced, which the idea of being free suggests, cannot be fulfilled, and that it is here also preferable to sever the more concrete and more manageable mode of thinking (that simply talks of different modes of influences) from the labyrinth of freedom. And the retrospective second thought would again be the recognition that this was not a slight, but that it, conversely, puts the discussion of what really is a de-humanizing way of being influenced and what is not on a more rugged base. But this should be clear enough by now, and we can therefore proceed to cast this same backward glance across the more recent parts of our thinking.

No, we would not advocate "more freedom" and for exactly the same reasons that would keep us from "translating" the reduction of obstacles into an increase of "freedom." Obstacles are obstacles, and calling them by their right name makes a clearer and more forceful thinking possible. In the same way, we would advocate everything that we have found to be right and sensible in this chapter in its own name and not in the name of freedom; just as we would object to everything that we have criticized in the plainer language we have used so far. As with obstacles and choices, we would not promise freedom nor raise that hope nor invoke that as our last and ultimate justification. The idea of freedom, even in the clarified and strengthened and refurbished re-interpretation of it we gave, is too beset by ambiguities and whirling questions. What we have said can stand much more vigorously on its own two legs. Nothing can be gained by referring it to that more mysterious abstraction. Greater lucidity and greater strength lie in the direction of the more concrete.

Our program, therefore, has already been spelled out. It has been formulated step by step in the details of our exploration and does not have to be tacked on at the end. It began when we said at the outset that suspending children in a vacuum is cruel and nonsensical, that it stifles the child and traps the parents in a vicious circle. It continued when we talked of the two ways of nursing and insisted that the less talented and skillful mother might afford her baby more of the indispensable experience of having wrought a change, of having produced some effect, of finding that the world sometimes responds. It was developed further in our criticism of some day-care centers and some open classrooms, when we suggested that the provision of mere physical mobility within the narrow confines of a room, combined with the merciless rote-training of a young mind through the rat-maze of "skill-books," was a very dubious advance. And we added on to it, when we maintained that the reasonable persuasion of a child, which seems so self-evidently more humane, must be reconsidered: that this relocates the conflict from the outside of the child, where it occurs between itself and an adult, into its own inner self, and splits the self apart and also intercedes in the formation of an impulse or a wish, even before it has had the opportunity properly to take shape.

We gave more of our answer to the question of what we would actually do when we compared the child or student to a juggler, who already performs an astounding feat, and the teacher to someone who has to add "the next plate" at exactly the right moment and in exactly the right way. That the wrong addition, the new idea for which the student is not ready, produces an effect like the crashing down of all the plates, which he so far managed to keep in the air, implied a radical revision of how one should teach and educate. And so did the idea that the "new plate" has to be assimilated to the rest, that the mere presentation of a new thought does not mean the act of teaching has as yet begun—that has only happened when the student or the child can play with the new fact or method or perspective as if it were its own.

We amplified still further what should and should not be done when we contrasted the "Japanese" with the "Prussian" mode of working in a garden. The cardinal division, far more important than the line between the harsh and the indulgent is not first to bulldoze flat a rectangular neat clearing, but to feel a kind of reverence for the immense subtlety of an already thriving nature: not to teach a child as if it were the philosopher's blank wax tablet, and especially not to erase until its mind indeed will match that metaphor; not to make the child study but instead to make a study of the child till one can, with knowledge of what is already there and with a high regard for it, undertake the act of working here and there a change.

Our long, one-sided dialogue with Neill also pointed up approaches which we heartily endorse. Our disagreements were particularly stressed because our concentration fell on the idea of freedom, more than on Neill's admirable relationships to children. But the many points on which we have agreed with him make up another part of our credo. Together with him we would say that nothing is quite as important as the homely fact that education is not the whole of living with a child; that neither schools nor parents nor theories of education can afford to blink at this basic truth; and that the one indispensable conviction is, therefore, that a child is not a piece of raw material which must be shaped and formed and tampered with at every moment. We thus share his insistence that much is already "there" before all teaching starts, and that much of it will grow best if it is left alone. And we could not be more with Neill than when he says that conflicts must be personal, that the parent should set his claims or his wishes directly against those of the child—that they should not be costumed in the robes of abstract rightness. To exile the child from the whole human world by saying "This was wrong!" and to form an alliance with a universal order, just so that it will give in to one's own preferences, creates a monstrous imbalance. It is easy to instill a permanent timidity and fearfullness in children, and Neill is right when he describes this as a sin against their spirit.

Another powerful concurrence between us and Neill is our disagreement with the fundamental premise that "socialization" is the task of education, and our view that the outside world is, if anything, so overwhelming that the "whisper" of subjectivity can be drowned out. The basic plot of the epic of bringing up a child is not for us the subjugation of its "egoistic" desires, but is an odyssey, a homeward journey. The endeavor is to assist the child in its search, away from the anonymous and neutral "public" world, towards the discovery and the creation of emotions and desires and ideas that are its own.

Again, we are at one with Neill when he makes a serious equality between the child and the grownup mandatory: we agree that the right sometimes to give orders must be earned; that one gains title to it only through a mutuality which places the child into a position where its wishes, too, are sometimes obeyed like commands.

And we would not hold back, but go with him fully, when he makes his most "extreme" demands: that "one be on the side of the child" when its own self-assertion is at stake, when it rebels against "authority" even, or especially, when the "authority" should be one's own. We share his belief that a child should not obey mere power or be browbeaten by the mere insignia of an institutional position, but that it should see the Other as no more and no less than another human being on an equal footing with itself. If a child had to throw mud at our freshly painted door to break out of a past of timidity, then we, too, would splatter mud against that door.

Though this is only a small part of the great deal which we value in Neill's practice, there are of course also the major disagreements which we marked out before, and these too define the detail of the position which we advocate. The kind of school that we envision is very different from Summerhill: it would not just pose the alternative between conventional "classes" and "being left alone"; and the teaching in the classes would be a radical departure from the kind of teaching with which Neill seems to be content. The fact that Neill makes no allowances for the cultivation of incisive thinking, but rather casts disparagements in that general direction, seems to us an awful flaw. For in the pandemonium of the modern world, in which on every corner mountebanks sell their intellectual liver pills and everybody is fair game to those who sell, the ability to question is needed to survive.

But the many points of opposition need not be recalled. The most crucial matter which needs to be re-emphasized and made a part of our new perspective is that Neill justifies the whole of what he does on the basis of his belief in freedom. His hope, goal and promise is that Summerhill gives freedom and raises children to become free human beings. Everything he advocates is ultimately advocated in the name of freedom. And on this score our disagreement with him is flat and unmitigated, and the full extent and force of our conflict with him in this regard could not have been seen prior to this looking backwards and to the summation of our reservations about the idea of freedom.

We would do none of this. Words have a social meaning against which all attempts at philosophical redefinitions are quite powerless, and part of the social meaning of freedom is that there will be no hindrances, that there will be an "open space," that one will not be influenced. Since none of this either can or should be done, and since without any question none of this is done at Summerhill, the raising of that promise is without excuse.

And we have straightforward philosophic reasons for why we would not either justify or promise or advocate these proposals "in the name" of freedom, even in the sense that we have urged upon that word. These reasons have by now been given and reiterated. They are the same as those which determined us to call obstacles by their right name, to reexamine the significance of choices, to distinguish different modes of being influenced and all the rest. Yet we can speak still more directly: we would not justify this "program" in the name of freedom, because that gives it only very weak support, when much stronger reasons can be given. We would not promise freedom, even in our sense, because no guarantee and no assurance could be given that its enactment would rear children who would possess a firm sense of their own identity and the ability to act from this sense of self and to express it. In short we would not advocate this approach "in the name" of freedom, because the names by which we called it are its own names and they are good enough.

None of this is in any sense meant to say that the concept of freedom has been rendered "meaningless," nor that the word should now be dismissed since it has lost its usefulness. We set out to dispel the magical mysteriousness of this idea, not the idea itself. A great deal of what it once seemed to comprise we discovered to be something else that we can grasp much more firmly with simpler names. The one thing that appeared to us to be its most essential substance, that truly deserved and needed that demanding title—the attribute of expressing one's own self—still has its magnificence, even after the pedestals have been removed, but it also has its flaws. It is not the one thing above all that one should hope to give to one's own children, though it is one of the many glorious possibilities of life. And there is no way of making sure that it will be theirs. There is no book of rules and no "environment" and no diet of regularly undertaken exercises that can guarantee a child will grow up to live a life that it will feel to be its own, that will fit it, and not be like a borrowed suit. Even this, which on the face of it does not seem much to ask, is a gift which cannot be extorted. It falls to some and is withheld from others without justice. But we can live with this, for there is much that can be struggled for and reached.

7

Freedom and Society

IMAGINE THAT LATE AT NIGHT you are walking through the deserted streets of a small town, and suddenly a man, dressed somewhat like a peddler, accosts you and waves you on to follow. In the spirit of one who has only recently arrived and wants to explore, you turn after him into an alley, climb up a staircase, and moments later you are in a large, bare and whitewalled room. A yoga class seems to be in progress. A number of young people lie on the floor, their bodies in a pose of relaxation. Their teacher, wearing a black leotard, appears to be in the middle of an explanation. You notice that everybody's eyes are not closed but extraordinarily wide open and alive; then you begin to listen:

"So you see," the yoga teacher says, "that there are situations, in which all this is obvious and evident and easy. You can walk around in it as if you were at home, in your own living room, in socks. You need not even look, it all goes without saying. And yet there are other contexts in which without any warning certain pictures capture our minds. It is strange, almost as if we had been hypnotized, for these images are crude and clumsy, but nonetheless possess great power. And they enthrall us not when we stay close to the ground, but when we rise up to the heights on which we theorize. The paradox is thus twofold: one layer of it is the sheer compartmentalization of our usual intelligence—that we should see so clearly from one angle and yet be so benumbed when we look from another. The second layer consists in the inversion: that we are stupider and much more mesmerized in our subtle theories, and for once (and perhaps not just for once) far more intelligent in our ordinary habits. So the pictures we discuss are childish; it is embarrassing to look at them; yet they are all the same deeper than the rest of our thinking.

"Take, for example, the most common saying, that under a democracy the people are naturally free, while this is not true under other dispensations, and ask yourself: What image seems to make this so self-evident? Is it not more than anything the notion that we are protected, that there are limits beyond which our government is not allowed to go; that it does not cover the whole ground like an inundation, but that there are checks, like dams, which hold it back? And does this not mean that we think freedom and the state exclude each other, that where one begins the other ends? And is it not true that this mythic or children's imagery lies only just below all kinds of axioms and philosophical appearing propositions? Man is born free, we say together with Rousseau, and conjure up the story of a cunning barter: this much, but no more of an original inheritance, a birthright, we surrender, in exchange for security, for protection, but some of that original endowment we hold back. We draw a line; the freedom on the far side of it we pay as a price, but the inner circle we would like to keep. And how do we think of rights? Are they, too, not like a moat around each individual keeping us at a proper distance from each other; and do they not enclose a plot of ground that is immune, a sanctuary in which we have license? But take this to its extreme. Where does it lead? Must it not reach its culmination in the idea that the government which governs least is best? Is this not the logical conclusion, the obviously most advantageous trade? Will that not leave intact the largest quantity of freedom, and give away a minimum of that immensely precious good? Is it not clear that the famous Jeffersonian dictum presupposes the images we just described? Could one come to this conclusion and experience it as evident if one had not been raised in a nursery in which these pictures hung?

"So let us take this sentence—the government that governs least is best—and look at it up close. What does it say? Imagine you told it to someone who never heard it, who had grown up in a completely different culture. What would be his reaction? Is it not likely that a traveler from far off might stare at you with bafflement and consternation; that he might blink and then burst into the response: 'What an unheard-of and weird thing to say! You would not say this of a doctor, would you? You would not think that a doctor who cured least was the best? Or that a gardener who gardened very little was the one to hire? Or that a worker who hardly worked was better than all others? So why do you hold such bizarre opinions when it comes to government? Maybe if a government barely governs, it only means that it does not perform its function, that it is a failure, a mistake?'

"And such a stranger might continue: 'If you really believe in this inverse proportion, why do you have any government at all? Surely, if the state marks the borderline of freedom, you would have still more freedom if there were no government whatever? Only the absence of government would be really least, and consequently best of all. So why do you not draw the logical conclusion and get rid of the state—or at least make sure it withers away gradually?'

"How would we reply," the yoga teacher asks, "if someone said this? Would we not respond that the results of such an abolition would be very different; that some few ruthless men perhaps would be still freer than under the most minimal of governments, but that the vast majority would be under the oppression of those few? But then, would you or I, mild as we are, not be among the latter? Would we not end up nearer to the bottom, with a much harsher life? Might not our existence be very like that of a dog, complete with bones from the table and a chain around our necks? So we owe a great deal to the interference of the state. Many of us would fall to a much lower level if it did not intercede.

"And this acknowledgment is important, for it implies that much of our picture-thinking has to be revised. Not all of us would be completely free in the 'natural condition' prior to the state. Some of us might be far more constrained than we are now, and the story that we have traded in some part of our freedom for security is therefore just a myth. But if this is true, if we never possessed this incommensurately precious good to barter it away, then our resisting and begrudging attitude also is not so obviously justified. Then at least some kinds of government—though certainly not all—give us not just material safety for a spiritual sacrifice, but do much more and should get their reward.

"Of course we know this. To our concrete thinking all this is very evident. If you work as a nurse's aide, you understand that your paycheck would be less if it were not for the minimum wage guarantees enforced by the state. The point is that from the clouds of our theoretical opinions our feet no longer touch this obvious ground. On that level a Pavlovian reflex jerks us back: authority, the state, makes us less free.

"Yet our traveler, recovered from his initial shock, might speak to us a second time. 'Why do you say that limiting the state makes people free? That word has such a grand and bell-like ring. But what real purpose does it serve when the facts are so very plain? A state imposes penalties and fines, and these are obstacles that hinder you in certain actions. But there are other obstacles besides those represented by the state—they surround you on all sides. Limiting the state reduces only some very few of all the obstacles you face. What of the remnant? How can the lowering of one kind of obstacle make you free? Why do you think of yourself in an open space when only one wall of your cage has been moved backwards by three feet?

" 'But in reality not even this occurred. You did not simply gain more space, for that ignores another and still more crucial fact: you cannot remove one obstacle in isolation. There is no fixed and stable sum from which you can subtract. A change in one place makes a difference in all others. The elements of the system interact. If you diminish hindrances in one sphere, those in other areas will go up. So your weakening of the state changed only one weight in a complicated clockwork mechanism. And what were the effects of this in other places?

" 'Consider the hindrances of poverty for instance. Go through a supermarket: not the asparagus because it costs too much. Not fresh bread but a loaf that is four days old. Where is the basket with the damaged cans? That's when the obstacles close in on you, and every step is up against a wall. Or take the barriers linked to work. You may not have the license to do the one thing which you could do best, and that can stop you cold—for then you cannot be insured; and there is the continuous control imposed on you within the work you do. Is it not as if your hands were strapped to a machine? Now put this block on top of the other, and now, like it or not, the next. Does not this grind you down more than all other pressures? Again, are you not impeded by ill health that could have been avoided; by a schooling that covers spontaneity with gravel, perhaps most of all by an indifference that spreads like a gas? But is it not likely that many of these obstacles grew larger as the direct result of the diminishment of others? You took the rocks that had pinned down someone's legs and lifted them from off his feet. But you piled them back on—and this time on his head!

" 'The one force in your culture on which most people have some influence you weakened. The state whose leaders are at least selected by elections you limited till it did least. But all the other powers you allowed to grow. Yet in their affairs you do not have a vote, and who their leaders are you hardly know. Is this not downright mad? To tie down and hold back the one force which in spite of all its flaws is somewhat open and accountable to you, and to give the advantage of this debility to elements which are inaccessible and closed? Is it not evident that this is upside-down; that you should have strengthened the one force over which you have some hold, so that through it you might have kept the rest in check? But this still misses the main point; for your state in actuality is not weak or limited at all! Your dictum that "least is best" must be a kind of game, like that with scissors, paper and a rock. For you accept compulsory education, do you not? But that allows the state to meddle with the raising of your children. And you apply for a license to get married. And it is the state that grants you a divorce; and there are even laws against homosexuality and fornication. So how large is your private territory? You can be arrested for having a too noisy party—that disturbs the peace, even if the country is at war. Sitting on a park bench can be a criminal offense. The government can tell you how big your bathroom has to be if you are building your own home. You even need a permit to bring your garbage to the dump! Just how far back have you pushed the state?

" 'Think of the slogan: the means of violence belong to the government. Spelled out this means that if your government betrays you, you can only sign petitions and write letters to your congressman. If you break a single window it is still a crime. But if the state decides that you were traitorous to it, then it can execute you. So whose hands are still tied, and who still throws the switches?

" 'Or take the measure of your deference to the law. From the time you watch Western movies: "He took the law into his own hands" is made to sound as if divinity had been defiled. The film cannot end, the sunset has to wait, till the law has been restored to the state. Your own beliefs count here for very little: if you disagree on a specific issue—on school busing or integrated housing, for example—you are wrong if you act on your own convictions. It is the law that has to be obeyed. You are more submissive than a child, for even parents say to their growing children: "These are my reasons. Weigh my arguments and then make your decision," but relative to laws your culture does just the reverse: this is right, because it is the law; no further questions—but laws are the voice of the state!

" 'No, you did not build a fence against the government so you could grow your own small garden. Your story has a very different plot. On the whole you were a very humble servant, but you did choose a single place—there you dug in your heels and drew a line: trade you made free; the economic you marked off; property became inviolable. The foundations for this predilection, for this one barricade against the state, were laid right from the start. They can be found in Hobbes and in Rousseau, and most especially in Locke. Their theories prepared the ground on which your institutions were erected. And that is still the single enclave you defend: What do you call it when the government stands helpless and has no control? In any area except for the economic this is Anarchy, and you associate it with pandemonium and slaughter. But in the economic the same condition has a different name: there it is Free Enterprise. And vice versa: if the state is vigilant in any other area, then that is Law and Order, but in the economic area the word for that is Socialism.

"'Your double standard stretches one's imagination. On one side you protest a total tax on incomes in excess of 80,000 dollars. That is an abridgement of your rights. You think the state has no claim on that money, and no prerogative to redistribute it. Here you forget that no one produces the value represented by 80,000 dollars quite by himself, that others must have lent a hand, and that all kinds of chance conventions and arbitrary social customs need to be observed for such a paycheck to materialize. You isolate a single fact: that someone has possession of that money, that it is his property, and then you wonder how anyone but him could have a right to it.

"'Yet, on the other side, you hardly question the right of governments to declare wars. Most of you condone the institution of conscription, and even the selection by lottery—a bingo game—of those the government will send to war. You refuse the government the right to property which is not even unambiguously yours. But to stake your life on the turning up of the right number, on a throw of dice, to that you give the state the right!

"'And with that we come to the real issue. The hindrances of poverty, of mindless labor and of disease you did not choose to fight. You only wanted to curtail the state, and that by no means generally but only in one segment, that of the economic, of Free Enterprise—on that short front you took your stand. But this one spot which you finally selected was the worst and most calamitous place you could possibly have picked. How great a toll in sacrifices would have been exacted if the state had intervened more in the sphere of property or business? What real loss in freedom—in genuine self-expression— would be imposed by regulating mergers and other similar transactions? How many actions vital to the self would that stop? Would the affected notice it in their own personal lives, or would the difference be known only to their accountants? So how much freedom is gained? But what a price is paid! For by putting that very small restraint on a mere handful (who could still have had their private yachts—just slightly shorter ones) you could turn around the lives of millions. A minimal increase in some obstacles faced by a very few would empower you to take down hindrances which daunt the great majority far more than abstract governmental regulations—obstacles so insurmountable and close that their will to be themselves capitulates in desperation.

"'Do not imagine therefore that your culture has granted you a high degree of freedom. The question of genuine freedom, of self-expression, has so far hardly ever been raised. That was not the measure by which your politics were judged. Your failures and successes, your long-range strategies and daily tactics can be assessed in the much plainer language of obstacles that either were removed or left to mount. Seen in that way, and coldly, your advances up to date are unimpressive and your retreats are very great. You have reduced some few hindrances, but only in that one most unintelligently chosen place, and other barriers grew higher than they were before. It is the waste of it, the crevasse between what you might have done and what you did, that seems most baffling and appalling. For no fundamental change, no total reconstruction was required. Minor adjustments might have sufficed. But you balked. You did not end that terrible imbalance. You watched its tilt grow steeper, but stood by and did not move.'"

After bringing the traveler's speech to this conclusion, the yoga teacher paced across the floor. Then he began anew: "This is the impression a visitor might form. That it is in some ways much too simple should be obvious. The lines are not that neat and sharp. Not only trade and finance were blocked off against incursions from the state. Speech, too, was protected, and so was religion and much else. And conversely: not the whole of the economic was off limits for the state. Far from it! The switch from resisting interference to inviting and submitting to all manner of controls—the double standard—occurred not only between the economic and the rest. It was also invoked inside the economic. Think of its blatant use in the relationship between the so-called mother countries and their colonies. In their dealings with each other the industrialized nations asked the state for the most nurturing protection. As long as their own plants were weak, a veritable greenhouse of differential customs, tariffs, and currency exchanges was put up. It was only when they were strong and ready, and 'open doors' to their advantage, that the ideology of Free Trade was hoisted to the mast. And the same shuttling between government control and laissez-faire was naturally also practiced inside each country's own domestic sphere, and often in exactly the same way: the powerful received the benefits of governmental interference, and the weak were told that freedom had to be preserved.

"So the borderline between the territory which one protected against intrusions from the state and the other areas in which the state was welcomed with red carpets was not fixed and drawn with a straight edge. It meandered and zigzagged and was continuously moved from place to place. The geometric picture in which only the economic was exempted is therefore certainly too crude. But we need not study the pressures which bent this line now this way and then back. Its exact location, and even that it sometimes disappeared is not to our purpose. We can admit that our traveler was mistaken on this score. That still leaves intact the lessons we can learn from him, and some of these we might compress into a list.

"The first comes to the fundamental irrationality of our prejudice against the state. Consider this in a psychological perspective: it seems a fact that we associate the establishment of rules, and especially the increase of government and regulations, with the idea that there will be more situations in which someone can tell us 'what to do,' and that we therefore will be less free. But this is actually an astonishing naiveté, and one should ask: What mistake delivers us into the arms of this conclusion? The answer is that it happens when we monopolize the stage. We slip into the fantasy that we are quite alone—like Robinson Crusoe on his small island—and we imagine that the only pertinent relationship is that between ourselves and these rules. If this were indeed the case, then our apprehension would be justified; then there really might be a proportionality between the increase of rules and our being hindered by them. But this would be true only if we were alone. As soon as this pretense is dropped and a genuinely social context is imagined, the absurdity of our fears becomes apparent: for with a multitude of others present most rules will far more often prevent them from infringing on me than they will impinge on me directly. The red traffic light which I have to obey keeps fifty others out of my way for every time it forces me to stop.

"So this mistake—this egocentric fallacy—is an arresting specimen, for in effect it constitutes a contradiction: precisely at the point at which we assess an instrument which is in its very essence social, i.e., a social rule or a government—and where a social thinking is mandatory, we relapse into a private, an asocial or even anti-social mode of thought.

"In the second place we can advance a summary critique of Anarchism. That word, too, has many meanings. Much of what it stands for inspires admiration and respect, but on one understanding of it freedom is to be achieved through the abolition or the gradual dismantling of the state. If this is taken literally and is not a hyperbole for a drastic decentralization and democratization of the state (a transformation with an outcome that many would no longer call a 'state'), then it is open to the following objections: (1) It singles out one obstacle—that of the state—and expects freedom from leveling this one to the ground, forgetting all the other obstacles which would still hem us in. (2) It overlooks that the various sets of obstacles interact with each other and that the abolition of the state would probably increase other barriers which might be even more debilitating than the state. (3) It commits the 'egocentric fallacy' for it thinks of the state as principally an obstacle or a limit on my freedom. But in a social context the right kind of state may increase my freedom rather than diminish it. In essence it is thus guilty of the very errors inherent in the 'least is best' conception, with the difference that Anarchism is consistent and carries them to their extreme.

"The third and most crucial lesson implicit in our traveler's reactions subsumes the two we have just detailed under a more comprehensive claim: in essence it constitutes a rejection of the framework in which these issues have been often posed.

"The pillars of this structure of assumptions were the notions that man as such was free before the state, that some of that primordial freedom was surrendered through the act of contracting into society or the state, and arising from this basis, the conception that freedom and the state exclude each other, that the territory given over to the state marks the borderlines of the preserved and to-be-defended sphere of our privacy.

"Our reasons for breaking with this mode of thought will stand out most clearly if we see it against the backdrop of the shift by now familiar, from the elusive and deceptive thought of freedom, to firmer and more incisive categories. As soon as we substitute the conception of facing obstacles for the idea of freedom, the discussion of man's condition prior to the state loses much of its mysteriousness. We can move away from postulating arbitrary myths that legitimate prearranged conclusions: from the story of a universal war in which life was nasty, brutish and short, which justifies gratitude and submission to the state, but also from its opposite, from the fable of the noble savage, which turns the whole of culture and society into a malady. If we ask not about freedom, but about the obstacles men faced, we can see at once that all men certainly faced some, and from there a discussion which compares societies that did not yet have a state to later ones that were so organized, can start.

"And the same holds for the rest. Once we think in terms of obstacles it becomes apparent that our joining of the state entailed not only a forfeiture of freedom, but that some barriers were lowered as others rose; and with that the picture of the two territories, where the state encroaches upon freedom, and freedom reigns only in the remnant, is brought to its collapse. For we are not free in the sphere from which government has been banished, since other barriers still remain and are apt to increase, and we are not unfree in areas over which the government has some control, for its interference might reduce the obstacles we otherwise would face.

"In essence this dispenses with a merely quantitative thinking that attempts only to measure the more or less of government, and makes room for a thinking that is qualitative in two different ways: government is for us only one of several modalities through which we and others act or can be influenced and hindered. It must be held up against other forces which may be less accessible to us, and which may have greater power over our lives. In addition it is the quality, the nature of government, that for us becomes all important: the material question is not whether it governs more or less or least, but how it governs: closed off from us or under our eyes, intelligently or with stupidity, a weapon in the hands of others, or a tool we all can use.

"Our fourth and last conclusion is that the identification of the absence of government interference with freedom is an ideological device whose function is very like the big brass gong in a certain ancient village. When a minimum of government was in the interest of some group, then they pronounced this to be freedom, and many others—deafened—acquiesced and fell into line. When a strong state was wanted, then Anarchy threatened at the gates, and many could again be herded in the opposite direction. The muffling of that gong was part of our aim.

"We began from the idea that crude and childish pictures sometimes mesmerize a part of our minds. Three separate charges have now been laid against the mode of thought which conjures up the one most hypnotizing image: (1) It talks as if the state were one undifferentiated force, and fails to recognize that the quality and nature of the state is far more important than its magnitude or strength. (2) It forgets that there are other obstacles besides those represented by the state. (3) It overlooks that the diversity of obstacles affect each other in a systemic way. To have recognized the threesome of these errors should break the spell this metaphor has cast. We can now take the picture which makes of the state the borderline of our freedom and turn it to the wall."

With these words the yoga teacher stopped.

II

Much of the time we talk as if freedom and democracy were one and the same thing. Someone just returned from Poland reports that freedom there is still as absent as it was five years ago. What he really means is that the government is still not democratic. The newspapers announce in a chorus that when Prime Minister Gandhi imposes censorship on the press, the subcontinent of India has been deprived of its freedom. What embarrasses us about the appellation, The Free World, is that so much of it is presided over by juntas and colonels. But that presupposes that nations ruled by parliaments do deserve the title: that freedom and democracy are equivalent.

This standard abbreviation is once more a consequence of the cloudiness of the idea of freedom. As long as that word does not stand for something one can grasp, it cannot function as a measure. There is no distinct and separate conception which one can set against an actual society, and thus the Free Society remains an easy and promiscuous honorific title.

But what if one committed a *faux pas* and grew serious? Would the implications not be very strange? Democracy has been a very rare phenomenon indeed. Even within the West it did not exist, apart from a brief span among the Greeks, until the eighteenth century, and then but precariously, hanging by its teeth. And prior to the rise of that one culture, and outside of it, democracy in our sense was not known at all. Are we prepared to single out these isolated spots and to differentiate them so radically from the rest? Could we—now that the actual shape and inner workings of that concept lie more exposed—still sustain the claim that no one possessed freedom for the longest part of mankind's history, but that just those peculiar arrangements which we associate with democracy transformed their beneficiaries and set them genuinely free?

However, we are not just dealing with an absent-minded manner of expression. How many "Histories of the World" have organized their story into a progression to that end? Are not the milestones, the Golden Ages, the developments included and ruled out and, therefore, the selection that gives shape to our idea of history determined by the vision of an emerging individuality? But on what actual evidence does this comforting schema rest? What could we offer apart from the fact that democracy became established?

A single, closer look would show how weak the legs of this conviction are. Commonly it is assumed, for instance, that only democracy guarantees the rights of individuals. That is how the nature and the origin of democracy is presented in almost every high school course: individuals banded together and laid down conditions to the government. The impression is created that one was helplessly exposed before. But this contains a laughable mistake, that a shift in the frame of reference makes at once evident. In "primitive" cultures the exact degree of deference to which another person is entitled is encoded in immensely complex and specific rules that go into such detail regarding the precise relationship and the particular occasion, that anthropologists are hard put to even summarize them. There is no question of not having any rights at all. On the contrary, once this comparison is made, it is the rights and privileges to which we are accustomed that seem disappointingly fatuous and vague. And similarly with certain crushing obstacles that block the fulfillment of the most elementary desires. If that is part of freedom, then again the standards of some of these cultures are if anything superior to our own. Among the Pygmies, for example (on Turnbull's account of them), every member of the tribe is entitled to his or her established customary portion after a successful hunt, even if the woman or the man in question did not share in the labor or the danger of the chase but instead stayed in the camp and slept. And Gregory Bateson reports that to the Balinese the thought of another human being left to starve would be "unutterably shocking." But more than that: many anthropologists maintain that these societies as a whole are far more egalitarian than any in the West have been in the periods in which they were democracies. In fact much of the current interest in the origin of the state derives from this perception: for genuine inequality may be as relatively recent as the hierarchically structured state. Now, admittedly shamans and head-men do not run for office. Still, does not this cursory glance reveal the ethnocentric arrogance of the conjunction of freedom with democracy? Does not the service performed by this equation start to show? Are not with one sleight-of-hand—with one definition—the connotations of the genuinely human cut loose and shifted, so that one side receives an unchallengable superiority, while the other side is irreparably demoted?

This, too, is one more symptom of a kind of schizophrenia. To one compartment of our minds nothing could be more transparent, but there are other contexts in which it is obscured, and our undertaking is therefore once more an insistence that what is known and understood in one department is not sealed off but is carried over as we move. Yet our question must be firmly understood: we do not sever the complacent bonds between democracy and freedom to prepare for an attack. The lines of thought which we began to trace through the less ideologically charged terrain of education now have to be extended: the catalog of doubts concerning freedom which we then compiled is still as long, and the strategy of *dis*-associating values and concerns from freedom so as to place them on a firmer base therefore still applies. Our general intent is not the erosion of the claims or of the justifications of democracy, but points in just the opposite direction. If we pry the ideas of freedom and democracy apart and suggest that democracy does not set people free, then this has to be coupled to our earlier refusal to advocate a form of education based on this hope. The underlying thought is that the rationale and the advantages offered by democracy are strong enough, and that the mummery with which the rhetoric of freedom cloaks them can be dropped—that "in their own name" they too will stand on sturdier ground.

A second motive prompting our disjunction of these two is the simple need for a more sensible assessment. If our minds snap shut once we are told that in a given country elections are not being held, the possibility of any kind of thinking is foreclosed. To forget what actual significance democracy might have for an Indian peasant, and to say simply that "India became unfree," and then to pass the same judgment about Chile to describe a reign of terrorism, obliterates indispensable distinctions. At bottom the relationship between freedom and democracy has to be questioned so as not to short-circuit thought.

But there is a third and more restricted reason. If one imagines that the establishment of democratic institutions already brings about man's liberation, then our culture has in a sense "arrived." Minor improvements on one score or another may still be in order, but on the whole it is as if the end of history were close at hand. Indeed, this general perspective underlies the famous "end of ideology" debate in which some took the position that the answer to the major questions had been reached, that larger confrontations were now a matter of the past, and that mainly technical adjustments remained to be made. But our culture need not be so moribund. The present phase may pass, and may turn out not to have been the beginning of retirement, when old men make tinkering repairs around the house. However, the energy for any future enterprise, for any real advance beyond the level we have reached, will not be found unless we can at least envision goals which point the way. And the blending of the two ideas forestalls this. We therefore must divide them so that the future is not closed.

As a first step, some long-secured results can be applied. If everyone alike is wholly influenced and passes nonetheless at every second from one choice to the next, then this means in the present context that our family upbringing and our schools and our pundits and TV commercials influence and condition us no less—though obviously by quite different means—than any Chinese peasant or Russian worker or even Nazi soldier was conditioned through military drills or sessions of self-criticism; just as it means that even under the most brutal totalitarian regime everyone still lives to the constant accompaniment of the "droning on" of choice. However vast the difference between life under a democracy and a dictatorship may be, they do not fit the fantasy that we are molded by our culture only up to a certain point, and that they are Frankensteinian robots propelled like windup toys. On these parameters the actual contrasts cannot be calibrated, for they mark out a commonality, a shared condition: on these two counts we really are all equal.

To face this is not just to dismiss the most ready-made seal of self-approval. It must be emphasized because it has serious implications. The reason most often cited by those who went willingly to fight in Vietnam was that they enlisted "to stop tyranny"; and even the most telling facts and the most fundamental differentiations between Vietnam and Russia and even Nazi Germany were blocked out by this one association of "tyranny" with the mindless, the mechanical and the no longer human. One small but memorable moment in which this categorization showed its power occurred during the so-called babylift, when in the last days of the war many here at home were shocked to discover that the NLF did have a program of child care of its own. What must they have imagined for this to come as a surprise?

So much of the human is crystallized in the idea of freedom that we can dehumanize the population of an entire country when we declare them to be unfree. Ironically this in turn betrays us into the commission of inhuman acts.

A second step takes us to the phrase "self-government." We think that people under a democracy are free because under that arrangement it is they themselves who govern and not someone else. But this plays on an ambiguity, and one might ask: Did not all people, long before democracy had been invented, govern themselves? Did they not evolve their own, often very satisfactory institutions? And is not this the meaning of the phrase which carried during most of history by far the greater weight? Did not one—more than anything—resist foreign domination so as to be governed by one's own kind? Has not the oppression by another nation been the contrast to what freedom meant, even from the times of the Old Testament? And is not this sense quite independent from democracy?

On the most opposite interpretation of the word, hardly anyone was ever literally governed by himself. With the exception of hermits, and possibly very small communities, this was always done at most by representatives who had been elected by the rest. Naturally this seems to indicate a deeply significant partition: that positions of rulership are not inherited or bequeathed through appointment, but are instead assigned on the basis of a competition for more votes. Yet doubts can be raised in regard to this distinction. If one holds the resounding abstract language which interprets an election as "the voice through which the people speak" and whose outcome therefore must be sacrosanct, against the appalling realities of actual practice, against even the most ordinary observation, such as that these days "images" are bought for sums of money which determine the results far more than the past performances or the convictions of the candidates, then this division, too, seems less than absolute. Moreover, one could add that elections offer us mostly a choice between two people, though we have very little control over the process through which these two are selected, and no end of similar well-worn cynicisms which erode the pedestal on which this division in theory is sometimes placed. Still further it could be pointed out that at least prior to the most recent times even the most non-democratic governments had to take some account of the will and the desires of their subjects. Those who did not, and became too mindless of the suffering they imposed were eventually, although sometimes only after a considerable period, overthrown. And it is not even true that only democratic systems explicitly stipulate for this contingency. Ancient and radically non-democratic forms of government also operated in a context that specified their possible removal: the Chinese conception of the "mandate of heaven" which an emperor could lose is only one of many such provisions.

The frequent definition of democracy as self-government thus invites misconstruction. In one sense all people, except for those subjugated under an empire, be it the Roman or the British, governed themselves. And in another sense people even within democracies are still governed by someone else, though they may have taken part in his election. The phrase "self-government" on one interpretation is therefore much too wide. Other forms of government and not only democracies can provide the good designated by it. On the opposite interpretation it is much too narrow; it promises far more than democracies can give. But it is the image which simply opposes those governed by themselves to those ruled by others, which leads us to think of the former as free, and of the latter as oppressed.

In the third place we could take the adage that people under a democracy "make their own decisions" and that this makes them free. Like the others, this sways us only in some contexts while it is quite transparent in most others. In response to it one could point out that in one sense all human beings everywhere—in Germany, in Russia or in China—have always made their own decisions. Just as no one can die in our stead or sleep or drink or eat for us, so no one can make a decision on behalf of us. Even a slave determines all by himself whether he will lift his shovel or speak one rather than another word, and in his case the difference between yes and no may entail either life or death. In another sense, none of us ever makes one decision which is wholly his own. Even the tools we use to reach it, the rules by which we judge its outcome, the steps of reasoning, the logic through which we arrive at a conclusion are not our own, but have been shaped and handed to us by the culture in which we were reared. We thus face once more the pattern of one sense in which what is offered is not a prerogative conferred only by democracies, and another sense in which more is suggested than even the best democracy could possibly provide.

A further and fourth example could be the phrase that people in a democracy should at least participate in the decisions "which affect their lives." Even this more modest goal is problematic. For if this dictum is taken literally, the aim set forth cannot possibly be reached. To see this, one has only to recognize that in the next two days decisions might be made in Africa or Japan or China which five years from now could easily have the most powerful effect on our lives—decisions that might, for example, direct an industry to produce a device which will eliminate the job we could have held some years from now. The interdependencies across all borderlines have become far too numerous for the dream of gaining through democracy a measure of control over our lives still to be believed—unless one at once admits that the measure might be miniscule. And this represents a problem not just on the global scale, but points to another gap between our actual conceptions and the justifications offered on their behalf. For even on the smallest scale, say in a philosophy department, democracy only requires that all its members vote on a decision. Yet that decision has effects not only on the families of department members, but if one were to take the language literally, on countless and extremely distant people who simply could not be consulted even if one tried. The notion that some influence is being granted to all who will suffer the consequences of a certain choice is therefore in principle unrealistic.

One could deal in a similar fashion with much else that is often said in justification or in definition of democracy. We have already indicated that the possession of rights does not distinguish the citizens of a democracy from other social systems. Compared to the greatest span of human history (though not to totalitarian countries), at most a kind of trade or an exchange has taken place. Some rights, like those associated with free speech and elections, represent impressive gains, but a great diversity of entitlements which were unquestioned in many "primitive" cultures and also in the Middle Ages, both in the West and outside it, have been lost—among them the right to sustenance.

The same holds of the thought that the power of governments is limited only in democracies. To anyone who as a child had to memorize the endless cabals and machinations, and especially the marriages of the various Habsburg emperors in the struggle for any power over the unruly counts, dukes, electors, bishops and even mayors in their realm, this conception has a humorous ring. History is surely more the story of the gradual increase of ever more centralized control over larger territories than the other way around.

The notion, finally, that only democracies provide a "public realm" in which "genuine action" becomes possible (Hannah Arendt) sounds like a desperate descent into a quasi-mysticism. Is there no "genuine action" in the plays of Shakespeare because they deal with kings? Is there no "public realm" at all in societies that lack a constitution? And what kind of "actions" happen in this realm? Are many of them not committee meetings? And is participation in their sessions quite as educational and ennobling as we are told?

After this clearing of the stage it should be easier to see the true characteristics and the real advantages democracies possess. Some of the largest of these do not appear in their full prominence till one distinction has been underscored: it is quite simply the opposition between an individual and a social point of view. Most philosophers and political theorists seem to look for the benefits which life in a democracy might hold for separate individuals. This preoccupation, however, is actually rather strange, for one could argue, as we did earlier in relation to the state, that it enacts a contradiction; that one refuses to apply a genuinely social thinking to an evidently social entity, and adopts a perspective which is "egocentric" when this is clearly out of place. We remarked in regard to the state that perceiving a rule primarily as a limitation of one's freedom is a crass example of this "egocentric fallacy," since a rule in any actual social context more likely diminishes the obstacles one may encounter. That all of the just rehearsed justifications of democracy operate from this same stance should now become apparent; and this is so principally because each of them tries to insist that the individual enjoys more freedom under a democratic form of government.

Now, paradoxically, it is only when this perspective is explicitly rejected, and a social or even "systemic" approach is adopted in its stead, that the far more telling assets of democratic forms of government come into view. In a formula: the first major superiority of democratic governments is not any benefit accruing directly to isolated individuals, but consists in the fact that as systems they are more intelligent.

To explain this an old presumption has to be reversed. One often hears the question whether "we can still afford democracy." This bluntly assumes that other systems—notably the totalitarian—are more "efficient," more organized and more productive, and that democracy is deficient on these scores but has been considered worth that sacrifice. In very special contexts—wars would be the prime example—this view contains some truth. But for most situations, and especially for those with a long range, it is patently mistaken. Nazi Germany was anything but the totally ordered, flawlessly functioning machine it seemed to be. Far more characteristic was the gradual breakdown of every semblance of coherence—which incidentally began even before Hitler came to power, as witnessed, for instance, by the infighting between the S.A. and the S.S.

With respect to Russia so very much has recently become common knowledge—not least through the books of Solzhenitsyn—that probably only very few remain who think of her totalitarianism as streamlined (think of the Russian bureaucracy) and well-coordinated (think of the many stories about the manipulation of "production quotas"—that managers set the goals purposefully low so that they can then receive a medal for exceeding them; or think of the anecdotes about tractors being shipped into the Ukraine, while their spare parts disappear in Siberia) or economically productive (think of the grain sales).

No summary statement gives perhaps a more vivid picture of the actualities than the famous *Appeal of Soviet Scientists to the Party Government Leaders of the USSR* which Andrei Sakharov issued, together with a fellow physicist and a historian in March 1970. A portion of it reads as follows:

> In the twenties and thirties the capitalist world underwent a period of crisis and depression. At that time we, by exploiting the

upsurge of national energy which had been unleashed by the Revolution, were creating industry at an unheard-of tempo. That was the time when the slogan "Overtake and Surpass America" was coined. And we were really overtaking it in the course of the next few decades. Then the situation changed. The second industrial revolution came along and now, at the onset of the seventies we can see that, far from having overtaken America, we are dropping further and further behind. . . .

Why is this? Why have we not only failed to become the pioneers of the second industrial revolution but, as it transpires, are we even incapable of keeping abreast of the developed capitalist countries in this revolution? Can it be that the socialist system does not present the same opportunities as the capitalist system for the development of productive forces. . . ?

Of course not. The source of our difficulty does not lie in the socialist system at all, but, on the contrary . . . in the anti-democratic traditions and norms of public conduct laid down during the Stalinist period. . . .

Our economy can be compared to traffic at an intersection. As long as there were only a few cars the man on point duty could cope and the traffic flowed freely. But the volume of traffic is growing unceasingly and so a traffic jam builds up. What can be done about it? . . . The only solution is to widen the crossing. The obstacles blocking the development of our economy lie beyond it, in the socio-political sphere. . . .

From our friends abroad we sometimes hear the USSR compared to a huge truck, whose driver presses one foot hard down on the accelerator and the other on the brake. The time has come to make more intelligent use of the brake! . . .

What has our country to expect if a course leading towards democratization is not taken? It can expect to lag behind the capitalist countries in the second industrial revolution and to gradually revert to the status of a second-rate provincial power. . . .

The overall conception that the democratization of a sphere of life represents a retardation, a slowing down, the adopting of a bungling, hamstrung process, which has to justify this sacrifice through compensating other values thus inverts the truth. Under normal circumstances (not those of war) and especially over extended periods of time it is precisely democratic procedures which are—as we often say—more responsive, more flexible, and therefore more efficient and more intelligent. And if evidence for this were needed one could refer to the most basic fact, namely, that the expansion of Western Culture from the small peninsula of Europe in which it barely held its own—recall the Mohammedan invasions—to every corner of the globe roughly coincided with the inauguration of democracy.

But why is this so? The most fundamental cause (and we realize that we are painting a portrait with a broom) derives directly from the one characteristic which from Plato's *Republic* on was regarded as the defining quality of a democracy, namely, that it is a government not just for and of but by the people. The promise this phrase holds out has to be properly understood, however. Its actual purpose and justification is not captured by the expectations we reviewed before. That it is a government by us, that we participate in it, means in the main that its eventual policies and decisions will be informed by the knowledge and the ideas which collectively we have brought to bear on it—not that it makes us free. One crucial difference between a totalitarian and an "open" government—and this seems the appropriate term—is thus the closedness of the former. In it often not even the relevant factual information is allowed to filter upwards towards the decision-making centers, and there is of course no question of subjugating governmental actions to forthright criticism and to assess them against possible alternatives. This is the sense in which a democratic government has at least the possibility of being more "intelligent"; the net effect of its much greater openness to every kind of information is the smaller likelihood of its "pushing with one foot down on the accelerator, and with the other on the brake."

Essential to the "openness" of a government is therefore the accountability of all levels of the government, and this is one central measure of the degree to which a government is democratic. The full exercise of this provision by the people cannot be found in other forms of political organization. Still, the concept of accountability omits one half of what we meant to stress. To realize the advantage implicit in the openness of democratic institutions requires more than just the opportunity for critical review. It demands that the knowledge—often of "details" inaccessible to any except those on the scene—and the new proposals arising from their more intimate acquaintance are used and put to work.

This has one decisive consequence, namely, that Freedom of Speech is anything but one privilege granted among others. It is not merely on a par with other rights. Its true significance, however, again does not appear as long as one maintains an "a-social" (egocentric) point of view. From that perspective it insures only that certain institutional penalties will not be among the countless painful consequences unavoidably entailed by anything we say. The cardinal importance of its status arises only for a genuinely social mode of thought: in essence, Free Speech protects the first main advantage democracies possess as systems; through the extension of certain guarantees to individuals it maintains the circulation of the blood throughout the body politic—so that the brain will stay alive.

The benefits for the individual are in contrast largely *in*direct. In receiving the qualified and partial immunity which Freedom of Speech bestows, the individual receives only the means which, properly employed, will bring about results of far greater weight. The fact that we need not mince our words is therefore an utterly mistaken measure of the energy with which that institution deserves to be protected. What we as individuals owe to it has to be weighed on a quite different scale: in actuality it is responsible for the sum total of the advantages which our living under a government of greater intelligence in the long run provides.

In less abstract language: the immediate impact of the guarantees associated with Freedom of Expression is admittedly far more momentous for politicians and intellectuals or other men of words than for a worker or a peasant. The question, How great a difference do they really make for an Indian peasant, or someone living in a squatter village outside of Rio de Janeiro? is quite justified. The point, however, is that the answer to it has to be given in two stages: immediately the significance may well be lower than that of a single bowl of rice, and lamentations for the loss of freedom for the peasant are therefore out of place. Yet one nonetheless may feel that the suspension of democracy in India imperils every last illiterate beggar. For if the sealing of the channels between the government and the people becomes chronic— and once closed they are not easily reopened—the cyclically mounting consequence of ignorance and dogmatism will pile up, and in time the impoverished peasant or squatter will feel them more than most.

The basic fact that the guarantees comprised in the democratic freedoms do not bestow large gifts upon the people, but that they on the contrary enable the people to render benefits to the government— that fact implies that the principle of participation by itself does not make a society already genuinely democratic. A second aspect, therefore, has to complement the first, and ensure that favors done to the state will be returned: this is one understanding of the role played by the ideal of equality.

The basic rights which a society grants to all of its members need not be interpreted as either "natural" or "God-given." One can regard them quite straightforwardly as a set of decisions on the part of those who make up a society, which resolve that no one in the community should be allowed to fall below the level which they specify. Seen in this fashion they represent attempts to set some limits to the degradations or calamities which those in the society will have to suffer.

This backdrop sets the meaning of equality into sharp relief. It was Kant who said that "All that is best, but also all that is worst has been advocated in the name of equality." This judgment is more severe than the platitude that complete equality would certainly be a disaster. It asserts that far less than this, namely, equality in the wrong respects, could be calamitous enough. This warning, however, does not raise either a serious conceptual difficulty or a major obstacle in practice. It only teaches that the selection of the scores on which members of a social group will be equal has to be made with care. On the just indicated interpretation of what rights in general represent, the task involved, though sometimes difficult, does not seem insurmountable. As long as it is firmly understood that the specific rights to some equalities have their foundation in a decision to abolish certain kinds of suffering or in the hope to realize a society with certain specified characteristics, and that they are not based on an independent, prior, "natural" standard—that they are no more than means for the achievement of certain ends—and as long as it is also clear that this inevitably requires the selection of some, perhaps very few equalities (namely, those which will serve these ends), their determination requires only knowledge and intelligence. To insist that everyone wear the same size shoes, eat the same amount of food, read the same books, laugh at the same jokes would entail unquestionable losses and no obvious gains, while the stipulations that everyone at least have a lawyer if he must go to court, or at least have a vote in the election of officials, or receive at least the same pay as others for his work, or be given some minimal attention in case of serious disease, and many others like it, appear appropriate once certain goals have been established.

Nothing within this general understanding prevents a society from changing the equalities from time to time. If equalities in some regards would have strained the resources at an earlier stage in its development, those can be added later; if others had unforeseen objectionable consequences, they can be dropped. And in the same spirit a society can naturally also establish *in*-equalities. If one agreed for instance that the society as a whole would be improved if some groups in it moved upwards in the social hierarchy, such in-equalities (needed perhaps only for a span of time) might be the best social instrument for the attainment of this end. Examples of this would be the so-called "affirmative action" programs for women and some minorities in our own society. Fundamentally, they involve the decision to employ a temporary in-equality so as to attain a more important and desirable equality in the end.

In adjudicating between various possible equalities one again would have to leave the "egocentric" for the social point of view, and therefore recognize that the establishment of a possible equality might benefit one in two separate ways: first, one might be among those who but for it would fall below the "minimum" for which it provides. (One's salary, to give a crude example, would be less if the society had not established that equality.) Secondly, one derives the advantage of living in a society in which fewer human beings have been spoiled by excessive privileges, and fewer are so wretched that their human qualities cannot unfold. The institution of equalities, therefore, does not constitute a sacrifice; one could agree to it on selfish grounds.

In rough summary we can say, therefore, that we perceive the outlines, both of the nature of democracy and of its benefits, under the aspects of openness (participation) and of equality. The conjunction of these two defines democracy and also gives us an overview of the advantages it holds. Decisive for us, however, is that the openness does not furnish to the individual the high-priced assets it is commonly thought to confer. In essence, we have been suggesting that the usual conception has to be reversed. Generally one assumes that the democratic freedoms and the other rights and institutions which together establish this openness and create the possibility for participation took prerogatives away from the larger system, that they even weakened it to some extent, and that they commensurately enhanced the position of the individual. But the opposite seems closer to the truth: this dimension of democracy makes the social body as a whole more flexible, resilient and, as it were, intelligent, so that it now can more than hold its own relative to other social entities. In contrast to this it does far less to strengthen the hand of the individual.

Examine a single feature for a moment under a magnifying glass. The most notable advantage which democratic institutions in theory confer upon the individual is the opportunity to "represent his own private interests" in debate and through his vote. On an abstract level this seems perfectly convincing. But if we move down to a microcosm, some of this self-evidence begins to fade. Imagine someone in an extremely democratic philosophy department. One day he proposes that his closest friend or wife should be given an appointment. When asked to speak in support of his motion he in no way mentions the professional virtues of his candidate, but instead maintains that the advantages of a favorable action to his own private person would evidently be immense, and then proceeds to give in great detail a description of how very much his personal or family life would be improved. What would be the reaction? An uproar? Laughter? Shock? But why? For does he not act according to the letter of the theory? Is this not exactly what representing his own interests would mean?

The contrast to the present practice is instructive. If the hiring of a close friend came up for discussion, one would usually disqualify oneself; one would say that one's personal interests were too much at stake. In other words, the actual interests of the individual are precisely not permitted to enter into the discussion. If an outsider overheard a department meeting, he could get the impression that all its members have only the department's interest in mind. And this seeming preoccupation with the welfare of the whole does not change as we move upwards to the university at large, or to the city, the state and beyond. Rare is the senator who openly admits that his bill is designed to benefit his friends, or even only his home state. Usually it is the national interest that is brought to the front.

This aspect of participation has been in the center of a protracted historical debate which goes back to the Greeks and was perhaps confronted most directly by Rousseau (particular interests have to be excluded if one is to act from the General Will), and it is emphatically not simple or clear-cut. Still, its meaning for us is that participation involves the danger that the individual's actual desires will be surrendered at the very moment at which they are finally to come upon the stage, that the society grants participation but that in accepting it the individual becomes an agent only for the group. The promise seems to be that the personal will be represented, but in actual practice the expectation seems to be precisely that it will be left behind—checked like a coat before one takes one's seat.

What larger perspective is this intended to convey? No one still needs to have a rehearsal of all the forces which discourage individuality and produce conformity and a mass society. We all know why the houses in developments look so alike, how great the pressures of advertising are, and the effects of massive "rationalization" (in Weber's sense) and the like. That depressing army does not have to be reviewed once more. Instead we wanted to add two new strokes to the picture.

The first was our reconsideration of the situation with regard to rights. We emphasized that democracy certainly did not bring a mere gain in rights, let alone their original acquisition; that all in all it offered an exchange, and that in comparison to other, earlier cultures the trade may not have been as advantageous as we are apt to think. One major contrast seems to be that in traditional cultures the totality of life was ordered and ameliorated through a coherent web of structures and ordering regularities. The economic was not a distinct and isolated segment but was thoroughly interwoven with the mythic and ritual and kinship orders of the culture. For the individual this meant that his sustenance and material existence were protected as an integral part of the extended fabric of the culture. In modern "mobilized" societies the economic sphere is by comparison far more divided from the rest; it obeys more its own logic of maximizing profits and production. On one side this did allow economic forces to be unleashed, but it also entailed, on the other, that the individual, in precisely the sphere in which he is most vulnerable and most in need, was more abandoned to his own devices.

But in addition to this there has also been a shift from the concrete and specific to the abstract. The individual lost a great diversity of particular, local privileges, which gave him status and security in more traditional societies, and received in compensation for this a set of far more abstract, universal, human rights. But these, just because of their abstractness, provide for less. Your claim as the member of a family or as a long-time local resident is stronger than your claim as just a citizen. Yet as a citizen you again have entitlements which you do not possess as a mere human being. So the individual lost ground, his position was weakened on two separate scores even with regard to rights which are supposed to be his shield.

The individual thus contends not only with massive leveling forces, but in addition his rights give him not more, but less support. Even the one seemingly strongest weapon in his arsenal—the prerogative of participation—is actually ambiguous, a kind of wooden sword. For it strengthens the larger system more than the individual, thus tilting the balance still further to his disadvantage, and it asks, moreover, that the genuinely private interests be surrendered, and it does this covertly, on the sly.

The accumulation of these losses explains the startling fact that while the fulfillment and realization of the individual was, from the beginning, the religion of modernity, its labor and sacrifices have so far engendered exactly the reverse. That the average, normal human being in our culture has turned out to be so sadly disappointing, and that this is true on all levels of the social scale from the blustering and frightened executive (described so marvelously in Heller's novel *Something Happened*) down to the bureaucrat or salesman or worker, is not surprising. How could the ambiguous instrument of participation, given this array of hostile forces, realize the expectation roused by the idea of a free human being? How could it possibly confer the pride, the independence, the courage in the face of life, the lightheartedness and ease, the sense of playfulness and self-possession, the cognizance of one's own amplitude which that idea originally held?

It goes without saying that participation should be expanded, and to begin with in less centralized and smaller units, where the impact of one's single voice would be not quite so vanishingly small, and where the gap between one's actual individual concerns and the professed weal of the group would be less great. Participation should advance from the political sphere into the economic, since the economic obstacles and risks affect the individual in his immediate life. Participation in the determinations of what is produced with his assistance, the working conditions he requires, the marketing aspects of the product, etc., would confer at least some power upon the individual in a vital area of his or her life. If we are right in the contention that increased participation in the long run raises the systemic efficiency and intelligence, then the closed and hierarchical organization of the productive apparatus of society is inexcusable. Under these circumstances, to argue for a measure of economic democracy on "humanitarian" grounds is an unnecessary imposition on one's patience, for now there are other arguments which should dent even those who pride themselves on the toughness of their minds. But that is not the issue. The question lies on the other side: it is, in short, whether the enlargement of participation is enough.

Certainly we know that political participation at present is hardly more than a veneer, that much of the time it only screens the literally murderous struggles that determine the direction of history from backstage. (Think of the assassinations of the sixties.) Still, even if we imagine such participation as having depth and being free of corruption, would full participation bring perfection to democracy or would it fall short? Can we not extrapolate from the degree of participation which we have to what the effects of its completion would be like? Unquestionably there would be an improvement, but how far would it carry us? In the light of all the limitations we enumerated: from the sceptical separation of participation from the rhetoric of freedom to the inherent sleight-of-hand that asks that the truly private not be brought into the public forum, down to such pragmatic doubts as whether participation ever can ensure control or inevitably leads to hidden agendas reserved for the back rooms, and beyond that even to such mundane questions as how much of an ordinary person's life would be spent in committee meetings—given all of this, can we not aim at a higher goal? Is the kind of society that maximal participation would engender all that is left of the great hopes in which the eighteenth century began? The impulse behind the reorganization of society through reason was, not so long ago, the hope for a new and more advanced form of life. There was the expectation that in freedom a nobler human being would develop, almost a higher species than the caged and oppressed former man. How can we deny that a mere increase in participation will only move us inches closer to this dream?

Some, seeing only the shortcomings of participation, dismiss it as a fig leaf that revolutionary politics can drop, and they sometimes look to China or to Cuba or even Russia as a "model" for the future. But apart from all else that could be said against this it should be evident that the basic task which these societies confronted, the single problem which they set themselves to solve, was their determination to industrialize— to "catch up with the West." Yet surely this task lies behind us. One therefore may have high respect for the astonishing and maybe unparalleled accomplishments of China in the last thirty years, and yet face the fact that it tells us next to nothing about the course that we must take. This is so not simply because of the great cultural divergencies or because one cannot shed one's "bourgeois values," but for the harder and, if you like, more "scientific" reason that China waged all-out war against its poverty, against the destitution, not of some group, but of the country. We as a nation, relative to other nations, stand exactly at the opposite extreme.

Others close their eyes to all the weaknesses of participation and talk as if, fully extended, it would bring on the millennium. But the image of a life half spent in committee meetings does not light sparkles in most people's eyes, and nearly everybody senses, even if in a duskier light, the doubts which we have raised. And that pulls us up short: it is a fact that we no longer have a vision of the future which is convincingly superior to the present, which has the feel and taste of an obviously better, more joyful and more exhilarating life.

Something more and radically different has to be undertaken, even without the hope of finally achieving genuine liberation. A drastic step has to be risked if even very much less than this is to be accomplished: if at least a tolerable, slightly more fulfilling, more nearly human life for the individual is to be attained.

III

The suggestion we are about to make is not involved, but it requires a large frame. Its rationale cannot be articulated unless we step far enough back to gain a quite encompassing perspective. Nothing short of a return to the beginnings of culture itself will do.

Our usual picture of Early Man sees him, above all, as a creature haunted by need. We imagine small roaming bands, finding a few nuts and berries, but having to press on; the hunters tracking a single beast for days, bringing it down finally with luck, yet with that soon consumed and hunger again on the rise, the little tribe is once more forced to move. Agriculture becomes an invention mothered by necessity: with the natural fruits exhausted and game still scarcer than before, man was forced to break the ground, to eke out a living.

Dominant in this story is the impression of scarcity. Struggle as one will, one never leaves it more than a few steps behind. But life seems to depend on the preservation of that fragmentary gain, and so one is driven on without respite; a maximal expense of effort seems barely to suffice.

This defines for us the progress we have made: we are shielded by a surplus, and the severity and strain has abated. It seems as if with the accumulation of knowledge and the ever wider distribution of inventions, the original weight has been relieved and a buffer has been created. We imagine that with the advent of modernity the possibility of leisure, not just for the few but for the many, was for the first time created.

One can assail this panoramic vista with exactly formulated arguments, and to a few of these we shall refer in a moment but it is more appropriate to our purpose to regard it first as yet another symptom of a compartmentalization of our minds, for although it passed for axiomatic in much of anthropology until fairly recently, it can be dissolved by a mere shifting of one's stance.

Confront the just sketched portrait of Early Man with our common understanding of the cultures developed in the South Pacific islands. Think, if you like, of Fiji or even of Hawaii. Unless our general sense is totally deluded this should be enough to raise the suspicion that something is quite wrong. If one substitutes tropical fruits—papayas, bananas and coconuts—for the berries and maybe hazelnuts, and if one thinks of fish instead of rabbits, the specter of scarcity becomes less grim, and with that the other features—the ceaselessly endangered margin, and the struggle at the brink of exhaustion—also start to fade.

In this instance, however, one need not be content with picturesque surmises. Very elegant and at the same time detailed and cautious work has been done on this question, most prominently by Marshall Sahlins in his book *Stone Age Economics*. The lead-off chapter of that volume is in fact a sustained assault on the gloomy traditional textbook interpretation of the early hunter's life. Under the title "The Original Affluent Society" it argues not only against the scarcity assumption, but systematically inverts a whole spate of other prevalent conceptions. It takes stock of reports on tribes from the most disparate geographical and climatic regions, and assembles evidence from early travelers' journals down to up-to-date, professional, quantitative studies. In one vignette, for instance, Sahlins cites the following statistics:

> In the total population of free-ranging Bushmen contacted by Lee, 61.3 percent (152 of 248) were effective food producers; the

remainder were too young or too old to contribute importantly. In the particular camp under scrutiny, 65 percent were "effectives." Thus the ratio of food producers to the general population is actually 3:5 or 2:3. *But*, these 65 percent of the people worked 36 percent of the time, and 35 percent of the people did not work at all! (Lee, 1969, p. 67)

For each adult worker, this comes to about two and one-half days labor each week. ("In other words, each productive individual supported herself or himself and dependents and still had 3-1/2 to 5-1/2 days available for other activities.") A "day's work" was about six hours; hence the Dobe work week is approximately 15 hours, or an average of 2 hours 9 minutes per day. (Sahlins, 1972, p. 21)

After putting many such mosaic stones together Sahlins eventually draws the following general conclusion:

Reports on hunters and gatherers of the ethnological present—specifically on those in marginal environments—suggest a mean of three to five hours per adult worker per day in food production. (p. 34)

The shortness of this time is startling, but the context adds even more to its significance. For the point is not only that hunters and primitive cultivators worked short hours. One has to stress that this is true even in "marginal environments," that even in the severest climates and under the most straitened circumstances—say, among the Eskimo—the figure is not sharply higher. Beyond this one must not forget that a deliberately maintained rhythm, periods of "on and off," sometimes lasting for only hours, but at other times for days and even months, is telescoped into these figures. This means that one could easily work far more, so that these hours represent a conscious choice not to work harder and not to produce, or gather as much as one evidently could. Behind these numbers thus stands an attitude: that work is onerous, that it is an irksome burden—one heartily dislikes it, and one prefers to spend one's time if at all possible in other ways.

Once this very different picture of the beginning is established, some of the later stages take on similar colors. Is it not likely that this posture of keeping work down to a minimum had some connection to the establishment of slavery? Would not a strong desire not to work be one among many motives for it? And would that institution not in turn reinforce one's contempt for labor? Surely the Greeks did not admire pedestrian industriousness. To rise above the need for work seems to have been their first condition for being a "free man." Closer to the present, in the Middle Ages, despite all other changes this much seems to have persisted. Indeed, Chayanov wrote his famous book *The Theory of Peasant Economics* in large part because peasants in general, true to the pattern handed down to them, did not conform to the axioms on which Adam Smith founded his (and our) theory of economics. Specifically, Chayanov holds, they do not indefinitely maximize their gains, but exert themselves only till a certain marginally comfortable level has been reached. Once on this plateau, their activity will diminish even if increased returns are in the offing.

This begins to turn the general perspective from which we started exactly upside down. It is not we who for the first time enjoy leisure, while throughout the preceding periods man worked at full capacity and strained against the limits set by his endurance. In broad terms it was more the other way around. For nearly the whole of man's long history he avoided work, and did as little of it as he could manage. He labored only when circumstances bore down on him and all escapes had been cut off. Moreover, Sahlins argues that it was not the ineptness of the hunter, or that he was not sufficiently inventive, or the scarcity of his resources that kept him from 'creating culture'—it seemed not worth the trouble. The Bushmen ask: "Why should we plant, when there are so many mongomongo nuts in the world?" (Sahlins, p. 27) Given all else there was to do, from the great feasts of eating, to the elaborate ritual dances, to the weeks spent on initiation, marriage and funeral ceremonies, or later, to the endless free entertainment offered by a medieval market, with its processions of flagellants passing through, its theatrical groups and jesters, its public hangings and the heraldry and costumes displayed in its cathedral, or to change the country, the rebellion against all ordinary life released by a Mexican fiesta, and yet again the month of costume balls and orgies that made up a Carnival, or even just the peasant dances Bruegel painted—to work no more than three hours on the average per day made sense. If more was not needed, and work was dull and strenuous and depressing, to keep it down to that level seemed right and sane and healthy.

So what occurred to change it? Measured by man's entire history (possibly 3.5 million years by Leaky's estimate), the work level stayed low for an immense duration and the increase brought on by the "neolithic revolution," the transition to agriculture, tilted the line upwards by only two or three degrees, and even after that it only barely rose. Essentially it climbed, if at all, only by imperceptible degrees till we come up to very recent times, really to the last few minutes compared to the previous eons, and only then, between two and three hundred years ago it suddenly turns sharply upwards and goes rapidly to 10 and 12 and even 16-hour days. Gone is the "on and off" rhythm, that with peasants extended over months—the whole winter was a slowing down, a period of recuperation—now work continues for many, and not just for the poor, for seven days a week—surprisingly the wealthy, too, take pride in their endurance.

From one perspective it seems like a madness, as if infected by a virus more and more people went berserk, like sheep in a St. Vitus dance, spinning about themselves, faster and faster, comic for a moment but then grotesque and horrifying. But from another side it seems like an awakening, like the emergence from a slumber. Whatever caused this turn to accelerated action, it would be wrong only to bemoan it, let alone to wish for the return of that more placid past. And not just because we can no more regain it than a chick can struggle back into its broken shell. Also because that heightened vitality, though it lost us some of the tranquillity we sometimes miss, released an immense potential, so far perhaps put to degrading uses but waiting to be redirected.

Max Weber in *The Protestant Ethic and the Spirit of Capitalism* gave at once a magnificent description of the before and after enclosing this transition, and also the single most celebrated explanation of what brought it about. One feature of his narration depicts the bordered scope of the Roman church. In Weber's mind it isolated and addressed a single sphere of life. In its own domain it reached great depths of intensity as well as of extravagance, but it acknowledged finally the separateness of the worldly life, to which it never bowed but which it also did not challenge. In a memorable passage Weber concludes with an analogy to Catholic monasteries: they stand isolated, sufficient unto themselves, in equanimity with the world around them; they fit into the landscape. The spirit of Protestantism, however, would not be confined. It had to carry its austere truth into every corner; it had to be consistent and cover the whole ground. With Protestantism, so Weber writes, "the whole world became a monastery."

But the fact that the spirit of religious asceticism and otherworldliness leapt across the monastic walls and invaded regions where the languid and loosely laced previously had its place only starts the drama. Weber focuses on Calvinism and his explanation selects for its base the doctrine of predestination. A stern rationality had forced the logical implications of this idea out of the shadows and insisted that some, prior to all trials, had been "elected" by God as those to be saved, while the remnant, through an equally inscrutable predetermination had been relegated to the damned. On this foundation happens the decisive step. For the relentlessness of that division leads to the desire that one should at least know to which side one had been consigned. Some telltale sign seemed called for, and strangely or not, the badge on which Calvinism lighted was that of worldly and material success: God made those who had been elected manifest to the world by the manner in which their business enterprises prospered.

The force and brilliance of Weber's thought, reduced to its minimal essentials, stands out most clearly if the total turn which it engendered is perceived. Poverty had been a calamity, but the proverb had it that one could be "poor but honest," and in Christianity, just as in Buddhism there had always been a current which linked the foreswearing of worldly possessions to saintliness. Not only was there ample scriptural support for this, but most of the Holy Orders also advocated begging as a religious practice. On the other end of the scale, the rich did weigh in as camels. Usury through most of the Middle Ages was so despised that the antisemitism of the time made of its practice a stigma branding Jews.

That fixes the about-face which Calvinism, on Weber's reading of it, worked. It is as if the prefixes had been inverted, the plusses and the minuses exchanged. Consider the extraordinary incentive for hard work which helped to break the pattern we have sketched: now one's worldly enterprises were not just the ladder to security, to comfort and pre-eminence among one's peers—and naturally that had always played some role, from the stone-age hunter to the seventeenth century serf—now one's eternal soul had been placed in the dock. Not just a handsome profit, or the interest on one's investment was at stake. An ultimate religious significance had been imposed on the skill and speed with which one moved one's hands, and on the cunning with which one bought and sold. (Anthropologists often define culture as a web of meanings, and frequently that sounds ethereal and vague, incommensurate to the hard factuality of the forces which seem to make a culture move. If one referred to this example, the efficacy of "mere" meanings would appear to be real enough.) How clumsy contemporary efficiency and speed-up devices seem by comparison! One is reminded of Voltaire: if this had not in fact occurred, could anything more fitted to the purpose have been possibly invented?

Weber, admittedly, meant to explain the origin of capitalism as a whole, and not just the metamorphosis of the significance of labor from the Biblical curse into a virtue and vocation. However, this does not affect the one most serious weakness of his famous book. As many have already argued, both the onset of capitalism and the sudden climb of labor occurred within a short span of time in widely separated parts of Europe that have no clear relationship to the few strongholds of Calvinism, and it is therefore practically certain that Calvinism alone cannot explain the transformation. Without entering into the much and subtly debated pros and cons of Weber's thesis, we ask: What might have been some of the other causes?

One major factor must have been the erosion of the traditional privileges that protected the members of earlier communities. Leaving aside how that breakup was engendered, the impact of being thrown back on one's own resources, of being isolated and no longer sheltered by a network of inherited relationships which included the obligation to assist in sickness and old age, must have been very powerful. If we do not shy away from a plain answer, then one large part of it must be, that we work harder because we must. Many peasants or small farmers either lost their land or discovered that the same harvest they had always grown now sold for much less; they abandoned the leisurely "on and off" rhythm, their weeks or months of hibernation and moved to the city just so that they could survive. This is no less true for the Indian who today finds himself inside the slums of Mexico than it was for the peasant whom the enclosure movement displaced to Birmingham.

Another factor probably played an equally important role. Every society—including those of animals—has intricate and highly regulated ways in which hierarchies are established. Many of these seem explicitly designed to minimize protracted conflict or overt aggression, and generally this economy involves the substitution of symbols which signify submission or dominance for actual bloody victories and defeats. In some human cultures symbolic superiority can be attained only through the explicit sacrifice of sheer material strength (e.g., the Indian potlatch, and the sponsoring of a Mexican fiesta, which assure higher status but leave the ennobled person poor). It is not hard to see that the stock of cultural arrangements which once performed this function—from rites of passage to the crassest instrument of passing status from father to son with a prefix before the family name—has gradually waned, and that this burden too has turned into a part of labor, so that we now earn our social rank with the sweat of our brow. Up to a considerable measure we are what we do, and therefore the price of higher status is often harder work. The added strain this places on the individual remains half hidden till another aspect of this major shift away from the symbolic is acknowledged. If higher status is conferred through one's participation in a ceremony, as in the dubbing of a knight, then the claim to that rank need not be established through the sheer physical performance that eventually makes one a boss; but also, once a knight—again because that rank is more symbolic and less utilitarian—always a knight, whereas the present-day boss is always subject to dismissal.

A far less obvious consideration, one that probably affected the meaning we now attach to work far more than the permutations of Calvin's theology, arises directly from our professed devotion to equality. It is tempting to speak for once of a "contradiction" in the Marxist sense. For on one level we subscribe, and not at all only as window-dressing but in earnest, to egalitarian ideals. But on another level there was never any question that some very major *in*-equalities were to be preserved—most notable that of owning property. But how was one to come to terms with the two horns of this dilemma? One certainly could not just turn one's back. So work had to come to the rescue. One needed a formula that would make peace between the colliding facts. This was found through the invention of the idea that those who possessed much deserved their wealth as long as they had worked for it, and that the poor in similar fashion had earned their fate through their own indolence.

To imagine that only complaisance or self-righteous callousness is expressed in this posture is a serious mistake. It actually carries a major structural burden. The notion that the application of work, really to anything at all which one might chance upon, transforms that object into property—a thought that could easily strike one as downright bizarre (but which significantly is fundamental to, e.g., Locke)—played the role of a switch in freight yards. It managed to reconcile blatant material inequity with the principle that all men nonetheless are equal. This service, not surprisingly, called for some compensation, and the price was yet another layer added to the significance, the heavy seriousness, of labor. One could hardly regard work as a gratuitous interference, or an irksome imposition, let alone as the consequence of God's curse, if the right to one's possessions hinged on it.

But we still may be too far in the woods to see the one most widely branching tree. If our question is why work fills a much greater portion of our time, then part of the explanation may be that an empty space had to be filled. Perhaps we work such long hours because there is nothing else that we conceivably could do. The choice is between labor and a vacuum that we abhor.

Some of my earlier descriptions should have given some impression of the clutter of activities, pastimes, obligations and entertainments that once crowded this now vacant space. Recall the blocks of time given over just to the religious sphere alone. One need not go back to tribal rituals and ceremonies. Until quite recently in South American or European villages a funeral or a wedding could easily occupy most of a week (compare this to the drive-in service of some morticians, where one need not even leave one's car), and naturally not only the immediate family but most of the community participated. In addition to baptisms, confirmations and the like, there was also the recurring annual cycle of religious holidays, none of which was quickly sandwiched in, but which were prepared for in elaborate ways that again filled days on end with musical rehearsals, the preparation of processions, the making of costumes, the arranging of flowers, not to forget the cooking, baking, and the slaughter of sheep or pigs. Beyond that one also lived in an often crowded extended family, and this enters our calculation with real force, for it would be hard to measure the time we save by living in neat foursomes, and the great energy formerly required to negotiate through these troubled waters. But there should be no need of illustrations. A short drive through any "bedroom community," in which the activities are as restricted as the name implies, gives us a direct, first-hand impression of how streamlined and simplified coexistence has become, and it stands to reason that the importance of work in the lives of many rose as the countless alternatives which once engaged one's interest and time declined.

I have not mentioned thus far the obvious fact that the disdainful attitude towards labor also went hand in hand with a greater frugality, and that we also work harder because the needs to which we have grown accustomed are much more opulent. That is of course true, but all the preceding factors should have shown that there is no direct correspondence, that a great deal of our labor is not done to meet our needs or to give us satisfaction. And this is where the actual problem starts. For the complaint is not that we exhaust ourselves while our predecessors through most of history lay on a sheepskin and rested. The point is not that people did nothing for long stretches, and bestirred themselves only for the three hours which anthropologists have calculated. The point is that they did much else besides work. (The presumption that the only alternative to work is to collapse into a semi-conscious drowsing, that there is only either work or "relaxation" is itself a product of the development we are describing.) We are not preaching a homily in praise of sloth.

The predicament, as we see it, has two sides: that so much of our life has been usurped by work, and that what was once complex and colorful and absorbing has been gradually destroyed, is only one half of the picture. The other half concerns the nature and quality of the labor which has occupied this disproportionate territory. The absurdity in which we are caught is that we have given over ever more ground to work, but that we also have allowed work to become progressively duller and more demeaning. The moral is not that we should do less, but that we should do something different, more exhilarating and more worthwhile.

If the progress of culture has brought our energies more to the surface, and if greater vitality and endurance now are available to us—and just possibly this has happened—then this would be all to the good and nothing could be further from my mind than the suggestion that this advance should be undone. On the contrary, not to waste this acquisition is the crux of the concern. At the moment most of it goes down the drain. To put it to work—though in a different sense of "work"—is our actual purpose.

The easiest and most trodden approach to any discussion of the degradation of work is the stock-comparison between the old-fashioned craftsman and the assembly line, and despite its nostalgic patina this contrast is not without validity. To make a whole shoe or table from start to finish requires judgment and intelligence and taste; it involves a sequence of diverse operations; one's skill can improve over time; some part of one's personal style and individuality can be expressed; and one can take pride in the result. None of this is true for the man who screws the same two bulbs into the same headlight casings all day long. Still, there is much that this comparison overlooks.

For one, it omits the shoddiness of the product. A recent documentary film argued, for instance, that the workers in one of the Rolls Royce factories in England perform their assignments in higher spirits, even though they too deal only with small, segmented tasks, just because they believe that a Rolls Royce is a superb machine. So the realization that one's energy goes into the making of badly designed, tawdry, deliberately obsolescent contraptions—into the manufacturing of trash—could be added as a factor. But so might the knowledge that no one really needs or wants many of the goods turned out; that it will take trickery and deception to sell them at all, and that soon after being purchased they will be thrown away in disappointment.

Yet there are also the effects dishonesty has had. Paul Goodman's *Growing Up Absurd* is full of memorable illustrations. In one he describes auto mechanics and writes that there is even a separate word, the word "wall-job," in vogue in garages. It means that one simply parks the car next to a wall after the customer's departure and does absolutely nothing except write the bill, since there is no way of checking whether the repairs have been made or not. We have all come to take such practices for granted, and it would take a major effort to gauge the shift in attitude, not just in the worker, but in his client, too, that their prevalence has brought about.

Still, one could pose the whole problem on a different plane. The craftsman-assembly-line-worker analogy is bound to limp just because the number of cabinet- or shoemakers was always rather small and the figure of factory workers also is declining. However, one should recall that until about fifty years ago approximately 90 percent of the population in all countries were farmers, and that this proportion has been exactly reversed in a stunningly short time. Where formerly all except 10 percent lived on the land, now only about 10 percent still remain there. And that casts a much stronger light on the magnitude of the impasse, for it means that the category of the jobholder, whose work is separated from the remainder of his life, who goes away to work from 9 to 5, is itself a relatively new invention.

What we are dealing with is therefore a far more radical change than the usual reference to the craftsman suggests. But the cliché of the assembly line belittles the problem on still another score: the malaise is much more widely spread. In fact it is a weakness of contemporary Marxists that their critique of labor still follows the lines laid down by Marx for the English factory worker. By now enough has been written on virtually every type of job or profession, from the salesman to the office worker to professional athletes, and of course to doctors, lawyers and politicians, including a spate of books on executives, and even a famous volume just on morticians (*The American Way of Death*) so that it is quite clear that the debauchery if anything is more advanced when the collar is not blue but white.

However, there should be no misunderstanding: we are not alleging that most people are unhappy or dissatisfied. It is the waste of human energy and endurance, the gap between the facts and easy possibilities that is at stake. If the majority are satisfied, then all the worse: then Dostoyevsky was right in saying that there is nothing to which human beings cannot become accustomed; then this adds to the accusation, for in that case the prevalent conditions have fostered the type of a human being who will make his peace and be content even with this!

There may be no solution to this dilemma, but consider some attempts.

The reduction in the sheer duration of labor hours which has been achieved in the last hundred years unquestionably represents a great step towards the more tolerable, but it nonetheless is very insufficient. While it alleviates the duration it does nothing to alter the character of work itself. One seems to accept the premise that work has to be "written off" but one makes efforts to amputate a smaller part. Yet if that portion is still anything like 40 hours in a week it, in effect, surrenders two-thirds of the energy of one's life, and to "give up" on that much seems grotesque. Moreover, this strategy also seems blind to the whole second side of this impasse: to the emptiness which we described before. So this merely shifts the dividing line between degrading work and vacuous leisure where one is not much better than the other, and it leaves the substance of both unrepaired.

The conception of self-management, developed principally in Yugoslavia, does face the magnitude of the dilemma; to transform the character of work itself is the explicitly acknowledged central purpose of that movement. One strategy sets off from the idea that a great many jobs might be engaging, and even fun, if one had to perform them only for three or six months, while they demean those who cannot escape from them for thirty years. Driving a bus or a taxi for one summer is (as many students know) not at all the same as doing it for the rest of one's life. Part of the charm of this notion to deliberately rotate people into and out of jobs for short periods (which was seriously practiced in Yugoslavia, though under various constraints) is that it accomplishes a good deal with a minimum of means. Another of its merits is the extent to which it deflates self-deception and empty arrogance. To realize that the secretary, after two weeks training, can very capably perform the job of the sales manager, puts both the secretary and the manager into their place. That some of the socially necessary but unappealing tasks—like the collecting of garbage—can be distributed more equitably is another, further boon. That some obvious limitations are encountered when it comes to the rotation of brain surgeons and potters, who need years to learn their skills, naturally must be admitted, but such exceptions help to prove the rule.

The more dramatic concept of "integrating work with the other aspects of life" led to the establishment of factories in Yugoslavia that were sharply different right down to their physical appearance. On entering them one could have gotten the impression that one was visiting a summer camp or an artist colony, till one was told that in one of the larger structures refrigerators were being built. The hope was to create a setting in which a great diversity of activities would be encouraged, and that any particular worker might, between working hours, practice in an orchestra or see a film or attend classes or spend time in a greenhouse and the like, all in one place and during the course of a single day. This extends the idea of rotating jobs and breaks the shibboleth that work has to be done in one grinding eight-hour stretch.

However, it is the management of the plants by the workers themselves through democratic participation that gave this approach its name. And here our earlier scepticism concerning participation is bound to reassert itself. Since so much has been said already, we can confine ourselves to two succinct reservations. For one, it seems unlikely that the prerogative to partake in discussion and cast a vote will affect the actual experience of work as decisively as many seem to expect. All of the doubts we have enumerated apply here as before, especially if the plant in question is fairly large. As long as the notion of self-management is closely allied with the ideas of self-determination and hence of freedom one is apt to anticipate a psychological revolution—a greater pride in one's work and a pervasive sense of the significance of it, and of one's engagement—but after our extended critique the disappointments on this count do not surprise us.

Self-management by the workers, if that is taken fairly literally, also limits the control too much. How deeply the conduct of an industry affects the embedding community is at last being recognized, with the consequence that many decisions require input from the community and not only from company employees. Perhaps there could be governing bodies somewhat like the boards which run the schools in a town or city. Citizens, directly elected by the public, might sit on such councils and supervise one or several local industries. On such boards should be representatives of the workers, of the management, of the stockholders, but also, and importantly, representatives of the community at large. I have no illusions about the resistance that would have to be overcome till each of these contingents was in possession of sufficient power to fulfill its intended function, but I would claim that a system aiming at this model would realize greater benefits than all other possible alternatives, if it were achieved. It also seems that this goal has the advantage that one could progress towards it in a gradual and systematic fashion, moving from an initially very small proportion of worker's and community representatives to an eventually quite different and more equitable balance, and that one could begin to advance towards this at once. Wholesale expropriation on our understanding is neither the essence nor the best first step towards a genuine socialism. If one thinks of ownership as a widely dispersed assortment of rights, one can be selective, and limit, step by step, the specific rights whose exercise is socially destructive. The most general task these "local management boards" would perform would be progressively to impose restrictions on the owners and managers of given industries till their actual conduct conformed to goals the community as a whole desired.

The Yugoslavian efforts—which tragically have now been interrupted and reversed—are, in spite of these criticisms, the most intelligent and daring responses to the problem so far put into practice. They, nonetheless, only ameliorate some of the symptoms of the deeper difficulty. We stepped back as far as we did so as to see the pattern of the larger forces, and we shall now sketch a response which hopes to meet it on a more basic level.

We shall start from a deliberately abstract formulation: fundamentally, the collision is the result of an extraordinarily powerful connection; we link work or employment to the right to obtain sustenance, and thus to survival. One works so as to earn a living. Labor, therefore, is performed under the threat that whatever one engages in must sell on a market and must fetch a certain price. On one side this means that much that might be socially most useful cannot be done, since the required work does not command a living wage. On the other side it has the consequence that a great deal of work which serves no real purpose is nonetheless undertaken. The way out of this impasse can be very simply stated: the tight connection between work and sustenance must at first be loosened and must in the end be cut.

To somersault from the most general to the most concrete: imagine the inauguration of a program—not at all necessarily by the government and, to begin with, of a modest size—which would offer one the following choice: one could either continue to live as one so far has, or one could opt for a much more frugal life—say at one half of one's current salary of $30,000—and in exchange for that one would be free, not to do nothing, but to do something, anything at all, that one really wants to do. Ideally it should also be of some, though by no means of immediate social use.

Initially the number opting for this "second life" might be quite small. Even if the choice were reversible (and there might be a minimum of say five years, to insure seriousness, but conceivably also a maximum, to guarantee that more could have a turn), many would not be ready to make the financial sacrifice, and others might find that there is nothing they either want or know how to do. Still, some no doubt would make the change, and given the conditions, the chances would be high that a good percentage of them would be people with vitality and imagination. They would start to live a sharply different life from the remainder of the culture. The expectation is quite uncomplicated: the kind of life taking shape in these enclaves might in time attract ever-growing numbers till there would be a gradual but in the end momentous shift towards a new configuration, a different balance: the "alternative" might grow till it would become the mainstream of the culture.

Look at this now more closely. Recall that the role of work has been in effect inverted: it is no longer a means but an end. In this inversion, people must have a job or else depend on welfare, therefore jobs and work must be created. Yet this requirement stands in direct contradiction to the entire thrust and potential of the technology we have developed, which is most basically designed to obviate human labor. So the obvious question: But how can we do that? The question, What will happen to us if gradually fewer and fewer people will still work for wages for their sustenance has a straightforward answer. No *necessary* work will have to be eliminated. Only the present huge excess will be pared off. The same quantity of goods could still be manufactured. The standard of living would not have to drop. And it really should be very easy to have both these goods and far less labor, for that is in fact the natural tendency already. The problem is that we have so far resisted it in a quite senseless way. But if sustenance and labor were no longer linked together, then one major force would not, as at present, cancel out the other. That technology and labor be brought into alignment with each other so that our conception of work no longer combats the drive towards its own reduction, but on the contrary pulls in that same direction and still escalates it—that is the heart of what we are suggesting.

No one, I imagine, would deny that this possibility exists in principle. But many might suppose that it lies in a science-fiction future. However, that is not the case, and to dispel this prejudice was one major purpose of the background we have sketched. That the sudden climb in the quantity of labor occurred so recently, and that most of the causes for it had nothing to do with increased needs, should show that this turn is far more realistic and closer to us than we are apt to imagine. The condition we envision is not at all a new, unheard-of summit to be scaled for the first time. On the contrary, it is more nearly a return to normalcy. In a large frame the brief span in which most had to work eight or ten hours every day will appear like a strange aberration. Not too long from now one might ask: What happened? Was it a fever, or an infection? Why was there this obsession, this frenzy, in just these two hundred years?

But one could also point to countless individual facts to demonstrate how imminent this recovery could be. Everyone knows of all manner of processes, tools and designs that of course could save labor, that in fact do endanger jobs, and that are barred precisely for that reason. Take as a single instance Buckminster Fuller's idea of the prefabricated bathroom. The clumsiness with which just the plumbing pipes have to be pieced together, if one builds a bathroom as it is now done, is itself an engineering scandal. But then add to this the gas lines, the electric wires, the installation of the tub and stool and shower, the dry-walling and the mortar work, and of course the fixtures, the tiles and the painting—keeping in mind that many of these tasks must be performed by different people under separate unions—and maybe some conception of the amount of wasted labor (and needlessly high cost) begins to take shape. For technically it has been possible for years to make a total bathroom out of one single piece, and to make it far more beautiful and individuated and incomparably less subject to breakdowns to boot. The owner could select a bathroom from hundreds of different models and the whole unit could be plugged into the prearranged space. Just that one solitary simplification could cut the labor hours required for the building of an average house by as much as 1/7th. Naturally it is not being used, for if it were, thousands of construction workers would lose their jobs. They fight it with the best of all possible justifications. But it still illustrates an absurd contradiction, and our aim is not just to palliate it, but to dismantle it down to the ground.

To give hundreds of other similar examples would be child's play. To concentrate only on the present moment: in just the last few weeks of this writing a battle has been fought over the computerization of type-setting, and since this again would obviate a sizeable percentage of jobs in the whole printing industry, the union won a—probably very short-lived—delay. The automation of the sorting and handling of bulk mail has also just begun in the last months, and that this could reduce the necessary labor force by 25 percent has been discussed in many papers. Bell Telephone has come up with a telephone that so easily separates into its individual components that one could trade the faulty part in at a store and the repairmen's calls would be eliminated. One obviously could go on for pages.

There is a genuine difficulty: the magnitude of the proportion of labor that is unnecessary, that is literally make-work and featherbedding, is so great that it cannot be conveyed through the mere piling up of individual examples. Any list of particulars, no matter how extended, would still fall ludicrously short and would not communicate how very drastic the change could be. So it might help to have recourse to more general categories. Focus, for instance, on the notorious built-in obsolescence, but construe it not in its current narrow meaning: how much working time could be abolished with one stroke if the saving of labor—and not "full employment"—were a principal consideration; if our engineering skills were deployed to make every item durable instead of self-destructible? What proportion could be cut if one added up the following broad classifications: (1) work levels artificially maintained through the efforts of labor organizations. (Think of the railroads, of the regulations that prevent one union member from doing another union member's job, of how much work is done at a deliberately slowed-down pace, etc., etc.) (2) Work levels maintained through governmental programs. (Not just "public service" jobs, but whole industries supported to slow down the advance of unemployment, especially the elaborate protective arrangements made for farming, etc.) and (3) the relationship between work levels and technology, where this last category should be divided into three sub-headings: (a) labor which is artificially maintained above the required level because already existing and operating technology is not fully used; (b) work which could be eliminated if technology now feasible and invented were not kept off the market, but were instead given the reins and installed; and (c) the amount of labor that could be obviated if the design and creation of future labor-saving technology were actively promoted and every step in that direction were perceived not as endangering the livelihood of many, but as bringing the whole culture closer to the moment of liberation from drudgery and degrading routine work.

Certainly one could argue this issue with a more technical apparatus and make a show of various statistics. Conceivably one could "prove" that 80 percent of the labor now performed could be avoided without a drop in actual production; but such pseudo-objectivity should be suspect, and we in any case do not need it. In fact, its use would be misleading on a very serious point: it might give the impression that technical feasibility is the pivot on which this whole transition would have to turn, and the opposite is our actual view. The higher obstacles to it seem to us clearly social and therefore we only want to say enough to indicate that the sheer material possibility is not the major hurdle. It should be clear that on this score the process could occur much more quickly than is at all likely from other points of view, so that the actual development will never be slowed down by this consideration, but in fact will permanently lag behind it.

The core of what we are proposing could be put in another way: basically, working for wages should become optional. Those who choose to live in relative material wealth would still be able to move upwards in a hierarchy of wages. That "incentive" would still operate, and would insure that the necessary work gets done, though many might do it only during certain periods of their lives, and jobs might be rotated on the Yugoslavian model. But a gradually increasing proportion of the population would be supported in a decent, though frugal style, even when they would not work for wages. (How this differs sharply from a "guaranteed minimum income" or the "Family Assistance Plan" will become apparent shortly.) One could think of it on the analogy to sabbatical years in universities, with the difference that it would not be one year off on half-pay every seventh, but between five and ten years off with say three years of work between, and that the system would be general; that it would be available to everybody and not only to college teachers. It goes without saying that this abolition of the necessity to work would reduce the pressure on the labor market, and that it would be relatively easy to insure that this would not occur either too slowly or too quickly. But it is important to get a sense of the more specific consequences.

Take, to begin with, as a small-scaled model instance, the conversion to mass-transportation. Despite the great diversity of reasons which speak for this (ranging from the ecological to traffic congestions and the flight from the cities of those who can afford it) no decisive progress can be made as long as we cannot "afford" to produce and sell fewer cars. But what turns a slump in car sales from a loss of profit for a few into a national disaster? We know the answer: that hundreds of thousands are thrown out of work. But this would not have to be the calamity it now represents. If the arrangement we have begun to sketch were sufficiently far advanced, the pressure might be by then in the opposite direction: there might be a very large backlog of applicants for the "alternative, second" life whose "furloughs" had to be denied as long as the present quantity of cars was needed, but who through the introduction of mass transportation and the labor this would save, now would be free to exercise the option they preferred.

We can stay with this example and trace some of its further implications. During the months of the so-called gasoline shortage people were simultaneously asked please to buy a new and preferably big car to help fight unemployment, but also not to drive it, so as to conserve fuel. This makes the connection: we cannot possibly reverse the trend in energy consumption and at the same time still cling to the notion that only those who earn a wage deserve to eat. This implicates not only the complex of problems for which the word ecology is now used as a label, but brings us also with one further step to the need to purchase foreign oil at current prices. The one way to decrease the need for foreign oil that is most at hand and would be most effective—to cut back on the use of cars—is again ruled out for the same reason. Yet it seems that one of the few points on which economists agree is that the continuing inflation has a direct relationship to the rising costs of raw materials such as oil. So that problem too has its root in the axiom that everyone must work.

And the same applies to military spending. Significant curtailments in the budget for defense are not likely as long as the closing of every military base threatens higher unemployment. This now compels us to acknowledge that there is a linkage all the way from the first premise, that if we run short of work, more of it has to be created, clear to the possibility of wars. But that presses us onwards to imperialism. For although the struggle for raw materials and markets may be immediately fired by an appetite for profits, a second, equal and perhaps even deeper force that makes constant expansion necessary derives from the need for work. How could the economy be allowed to level off if jobs inevitably are eliminated, and therefore new ones continuously must be found in compensation for this loss? The tendency to perpetual aggrandizement can therefore not be blamed on just the logic that inheres in capital alone. There is a parallel logic of work—and the two go hand in hand.

None of these issues can be resolved on the now prevailing terms. Each of these cycles spirals upwards to meet the demand for jobs and there is only one way out: to pull the pivot around which these wheels turn, and doing this means abolishing the necessity of work.

One could make the same argument for the welfare-unemployment problem. That over the long run unemployment is bound to increase by staggering proportions, and that the present means to combat it are laughably inadequate has already been established by our overall perspective. Yet our larger picture suggests also that one could see the dilemma in a different light. Is not the fact that unemployment constitutes a "problem," that it is perceived as symptomatic of a social disease, itself bizarre? What is the underlying structure which forces us to say, "Eight percent *cannot* work," when we might say instead, "They no longer *must*"? Why is our ability to produce more than enough without their assistance not an achievement, a hopeful sign that the day may not be too far off when perhaps no one will have to work (for money) for more than three or four hours every week, or maybe one year out of every seven? Must what should be an advance remain a calamity?

It need not, but leprosy cannot be cured with baby powder. A major general reorientation is required, and not just slightly increased alms. One key feature of our overall design would be that not only those hired last would be out of work. The opposite would be the case: many who formerly held positions of prestige would choose the "alternative" life, free from wage-earning. There would therefore be a gradually waxing exodus in the middle strata, and those closer to the top, and the empty space created could be filled by those who hitherto were kept down. So far, all of the attempts to raise the really poor have branded them with the stigma of their dependence and their inferiority, and tinkering changes in the administration of these programs will not change this fact. The alternative we have in mind is therefore drastically different. The scheme we are proposing is deliberately not tailored to those on the lowest rungs of the social ladder. Instead it would draw a proportion of those who have held reasonably paid positions away from the labor market, so that the now destitute would have a chance to enter it. Free of onus they could then rise up to the level on which they in turn could opt for our "second" economically noncompetitive existence.

Those not working for a wage would thus be in an entirely different position from today's recipients of welfare payments or unemployment compensation—or, for that matter, from those obtaining any future guaranteed minimum income. For one, they would have an altogether different past. They might range from factory workers who after fifteen years on the assembly line decided that this was enough, to former plumbers, salesmen or beauticians, and of course also to professors, lawyers, dentists and executives. In addition, there would be no doubt that their more frugal life did not fall upon them as a fate, but that they chose it because they regarded it as preferable. This would not only place their own self-respect on a firm foundation and afford some protection against the insolence of others; it would alter the material actualities at their disposal. The alternative of those on welfare is starvation, and therefore they can only plead. But those who had joined the "second" culture could demand that their life not become too frugal and warn that they might otherwise again compete for work. (Those still working would be in the converse position: their conditions would have to be met since they would no longer be obliged to work. Employers would have to compete for labor, and therefore make the work they offered more attractive.) Moreover, they would not encounter the notorious resentment with which welfare clients have to cope. They could always say: "If our life seems enviable to you, then by all means join up; it will not be just to your own advantage but you will have done the whole society a service, for there will be one pair of hands fewer for whom work—for wages—will have to be drummed up."

Still, these differences are minor compared to the most basic contrast in how each would spend an average day. The image of the currently unemployed is formed from the waiting lines in hiring halls, and from the daily pilgrimage to the local bar with its game of pool. But those stepping off the economic escalator in the future would have done it with a purpose, with a definite conception of something that they want to do. They would be off on their own projects, alone or with a group, growing a new kind of plant, designing fabulous mechanical contraptions, sawing, hammering, or nailing, learning anything from Chinese poems to the neurology of frogs, and teaching all of that—they would cure and build and think—they would do the one thing which they above all others chose to do.

Despite these glowing assets, what we are suggesting would not be at all likely to succeed—in fact it could not even start—unless a sustained and, in its size perhaps incomparable, effort in educating the whole country were launched in advance, and accompanied the gradual transition with both critique and explanation. Nothing could be further from our conception of what needs to be done than the stereotype of yet another massive, highly centralized governmental "program"—a kind of Social Security for the middle-aged—entombed in yet another set of bureaucratic pyramids and financed by a general tax. What we are advocating is at the opposite extreme: one imaginatively conceived step in this general new direction organized in one community or plant or institution, and a quite different tactic developed somewhere else. But if it is to happen in this fashion then explanation, teaching—the undoing of encrusted prejudices about work, about economics, about democracy and freedom, and about the goals our culture could attain, is the only lever with which this giant wheel could be made to turn.

Other cultures in this century have had to break with their whole past and begin anew—and mostly with bought seeds. Compared to their enterprises, the change before us is a mere practice jump. Yet, if it is agreed that nothing of any value can occur unless it is comprehended and actively desired and in its detail executed by a preponderant majority and that we also cannot simply float down the same stream, but must steer at new goals, then to explain them and to teach how they can be attained is first on the agenda.

This dictates the one most important preparatory action for this turnabout. As long as the media of mass communication are in league with those whose power this re-direction would curtail, the change will not occur. The crucial opening move would therefore have to be the gaining of far greater access to the mainline newspapers and magazines and TV stations. If one could get a foot, and not just a toe, into that one door (and surely this is feasible), the imperative need for a general reorganization could be proposed, the advantages and difficulties could be considered in detail, modifications and revampings could be incorporated and the problems of the actual implementation debated and resolved. But nothing short of a decisive alteration in the climate of opinion, a kind of coming to a halt in which the path before us can be re-evaluated, would suffice.

However, we by no means put our faith into a publicity campaign on a yet grander scale. The idea is more that the presently one-sided campaign has the power to lull most everyone to sleep and that its monotony has to be interrupted to bring the somnambulism to a stop. The opening move would only aim at a waking up. The actual reconsideration would have to happen in a quite different way.

Up to this point we have really only looked at one side of the coin. Its whole other side consists of the positive contributions which those relieved from wage-labor would then be free to make. Any attempt to summarize these in three or four paragraphs would be grotesque. It would be as vain as an endeavor to describe in the same space what a quarter, and maybe before long seven-eighths of the total population do now with their energy and time. One can only say that the net effect would be incalculable, for how could one form an accurate conception of the degree to which the quality of our social life would be transformed if, instead of giving a year's leave, on the basis of a proposal, to a few thousand scholars and artists, one-third of the now working population had submitted their plan for a project—which could be anything from the handcrafting of furniture to the planting of trees along a highway, from working with the sick and aged to the tending of a well-kept vegetable garden, from teaching magic tricks to a small group of children to the development of a new art-form—and had been given leave (not for one year but for five, and not by one central agency but by their union or their employer or their town or city) to pursue it? Not a new rainfall from the mass media but the constant observation of those who had begun to live the "second" life—the daily seeing of what good it did to them, and of whether they were good for others—would create the different cultural climate.

Maybe the question, But can we afford it, and who will pay for it? is by now overdue. The briefest answer might be that for the society as a whole it would be far more economical than our present course, and that this shoe therefore fits more snugly on the other foot: can we afford what we are doing now? To decrease some of the enormous wastefulness of our present practice is one of our major motives, not to "spend more."

Consider the unemployment-welfare situation. Those now fired or laid off are in no position to add anything of real value to society. On our plan many of these might work for wages (not forever, but until they too might choose the "second" life), and those freed from work-for-wages would of course receive a higher stipend, but they also would not be condemned to idleness. They would improve the society and make it richer, by performing tasks that now do not pay.

Or go back to the requirement to purchase foreign oil and other raw materials, which could be conserved if a more economical technology (e.g., mass transportation) took the place of the extravagant devices we now must condone, since there might be less work without them. How many families could be supported out of the savings, out of the sums not spent, if the level of those wanting to work for wages had fallen to a point where excess production and the need for raw materials could subside?

But this still does not cut to the bone. What we are proposing is that a steadily increasing number be allowed to work at what and how and when they please in exchange for a more modest life—so why should the society find that expensive? The supposition is bizarre. A superstition forced us to eat cake—surely we will not go bankrupt because some decide to go back to bread.

However, admittedly, the benefits to society are somewhat beside the point. *Who* will pay for it is the real issue. The answer need not be the obviously rich.

Some equalization of incomes would of course occur, but it would follow more from a raising of the poor than from a lowering of the wealthy for they would have the option to remain in their present life, and it is not settled that the profit margin of their enterprises—if they were more automated and operated with only a fraction of the current labor force—would have to be much smaller. Is not the reduction of labor costs one of their own main goals? Not income, but power would be much more seriously equalized. For even if the payment of half-salaries to those on long furloughs in the "second" life were in the long run to the advantage of a corporation, it would naturally do far less, as long as it could. Which means that the prerogatives of some would have to be curtailed, and certainly that cannot be done without a struggle. Still, if we imagined that the rationale and the goals of this plan had been thoroughly debated, and that over a period of years many from all walks of life had gradually begun to see its plausibility, and if we further bear in mind that the beginning need not be dramatic but could be as inconspicuous as one labor union including the option of a sabbatical year in its demands, then it is not completely hopeless. Furthermore, we could simultaneously move in the direction of the "local management boards" we discussed before, and, finally, if enough people really wanted this, even the government might help in a small way.

The mild language in which our proposal was explained and our insistence on moving gradually and with caution should not be misconstrued. Though we eschewed all suggestions of military rhetoric and did not speak of a warfare among classes or of a condition in which only chains are to be lost, the metamorphosis we envision would be far more drastic than any hoped for from all the various forms of socialism. For Marx accepted not only the necessity of work, which we reject, but made work the axle around which his own thinking and the society he projected turned. Labor became for him the general source of value. True, it was his intention to destroy the claims of those who possessed much while they performed no labor, and to establish the right to the product of their labor of those who worked. Still, against the backdrop of the panoramic history we sketched, labor became in that process undeniably more central. The future would bring a society of *workers*. Socially they would be the only class, and individually their work would give them their primary self-definition. The valuation of work thus was raised to a yet higher plane. The Calvinistic sanctity of the vocation was secularized and enveloped manual labor in its mystique. Yet if the natural and normal place of work through most of human history was marginal then this drives an aberration to extremes.

If men through their pre-history were largely equal, then history brought first the servitude of the many under the lordship of the few, and then the servitude of all under the tyranny of work. We mean to reverse the long march in this one direction, and right the inversion of means and ends. The subordination of human life to work for wages could be the last link in a chain of subservience; with it broken, the enhancement of human life could again become the end.

A social order in which the fear of falling below the level of a frugal sustenance was permanently lifted, and in which wage labor was reduced to a minimum would provide more freedom across the range of its entire population than any other possibility on the horizon. It certainly would not eliminate all obstacles, but we have already seen how the granting of *that* wish would be dreadful. Only the reduction of obstacles which stunt the self, undermine the possibility of its expression, and extinguish the "whisper of subjectivity" furthers freedom. The termination of the struggle for mere sustenance would finally bring down these hindrances. More crucial still, under this new dispensation the time and energy now spent on one's job would be given to the one activity each individual preferred to all others. This large portion of the life of many would thus become a form of self-expression. It would be free in the strict sense of our definition.

Marvellous as this advance—if it should come to pass—would be, for us it would still not be an end-point and a last fulfillment. Not only because it would leave us far from complete freedom, but also because freedom itself is for us now a measured value: neither a sacred absolute, nor a burden to which man has been condemned. And to attain the balance where we can see freedom fully for what it is—that has been our purpose.

Appendix
Freedom and Determinism

WE CONSIGN OUR DISCUSSION of this question to a mere postscript so as to leave no doubt that we shall not attempt a full-dress treatment of the awesome complexities in the literature on this problem. A chapter on this topic might have raised that expectation, but we mean to draw only a few lines to indicate the general approach we would adopt.

The dilemma between freedom and determinism was first framed as a paradox by theologians. How could God's omniscience, which encompasses knowledge of our future actions, and God's omnipotence, which includes power over our deeds, be reconciled with man's possession of free will? How could we be held responsible and damned for sins if God knew in advance that we would commit them, and had control over our undertakings? Are our choices not reduced to mere illusions by these attributes of God?

The secular and more modern version of the issue resulted in large part from the impact of Newtonian physics, and reformulated essentially the same questions in terms of mechanistic causal laws. How could our wills be free, how could we be responsible for our actions and our choices not be mere deceptions if the relevant causal laws could give us a similar fore-knowledge, and if these causal laws exercised an, analogous control?

I stress the resemblance between the theological and the secular posing of the difficulty to suggest two questions: (1) How indebted is the causal formulation of the paradox to its theological antecedent? Would these conflicts have been cast in quite this way in response to Newton if they had not lain ready-made in wait? (2) Is the substitution of cause and effect for God unproblematic? Is causality an agency *separate from us* like a God, and could it deprive us of our responsibility in the same fashion?

231

The classical and most familiar attack on the non-religious version of the problem tries to show that there are limits beyond which causal determinacy cannot go. Implicitly one grants that freedom and determinism do exclude each other, and then pursues the tactic of setting borders to causality with the presumption that in the salvaged territory man will be free. The metaphor which underlies this enterprise is thus extremely reminiscent of the "narrow hallway." Once more the picture of a corridor is conjured up in which one cannot move either to the left or right, but can only take the single pre-determined next step forward. One imagines that to act from causes is somehow analogous to being so constrained—that each cause "pushes" us a little further along this confined path—and one conceives indeterminacy on the analogy of a place where one can move in several possible directions.

We shall make two preliminary observations before we focus on the center of the difficulty. For one, many writers have been so preoccupied with the demonstration that some indeterminacy does indeed exist that the second step—from the absence of causality to freedom—is assumed to follow without saying. But even on the face of it there seems to be a gap. To call someone "free" initially suggests far more than just that there is some small margin in which his actions are not quite determined. It is as if one tied a person into chains but called him "free" because he still can turn his head. Similarly in the reverse direction: if one substitutes "caused" for the more highly charged "determined" the leap involved becomes more noticeable. To conceive of an action as "determined" seems to preclude its freedom, but is it self-evident that an act cannot be free because it had an antecedent "cause"?

Our second prefatory caution hinges on the development of science, particularly that of physics. Much has been made of Heisenberg's "Principle of Indeterminacy," but in the crudest terms it asserts only that two separate magnitudes cannot both be measured at one and the same time, and whether this has any relevance to freedom is extremely doubtful. So this is not what we have in mind, nor are we thinking of any other specific recent theory or concept. The more pertinent transformation is quite general and involves our conception of the whole enterprise of physics and the expectations we attach to it. Even the layman has come to understand that the relationship between the often independently developed mathematical "models" and the realities which they are intended to explain has progressively become more tenuous and stretched. Gone is the sense that our theories have a direct correspondence and move on solid and firm ground. The expectation that a relatively simple and at the same time complete explanation of the material universe may be close at hand has thus receded into an ever greater and more baffling distance. This shift in our over-all perception has been so great that one could meaningfully ask whether someone who had never heard of the conflict between freedom and determinism, and was familiar only with the condition in which physics finds itself today, would come to feel this as a serious and urgent problem.

To prevent a possible misunderstanding: I only mean to regain a sense of proportion, a sense of the actual distances at stake before we enter into the core of the philosophical debate. To put it bluntly: in many discussions of determinism a genuine fear of science seems to grip the partisans of freedom. One gets the impression that they want to protect a tiny island against the rising tide of a surrounding ocean, that in their view almost everything is by now subected to the laws of science and can be explained and predicted. But that is surely wrong. One should recall that in most of the social sciences even the terminology of cause and effect has been gradually abandoned, and that one withdrew to the more cautious search for "significant correlations" because one could so rarely give straightforward causal explanations of any phenomena at all. We still cannot predict even such crude and physical events as earthquakes, or what kind of weather we will have four days from now, and many linguists are agreed that in actual practice we may never reach the point where even the simplest sentence uttered by a living speaker could be reliably predicted. A more accurate picture of the existing situation would therefore reverse the island and the ocean: our scientific knowledge has barely gained a foothold. There is no danger that nothing inexplicable will soon remain. Naturally, this does not begin to settle any of the theoretical concerns we face, but it should clear the air of some emotional clouds.

To advance now our first genuinely philosophic argument: We already indicated that the traditional debate converged on the question of the existence of some indeterminacy. In often very technical and complicated ways the partisans of one side have tried to prove that there are some events which *in principle* cannot be predicted, while their opponents have argued that this is not the case. Both parties thus tacitly accepted one key assumption: namely that the establishment of indeterminacy guarantees the possibility of freedom. Our strategy will be quite different. We shall not attempt to demonstrate either the existence or the non-existence of indeterminacy. Precisely this most controverted question we shall set aside and address instead the agreed upon presupposition. Our question will be: What is the relationship between *in*determinacy and freedom? Would indeterminacy, even if its existence could be demonstrated, really vouchsafe freedom, or would it not fulfill this expectation?

The shift to this new question is our first step. Our second step narrows the specific point down to the location of the indeterminacy. Where or when would it have to occur to provide us with freedom? Evidently some measure of indeterminacy might, for example, take place on the moon and yet be of no benefit to us whatever. We need to know at what exact juncture the causal sequence would have to be broken to furnish us the opening for the exercise of our freedom.

Take a concrete example. Imagine Raskolnikov walking up the steps to the old pawnbroker woman's room and assume that his mind still vacillates, that with every tread he climbs his thinking alternates from one side to the other. Like someone pulling the petals off a flower while saying "she loves me," "she does not," he mounts the staircase thinking "I shall kill her," "no, I shall not." This continues till he stands right before her door. Now let us hypothesize that his last thought just as he pushes the door open is "no, I shall not do it" and that the sought-for indeterminacy occurs right after these words crossed his mind. The thinking of this thought is the last link in a causal chain, but now there is a gap between this and the next event, which is his bringing the axe down on her head.

What would this mean? Would the occurrence of a disjuncture in this place render Raskolnikov's act more free; would it provide him with a power or a control that he lacks otherwise? It seems that once the situation has been made sufficiently concrete and is looked at through a magnifying glass the answer is quite obvious. The implication, if anything, would be the reverse. If his last thought really is "no, I shall not do it" and this thought is somehow disconnected from the next event so that it has no causal influence on it and he then kills her, then one could only say that the indeterminacy has rendered his will ineffectual, that instead of giving him greater power or control the causal gap *decreased* it. If a moment of indeterminacy severed his last thought from the subsequent events then this means only that his last thought has been isolated and was rendered impotent.

If one wanted to picture the crucial episode in still more detail one could envision two alternatives: either something other than his own last thought "influences" him so that he does commit the murder, or this last reversal was quite strictly not effected by anything whatever and occurred entirely "by chance." Both of these options have the, for us, crucial element in common: in either case it was not *he* that made the decision, and *he* certainly did not exercise his freedom. We therefore can conclude that the occurrence of a causal gap in this particular location—between his last thought and his action—would not furnish him with freedom, but on the contrary would undermine the agent, and make him a victim.

Would it be more of an advantage if the indeterminacy happened in a different location? Would Raskolnikov have been more of a free agent if the causal gap had occurred somewhat sooner, while he climbed the staircase, between two of his opposing resolutions, for example? If we focus on the immediately contiguous next moment, on the "yes, I will do it" that follows on the heels of the "no, I will not" then we have of course once more exactly the same pattern, only that it will now be the occurrence of the "yes" over which Raskolnikov has *less* control. And for the more distant action of his murder the earlier moment of indeterminacy on the staircase will simply be irrelevant: certainly Raskolnikov will not be *more* responsible for a deed he performs five minutes later because an earlier shift from a "no" to a "yes" happened mysteriously and less subject to his influence. All other conceivable locations of the indeterminacy therefore make matters only worse. But if a causal gap immediately prior to the action would be in the one most promising location and would yet fail to provide him freedom then we can conclude that no indeterminacy—regardless of its location—could ever render an act free. If the best position fails, then *a fortiori* all other, weaker, places will fail all the more.

We now can turn the table and raise the converse question: not Will indeterminacy create freedom? but What would be required to produce the kind of freedom that a causal gap was expected to provide? What circumstances would one have to imagine to satisfy the implicit hope? Evidently one would have to go to extremes. If a mere interruption in the causal sequence only turns Raskolnikov into a victim then we would have to fall back on the fantasy of a second, internal, ghost-like, little midget self. And even then a momentary suspension of causality would not be enough. The homunculus would only have the opportunity for a "free choice" if the whole of time stopped for a few seconds and everything froze in place so that he could survey the situation, could consider the alternatives, select one, and then intervene to bring about one of the options. Notice that the inner self here must be a complete replication that could think and speculate and arrive at a decision while all else—including the thoughts of the actual Raskolnikov—did not move.

This caricature makes explicit the fantasy which gives us the impression that indeterminacy would set us free. That it is grotesque is very much the point. For nothing less than this would turn indeterminacy into an occasion in which freedom could be exercised, and just because this is undeniably a piece of science fiction a causal gap does *not* create the possibility of freedom. (One could add that even if all this miraculously were the case, it would still give freedom only to the small homunculus, and not to the flesh and blood Raskolnikov.)

This brings us to a third question: Does the fact that an act has causes really render it unfree? If we once more look at an actual situation through a magnifying glass it is not at all apparent why this should be so. Take the instance of my teaching philosophy. There are a diversity of expectations and hopes and desires which do cause me to teach. But does the supposition that these causes make my teaching unfree seem convincing? Would it not be very strange to suppose that I am coerced to teach because I do have these feelings, and because they prompt me to refuse alternative professions? Is not exactly the reverse the case? Is my teaching not something which I do freely just because I have these desires, and because it is they who cause me to teach and not some external exigencies or requirements?

In summary this shows that the absence of causation does not furnish us with freedom, while the presence of causation does not rule it out. The schema which assumes causality to be decisive is therefore a mistake. The criterion on which the freedom or unfreedom of an act depends is different from this: it was the core of our definition from the start. An action may be caused and free in spite of that. The fulcrum on which the issue turns is the concept of identification: if I accept the causes of the action as part of my genuine self, if whatever prompts the action is *me*, if it is caused by my wish, or a hope of mine, then it is free. And conversely: regardless of whether the act is strictly caused or not, if whatever causes it or generates it in some other fashion is not me, the action is not free. The principle of identification is thus in a specific sense "stronger" than that of causality. It overrides causality in both directions.

This subsumes the issue of determinism under our general definition, and this definition stands therefore now more firmly than it ever did before. Up to this point one might have thought that there is after all one other major sense of freedom not covered by it. But this we have now shown not to be the case. An action is not free in some other meaning of the word when it is indetermined, and unfree in that other sense when it is caused. We can apply our criterion and follow it in this as in other situations: if an action is prompted by an aspect of myself with which I identify then it is free even if that part of me is the cause of the action. If the act is prompted by something other than myself it is unfree, regardless of whether this disassociated element is a cause of the act or not.

So far we have adduced three main considerations. We asked first exactly where or when indeterminacy would have to occur for it to create the opportunity for freedom. The answer turned out to be that there was no such location, that a causal gap no matter where it might be postulated would not increase our freedom but would render us ineffectual instead. Secondly, we argued that only a patently fictitious homunculus could take advantage of a breach in the causal sequence, and that this fantasy lies behind the dream that indeterminacy would set us free. In the third instance we insisted that we can be free even when our acts are caused as long as we ourselves cause our acts to come into being, and that we are unfree when the cause lies outside of our "genuine" or "real" self.

One last thought should now still be added. There is a close resemblance between those who are convinced that they are coerced by causality and the Undergroundman. Dostoyevsky's clerk disassociates himself from everything, and everything therefore has the power to constrain him. Those who disassociate themselves from all causality, who experience every causal nexus as something they oppose, are similarly coerced by all causes. In that sense the incompatibility between freedom and causality is not an illusion. If one adopts a certain identification then all causes do indeed make one unfree. But this is only one of many possible identities, and the conflict is therefore neither inescapable nor universal. One can accept elements which have causes and effects as part of one's "true" self. For those who adopt such an identification the problem of determinism is resolved. Only Undergroundmen are made unfree by *every* cause; those who accept anything real as part of their "true" self are free if they identify with the cause of their action.